Network Security Through Data Analysis

Building Situational Awareness

Michael Collins

Beijing · Cambridge · Farnham · Köln · Sebastopol · Tokyo

Network Security Through Data Analysis

by Michael Collins

Copyright © 2014 Michael Collins. All rights reserved.

Printed in the United States of America.

Published by O'Reilly Media, Inc., 1005 Gravenstein Highway North, Sebastopol, CA 95472.

O'Reilly books may be purchased for educational, business, or sales promotional use. Online editions are also available for most titles (*http://my.safaribooksonline.com*). For more information, contact our corporate/institutional sales department: 800-998-9938 or *corporate@oreilly.com*.

Editors: Andy Oram and Allyson MacDonald	**Indexer:** Judy McConville
Production Editor: Nicole Shelby	**Cover Designer:** Randy Comer
Copyeditor: Gillian McGarvey	**Interior Designer:** David Futato
Proofreader: Linley Dolby	**Illustrators:** Kara Ebrahim and Rebecca Demarest

February 2014:   First Edition

Revision History for the First Edition:

2014-02-05:   First release

See *http://oreilly.com/catalog/errata.csp?isbn=9781449357900* for release details.

ISBN: 978-1-449-35790-0

[LSI]

Table of Contents

Part II. Tools

Part III. Analytics

Preface

This book is about networks: monitoring them, studying them, and using the results of those studies to improve them. "Improve" in this context hopefully means to make more secure, but I don't believe we have the vocabulary or knowledge to say that confidently —at least not yet. In order to implement security, we try to achieve something more quantifiable and describable: *situational awareness*.

Situational awareness, a term largely used in military circles, is exactly what it says on the tin: an understanding of the environment you're operating in. For our purposes, situational awareness encompasses understanding the components that make up your network and how those components are used. This awareness is often *radically* different from how the network is configured and how the network was originally designed.

To understand the importance of situational awareness in information security, I want you to think about your home, and I want you to count the number of web servers in your house. Did you include your wireless router? Your cable modem? Your printer? Did you consider the web interface to CUPS? How about your television set?

To many IT managers, several of the devices listed didn't even register as "web servers." However, embedded web servers speak HTTP, they have known vulnerabilities, and they are increasingly common as specialized control protocols are replaced with a web interface. Attackers will often hit embedded systems without realizing what they are— the SCADA system is a Windows server with a couple of funny additional directories, and the MRI machine is a perfectly serviceable spambot.

This book is about collecting data and looking at networks in order to understand how the network is used. The focus is on analysis, which is the process of taking security data and using it to make actionable decisions. I emphasize the word *actionable* here because effectively, security decisions are restrictions on behavior. Security policy involves telling people what they shouldn't do (or, more onerously, telling people what they *must* do). Don't use Dropbox to hold company data, log on using a password and an RSA dongle, and don't copy the entire project server and sell it to the competition. When we make security decisions, we interfere with how people work, and we'd better have good, solid reasons for doing so.

All security systems ultimately depend on users recognizing the importance of security and accepting it as a necessary evil. Security rests on people: it rests on the individual users of a system obeying the rules, and it rests on analysts and monitors identifying when rules are broken. Security is only marginally a technical problem—information security involves endlessly creative people figuring out new ways to abuse technology, and against this constantly changing threat profile, you need cooperation from both your defenders and your users. Bad security policy will result in users increasingly evading detection in order to get their jobs done or just to blow off steam, and that adds additional work for your defenders.

The emphasis on actionability and the goal of achieving security is what differentiates this book from a more general text on data science. The section on analysis proper covers statistical and data analysis techniques borrowed from multiple other disciplines, but the overall focus is on understanding the structure of a network and the decisions that can be made to protect it. To that end, I have abridged the theory as much as possible, and have also focused on mechanisms for identifying abusive behavior. Security analysis has the unique problem that the targets of observation are not only aware they're being watched, but are actively interested in stopping it if at all possible.

The MRI and the General's Laptop

Several years ago, I talked with an analyst who focused primarily on a university hospital. He informed me that the most commonly occupied machine on his network was the MRI. In retrospect, this is easy to understand.

"Think about it," he told me. "It's medical hardware, which means its certified to use a specific version of Windows. So every week, somebody hits it with an exploit, roots it, and installs a bot on it. Spam usually starts around Wednesday." When I asked why he didn't just block the machine from the Internet, he shrugged and told me the doctors wanted their scans. He was the first analyst I've encountered with this problem, and he wasn't the last.

We see this problem a lot in any organization with strong hierarchical figures: doctors, senior partners, generals. You can build as many protections as you want, but if the general wants to borrow the laptop over the weekend and let his granddaughter play Neopets, you've got an infected laptop to fix on Monday.

Just to pull a point I have hidden in there, I'll elaborate. I am a firm believer that the most effective way to defend networks is to secure and defend *only* what you need to secure and defend. I believe this is the case because information security will always require people to be involved in monitoring and investigation—the attacks change too much, and when we do automate defenses, we find out that attackers can now use them to attack us.[1]

I am, as a security analyst, firmly convinced that security should be inconvenient, well-defined, and constrained. Security should be an artificial behavior extended to assets that must be protected. It should be an artificial behavior because the final line of defense in any secure system is the *people* in the system—and people who are fully engaged in security will be mistrustful, paranoid, and looking for suspicious behavior. This is not a happy way to live your life, so in order to make life bearable, we have to limit security to what must be protected. By trying to watch everything, you lose the edge that helps you protect what's really important.

Because security is inconvenient, effective security analysts must be able to *convince* people that they need to change their normal operations, jump through hoops, and otherwise constrain their mission in order to prevent an abstract future attack from happening. To that end, the analysts must be able to identify the decision, produce information to back it up, and demonstrate the risk to their audience.

The process of data analysis, as described in this book, is focused on developing security knowledge in order to make effective security decisions. These decisions can be forensic: reconstructing events after the fact in order to determine why an attack happened, how it succeeded, or what damage was done. These decisions can also be proactive: developing rate limiters, intrusion detection systems, or policies that can limit the impact of an attacker on a network.

Audience

Information security analysis is a young discipline and there really is no well-defined body of knowledge I can point to and say "Know this." This book is intended to provide a snapshot of analytic techniques that I or other people have thrown at the wall over the past 10 years and seen stick.

The target audience for this book is network administrators and operational security analysts, the personnel who work on NOC floors or who face an IDS console on a regular basis. My expectation is that you have some familiarity with TCP/IP tools such as *netstat*, and some basic statistical and mathematical skills.

In addition, I expect that you have some familiarity with scripting languages. In this book, I use Python as my go-to language for combining tools. The Python code is illustrative and might be understandable without a Python background, but it is assumed that you possess the skills to create filters or other tools in the language of your choice.

---

1. Consider automatically locking out accounts after *x* number of failed password attempts, and combine it with logins based on email addresses. Consider how many accounts you can lock out that way.

In the course of writing this book, I have incorporated techniques from a number of different disciplines. Where possible, I've included references back to original sources so that you can look through that material and find other approaches. Many of these techniques involve mathematical or statistical reasoning that I have intentionally kept at a functional level rather than going through the derivations of the approach. A basic understanding of statistics will, however, be helpful.

Contents of This Book

This book is divided into three sections: data, tools, and analytics. The data section discusses the process of collecting and organizing data. The tools section discusses a number of different tools to support analytical processes. The analytics section discusses different analytic scenarios and techniques.

Part I discusses the collection, storage, and organization of data. Data storage and logistics are a critical problem in security analysis; it's easy to collect data, but hard to search through it and find actual phenomena. Data has a footprint, and it's possible to collect so much data that you can never meaningfully search through it. This section is divided into the following chapters:

Chapter 1

This chapter discusses the general process of collecting data. It provides a framework for exploring how different sensors collect and report information and how they interact with each other.

Chapter 2

This chapter expands on the discussion in the previous chapter by focusing on sensors that collect network traffic data. These sensors, including *tcpdump* and NetFlow, provide a comprehensive view of network activity, but are often hard to interpret because of difficulties in reconstructing network traffic.

Chapter 3

This chapter discusses sensors that are located on a particular system, such as host-based intrusion detection systems and logs from services such as HTTP. Although these sensors cover much less traffic than network sensors, the information they provide is generally easier to understand and requires less interpretation and guess-work.

Chapter 4

This chapter discusses tools and mechanisms for storing traffic data, including traditional databases, big data systems such as Hadoop, and specialized tools such as graph databases and REDIS.

Part II discusses a number of different tools to use for analysis, visualization, and reporting. The tools described in this section are referenced extensively in later sections when discussing how to conduct different analytics.

Chapter 5

System for Internet-Level Knowledge (SiLK) is a flow analysis toolkit developed by Carnegie Mellon's CERT. This chapter discusses SiLK and how to use the tools to analyze NetFlow data.

Chapter 6

R is a statistical analysis and visualization environment that can be used to effectively explore almost any data source imaginable. This chapter provides a basic grounding in the R environment, and discusses how to use R for fundamental statistical analysis.

Chapter 7

Intrusion detection systems (IDSes) are automated analysis systems that examine traffic and raise alerts when they identify something suspicious. This chapter focuses on how IDSes work, the impact of detection errors on IDS alerts, and how to build better detection systems whether implementing IDS using tools such as SiLK or configuring an existing IDS such as Snort.

Chapter 8

One of the more common and frustrating tasks in analysis is figuring out where an IP address comes from, or what a signature means. This chapter focuses on tools and investigation methods that can be used to identify the ownership and provenance of addresses, names, and other tags from network traffic.

Chapter 9

This chapter is a brief walkthrough of a number of specialized tools that are useful for analysis but don't fit in the previous chapters. These include specialized visualization tools, packet generation and manipulation tools, and a number of other toolkits that an analyst should be familiar with.

The final section of the book, Part III, focuses on the goal of all this data collection: analytics. These chapters discuss various traffic phenomena and mathematical models that can be used to examine data.

Chapter 10

Exploratory Data Analysis (EDA) is the process of examining data in order to identify structure or unusual phenomena. Because security data changes so much, EDA is a necessary skill for any analyst. This chapter provides a grounding in the basic visualization and mathematical techniques used to explore data.

Chapter 11

This chapter looks at mistakes in communications and how those mistakes can be used to identify phenomena such as scanning.

Chapter 12

This chapter discusses analyses that can be done by examining traffic volume and traffic behavior over time. This includes attacks such as DDoS and database raids, as well as the impact of the work day on traffic volumes and mechanisms to filter traffic volumes to produce more effective analyses.

Chapter 13

This chapter discusses the conversion of network traffic into graph data and the use of graphs to identify significant structures in networks. Graph attributes such as centrality can be used to identify significant hosts or aberrant behavior.

Chapter 14

This chapter discusses techniques to determine which traffic is crossing service ports in a network. This includes simple lookups such as the port number, as well as banner grabbing and looking at expected packet sizes.

Chapter 15

This chapter discusses a step-by-step process for inventorying a network and identifying significant hosts within that network. Network mapping and inventory are critical steps in information security and should be done on a regular basis.

Conventions Used in This Book

The following typographical conventions are used in this book:

Italic

Indicates new terms, URLs, email addresses, filenames, and file extensions.

`Constant width`

Used for program listings, as well as within paragraphs to refer to program elements such as variable or function names, databases, data types, environment variables, statements, and keywords.

`Constant width bold`

Shows commands or other text that should be typed literally by the user.

`Constant width italic`

Shows text that should be replaced with user-supplied values or by values determined by context.

## PART I

Data

This section discusses the collection and storage of data for use in analysis and response. Effective security analysis requires collecting data from widely disparate sources, each of which provides part of a picture about a particular event taking place on a network.

To understand the need for hybrid data sources, consider that most modern bots are general purpose software systems. A single bot may use multiple techniques to infiltrate and attack other hosts on a network. These attacks may include buffer overflows, spreading across network shares, and simple password cracking. A bot attacking an SSH server with a password attempt may be logged by that host's SSH logfile, providing concrete evidence of an attack but no information on anything else the bot did. Network traffic might not be able to reconstruct the sessions, but it can tell you about other actions by the attacker—including, say, a successful long session with a host that never reported such a session taking place, no siree.

The core challenge in data-driven analysis is to collect sufficient data to reconstruct rare events without collecting so much data as to make queries impractical. Data collection is surprisingly easy, but making sense of what's been collected is much harder. In security, this problem is complicated by rare *actual* security threats. The majority of network traffic is innocuous and highly repetitive: mass emails, everyone watching the same YouTube video, file accesses. A majority of the small number of actual security attacks will be *really stupid* ones such as blind scanning of empty IP addresses. Within that minority is a tiny subset that represents actual threats such as file exfiltration and botnet communications.

All the data analysis we discuss in this book is I/O bound. This means that the process of analyzing the data involves pinpointing the correct data to read and then extracting it. Searching through the data costs time, and this data has a footprint: a single OC-3 can generate five terabytes of raw data per day. By comparison, an eSATA interface can read about 0.3 gigabytes per second, requiring several hours to perform *one* search across that data, assuming that you're reading and writing data across different disks. The need to collect data from multiple sources introduces redundancy, which costs additional disk space and increases query times.

A well-designed storage and query system enables analysts to conduct arbitrary queries on data and expect a response within a reasonable time frame. A poorly designed one takes longer to execute the query than it took to collect the data. Developing a good design requires understanding how different sensors collect data; how they complement, duplicate, and interfere with each other; and how to effectively store this data to empower analysis. This section is focused on these problems.

This section is divided into four chapters. Chapter 1 is an introduction to the general process of sensing and data collection, and introduces vocabulary to describe how different sensors interact with each other. Chapter 2 discusses sensors that collect data from network interfaces, such as *tcpdump* and NetFlow. Chapter 3 is concerned with host and service sensors, which collect data about various processes such as servers or operating systems. Chapter 4 discusses the implementation of collection systems and the options available, from databases to more current big data technology.

## CHAPTER 1

Sensors and Detectors: An Introduction

Effective information monitoring builds on data collected from multiple sensors that generate different kinds of data and are created by many different people for many different purposes. A sensor can be anything from a network tap to a firewall log; it is something that collects information about your network and can be used to make judgement calls about your network's security. Building up a useful sensor system requires balancing its completeness and its redundancy. A perfect sensor system would be complete while being nonredundant: complete in the sense that every event is meaningfully described, and nonredundant in that the sensors don't replicate information about events. These goals, probably unachievable, are a marker for determining how to build a monitoring solution.

No single type of sensor can do everything. Network-based sensors provide extensive coverage but can be deceived by traffic engineering, can't describe encrypted traffic, and can only approximate the activity at a host. Host-based sensors provide more extensive and accurate information for phenomena they're instrumented to describe. In order to effectively combine sensors, I classify them along three axes:

Vantage

The placement of sensors within a network. Sensors with different vantages will see different parts of the same event.

Domain

The information the sensor provides, whether that's at the host, a service on the host, or the network. Sensors with the same vantage but different domains provide complementary data about the same event. For some events, you might only get information from one domain. For example, host monitoring is the only way to find out if a host has been physically accessed.

Action

> How the sensor decides to report information. It may just record the data, provide events, or manipulate the traffic that produces the data. Sensors with different actions can potentially interfere with each other.

Vantages: How Sensor Placement Affects Data Collection

A sensor's *vantage* describes the packets that a sensor will be able to observe. Vantage is determined by an interaction between the sensor's placement and the routing infrastructure of a network. In order to understand the phenomena that impact vantage, look at Figure 1-1. This figure describes a number of unique potential sensors differentiated by capital letters. In order, these sensor locations are:

A

> Monitors the interface that connects the router to the Internet.

B

> Monitors the interface that connects the router to the switch.

C

> Monitors the interface that connects the router to the host with IP address 128.2.1.1.

D

> Monitors host 128.1.1.1.

E

> Monitors a spanning port operated by the switch. A spanning port records all traffic that passes the switch (see the section on port mirroring in Chapter 2 for more information on spanning ports).

F

> Monitors the interface between the switch and the hub.

G

> Collects HTTP log data on host 128.1.1.2.

H

> Sniffs all TCP traffic on the hub.

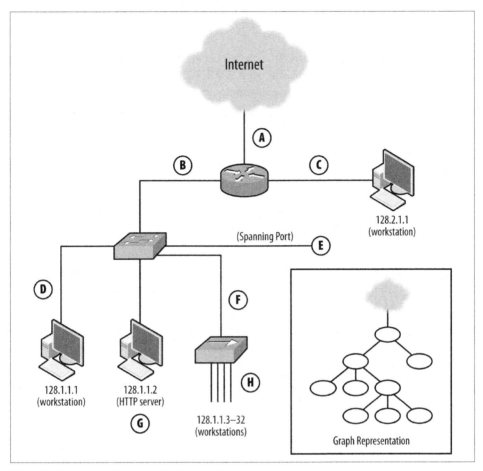

Figure 1-1. Vantage points of a simple network and a graph representation

Each of these sensors has a different vantage, and will see different traffic based on that vantage. You can approximate the vantage of a network by converting it into a simple node-and-link graph (as seen in the corner of Figure 1-1) and then tracing the links crossed between nodes. A link will be able to record any traffic that crosses that link en route to a destination. For example, in Figure 1-1:

- The sensor at position A sees only traffic that moves between the network and the Internet—it will not, for example, see traffic between 128.1.1.1 and 128.2.1.1.

- The sensor at B sees any traffic that originates or ends in one of the addresses "beneath it," as long as the other address is 128.2.1.1 or the Internet.

- The sensor at C sees only traffic that originates or ends at 128.2.1.1.

- The sensor at D, like the sensor at C, only sees traffic that originates or ends at 128.1.1.1.

- The sensor at E sees any traffic that moves between the switches' ports: traffic from 128.1.1.1 to anything else, traffic from 128.1.1.2 to anything else, and any traffic from 128.1.1.3 to 128.1.1.32 that communicates with anything *outside* that hub.

- The sensor at F sees a subset of what the sensor at E sees, seeing only traffic from 128.1.1.3 to 128.1.1.32 that communicates with anything *outside* that hub.

- G is a special case because it is an HTTP log; it sees only HTTP traffic (port 80 and 443) where 128.1.1.2 is the server.

- Finally, H sees any traffic where one of the addresses between 128.1.1.3 and 128.1.1.32 is an origin or a destination, as well as traffic between those hosts.

Note that no single sensor provides complete coverage of this network. Furthermore, instrumentation will require dealing with redundant traffic. For instance, if I instrument H and E, I will see any traffic from 128.1.1.3 to 128.1.1.1 twice. Choosing the right vantage points requires striking a balance between complete coverage of traffic and not drowning in redundant data.

When instrumenting a network, determining vantage is a three-step process: acquiring a network map, determining the potential vantage points, and then determining the optimal coverage.

The first step involves acquiring a map of the network and how it's connected together as well as a list of potential instrumentation points. Figure 1-1 is a simplified version of such a map.

The second step, determining the vantage of each point, involves identifying every potentially instrumentable location on the network and then determining what that location can see. This value can be expressed as a range of IP address/port combinations. Table 1-1 provides an example of such an inventory for Figure 1-1. A graph can be used to make a first guess at what vantage points will see, but a truly accurate model requires more in-depth information about the routing and networking hardware. For example, when dealing with routers it is possible to find points where the vantage is asymmetric (note that the traffic in Table 1-1 is all symmetric). Refer to "Network Layering and Its Impact on Instrumentation" on page 16 for more information.

Table 1-1. A worksheet showing the vantage of Figure 1-1

Vantage point	Source IP range	Destination IP range
A	Internet	128.1, 2.1.1-32
	128.1, 2.1.1-32	Internet
B	128.1.1.1-32	128.2.1.1, Internet
	128.2.1.1, Internet	128.1.1.1-32

Report

Simply provide information on all phenomena that the sensor observes. Reporting sensors are simple and important for baselining. They are also useful for developing signatures and alerts for phenomena that alerting and blocking sensors haven't yet been configured to recognize. Reporting sensors include NetFlow collectors, *tcpdump*, and server logs.

Event

An event sensor differs from a report sensor in that it consumes multiple data to produce an *event* that summarizes some subset of that data. For example, a host-based intrusion detection system might examine a memory image, find a malware signature in memory, and send an event indicating that its host was compromised by malware. At their most extreme, event sensors are black boxes that produce events in response to internal processes developed by experts. Event sensors include IDS and antivirus (AV).

Control

A controlling sensor, like an event sensor, consumes multiple data and makes a judgment about that data before reacting. Unlike an event sensor, a controlling sensor modifies or blocks traffic when it sends an event. Controlling sensors include IPSes, firewalls, antispam systems, and some anti-virus systems.

A sensor's action not only affects how a sensor reports data, but also how it affects the data it's observing. Controlling sensors can modify or block traffic. Figure 1-3 shows how these three different types of action interact with data. The figure shows the work of three sensors: *R*, a reporting sensor; *E*, an event sensor; and *C*, a controlling sensor. The event and control sensors are signature matching systems that react to the string ATTACK. Each sensor is placed between the Internet and a single target.

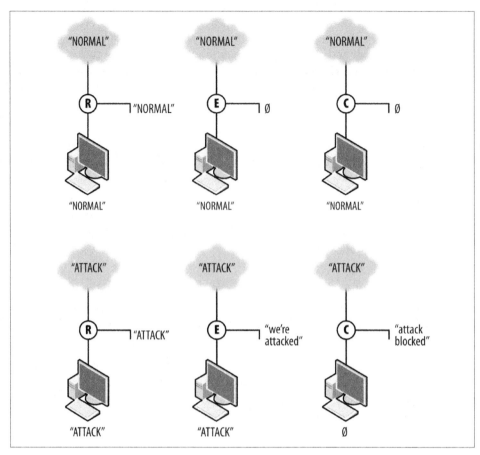

Figure 1-3. Three different sensor actions

R, the reporter, simply reports the traffic it observes. In this case, it reports both normal and attack traffic without affecting the traffic and effectively summarizes the data observed. E, the event sensor, does nothing in the presence of normal traffic but raises an event when attack traffic is observed. E does not stop the traffic; it just sends an event. C, the controller, sends an event when it sees attack traffic and does nothing to normal traffic. In addition, however, C *blocks* the aberrant traffic from reaching the target. If another sensor is further down the route from C, it will never see the traffic that C blocks.

Aggregation and Transport Tools

When evaluating a logging package, make a point of checking to see if it provides software that aggregates or transports records. These capabilities don't add data in response to phenomena, but they may modify the format and content of records.

Some examples include the use of aggregation in Cisco NetFlow and the various redirection and transport tools in *flow-tools*.[1] Historically, NetFlow records in their basic format (raw flows) were sent to a *collector*, which would then aggregate them into various reports. *flow-tools* provides a number of tools that can take flow data and route it to different sensors as needed.

Conclusion

The taxonomy introduced in this chapter should be sufficient to describe any sensors available for security monitoring and explain how they can potentially interact. This description is intended to be at a high enough level that an operator can start classifying sensors without getting mired in details. In Chapter 2 and Chapter 3, we discuss vantage, domain, and action in-depth in order to provide a more precise enumeration of how they relate to real systems.

---

1. The flow-tools mailing list and repository are both available for free download (*http://bit.ly/flow-tools*).

## CHAPTER 2

Network Sensors

A *network sensor* collects data directly from network traffic without the agency of an intermediary application, making them different from the host-based sensors discussed in Chapter 3. Examples include NetFlow sensors on a router and sensors that collect traffic using a sniffing tool such as *tcpdump*.

The challenge of network traffic is the challenge you face with all log data: actual security events are rare, and data costs time and storage space. Where available, log data is preferable because it's clean (a high-level event is recorded in the log data) and compact. The same event in network traffic would have to be extracted from millions of packets, which can often be redundant, encrypted, or unreadable. At the same time, it is very easy for an attacker to manipulate network traffic and produce legitimate-looking but completely bogus sessions on the wire. An event summed up in a 300-byte log record could easily be megabytes of packet data, wherein only the first 10 packets have any analytic value.

That's the bad news. The good news is that network traffic's "protocol agnosticism," for lack of a better term, means that it is also your best source for identifying blind spots in your auditing. Host-based collection systems require knowing that the host *exists* in the first place, and there are numerous cases where you're likely not to know that a particular service is running until you see its traffic on the wire. Network traffic provides a view of the network with minimal assumptions—it tells you about hosts on the network you don't know existed, backdoors you weren't aware of, attackers already inside your border, and routes through your network you never considered. At the same time, when you face a zero-day vulnerability or new malware, packet data may be the only data source you have.

The remainder of this chapter is broken down as follows. The next section covers *network vantage*: how packets move through a network and how to take advantage of that when instrumenting the network. The next section covers *tcpdump*, the fundamental network traffic capture protocol, and provides recipes for sampling packets, filtering them, and manipulating their length. The section after that covers NetFlow, a powerful traffic summarization approach that provides high-value, compact summary information about network traffic. At the end of the chapter, we look at a sample network and discuss how to take advantage of the different collection strategies.

Network Layering and Its Impact on Instrumentation

Computer networks are designed in *layers*. A layer is an abstraction of a set of network functionality intended to hide the mechanics and finer implementation details. Ideally, each layer is a discrete entity; the implementation at one layer can be swapped out with another implementation and not impact the higher layers. For example, the Internet Protocol (IP) resides on layer 3 in the OSI model; an IP implementation can run identically on different layer 2 protocols such as Ethernet or FDDI.

There are a number of different layering models. The most common ones in use are the OSI's seven layer model and TCP/IP's four layer model. Figure 2-1 shows these two models, representative protocols, and their relationship to sensor domains as defined in Chapter 1. As Figure 2-1 shows, the OSI model and TCP/IP model have a rough correspondence. OSI uses the following seven layers:

1. Physical: The *physical* layer is composed of the mechanical components used to connect the network together—the wires, cables, radio waves, and other mechanisms used to transfer data from one location to the next.

2. Data link: The *data link* layer is concerned with managing information that is transferred across the physical layer. Data link protocols, such as Ethernet, ensure that asynchronous communications are relayed correctly. In the IP model, the data link and physical layers are grouped together as the *link layer*.

3. Network: The *network layer* is concerned with the routing of traffic from one data link to another. In the IP model, the network layer directly corresponds to layer 2, the Internet layer.

4. Transport: The *transport* layer is concerned with managing information that is transferred across the network layer. It has similar concerns to the data link layer, such as flow control and reliable data transmission, albeit at a different scale. In the IP model, the transport layer is layer 3.

5. Session: The *session* layer is concerned with the establishment and maintenance of a session, and is focused on issues such as authentication. The most common example of a session layer protocol today is SSL, the encryption and authentication layer used by HTTP, SMTP, and many other services to secure communications.

6. Presentation: The *presentation* layer encodes information for display at a higher level. A common example of a presentation layer is MIME, the message encoding protocol used in email.

7. Application: The *application* layer is the service, such as HTTP, DNS, and SSH. OSI layers 5 through 7 correspond roughly to the application layer (layer 4) of the IP model.

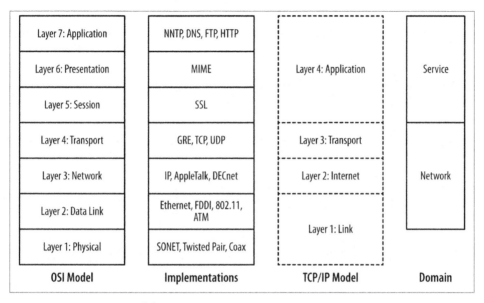

Figure 2-1. Layering models

The layering model is just that: a model rather than a specification, and models are necessarily imperfect. The TCP/IP model, for example, eschews the finer details of the OSI model, and there are a number of cases where protocols in the OSI model might exist in multiple layers. Network interface controllers (NICs) dwell on layers 1 and 2 in the model. The layers do impact each other, in particular through how data is transported (and is observable), and by introducing performance constraints into higher levels.

The most common place where we encounter the impact of layering on network traffic is the *maximum transmission unit* (MTU). The MTU is an upper limit on the size of a data frame, and impacts the maximum size of a packet that can be sent over that medium. The MTU for Ethernet is 1,500 bytes, and this constraint means that IP packets will almost never exceed that size.

The layering model also provides us with a clear difference between the network and service-based sensor domains. As Figure 2-1 shows, network sensors are focused on layers 2 through 4 in the OSI model, while service sensors are focused on layers 5 and above.

Layering and the Role of Network Sensors

It's logical to ask why network sensors can't monitor everything; after all, we're talking about attacks that happen *over a network*. In addition, network sensors can't be tampered with or deleted like host logs, and they will see things like scans or failed connection attempts that host logs won't.

Network sensors provide extensive coverage, but recovering exactly what happened from that coverage becomes more complex as you move higher up the OSI model. At layer 5 and above, issues of protocol and packet interpretation become increasingly prominent. Session encryption becomes an option at layer 5, and encrypted sessions will be unreadable. At layer 6 and layer 7, you need to know the intricacies of the actual protocol that's being used in order to extract meaningful information.

Protocol reconstruction from packet data is complex and ambiguous; TCP/IP is designed on end-to-end principles, meaning that the server and client are the only parties required to be able to construct a session from packets. Tools such as Wireshark (described in Chapter 9) or NetWitness can reconstruct the contents of a session, but these are approximations of what actually happened.

Network, host, and service sensors are best used to complement each other. Network sensors provide information that the other sensors won't record, while the host and service sensors record the actual event.

Recall from Chapter 1 that a sensor's vantage refers to the traffic that a particular sensor observes. In the case of computer networks, the vantage refers to the packets that a sensor observes either by virtue of transmitting the packets itself (via a switch or a router) or by eavesdropping (within a collision domain). Since correctly modeling vantage is necessary to efficiently instrument networks, we need to dive a bit into the mechanics of how networks operate.

Network Layers and Vantage

Network vantage is best described by considering how traffic travels at three different layers of the OSI model. These layers are across a shared bus or collision domain (layer 1), over network switches (layer 2), or using routing hardware (layer 3). Each layer provides different forms of vantage and mechanisms for implementing the same.

The most basic form of networking is across a *collision domain*. A collision domain is a shared resource used by one or more networking interfaces to transmit data. Examples of collision domains include a network hub or the channel used by a wireless router. A collision domain is called such because the individual elements can potentially send data at the same time, resulting in a collision; layer 2 protocols include mechanisms to compensate for or prevent collisions.

The net result is that layer 2 datagrams are broadcast across a common source, as seen in Figure 2-2. Network interfaces on the same collision domain all see the same datagrams; they *elect* to only interpret datagrams that are addressed to them. Network capture tools like *tcpdump* can be placed in promiscuous mode and will then record all the datagrams observed within the collision domain.

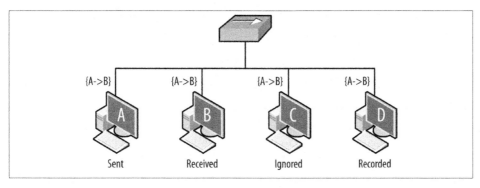

Figure 2-2. Vantage across collision domains

Figure 2-2 shows the vantage across a broadcast domain. As seen in this figure, the initial frame (A to B) is broadcast across the hub, which operates as a shared bus. Every host connected to the hub can receive and react to the frames, but only B should do so. C, a compliant host, ignores and drops the frame. D, a host operating in promiscuous mode, records the frame. The vantage of a hub is consequently all the addresses connected to that hub.

Shared collision domains are inefficient, especially with asynchronous protocols such as Ethernet. Consequently, layer 2 hardware such as Ethernet switches are commonly used to ensure that each host connected to the network has its own dedicated Ethernet port. This is shown in Figure 2-3.

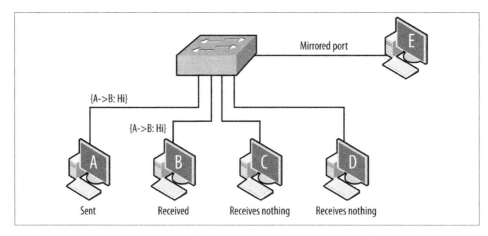

Figure 2-3. Vantage across a switch

A capture tool operating in promiscuous mode will copy every frame that is received at the interface, but the layer 2 switch ensures that the only frames an interface receives are the ones explicitly addressed to it. Consequently, as seen in Figure 2-3, the A to B frame is received by B, while C and D receive nothing.

There is a hardware-based solution to this problem. Most switches implement some form of *port mirroring*. Port mirroring configurations copy the frames sent between different ports to common mirrored ports in addition to their original destination. Using mirroring, you can configure the switch to send a copy of every frame received by the switch to a common interface. Port mirroring can be an expensive operation, however, and most switches limit the amount of interfaces or VLANs monitored.

Switch vantage is a function of the port and the configuration of the switch. By default, the vantage of any individual port will be exclusively traffic originating from or going to the interface connected to the port. A mirrored port will have the vantage of the ports it is configured to mirror.

Layer 3, when routing becomes a concern, is when vantage becomes messy. Routing is a semiautonomous process that administrators can configure, but is designed to provide some degree of localized automation in order to provide reliability. In addition, routing has performance and reliability features, such as the TTL, which can also impact monitoring.

Layer 3 vantage at its simplest operates like layer 2 vantage. Like switches, routers send traffic across specific ports. Routers can be configured with mirroring-like functionality, although the exact terminology differs based on the router manufacturer. The primary difference is that while layer 2 is concerned with individual Ethernet addresses, at layer 3 the interfaces are generally concerned with blocks of IP addresses because the router interfaces are usually connected via switches or hubs to dozens of hosts.

Layer 3 vantage becomes more complex when dealing with multihomed interfaces, such as the example shown in Figure 2-4. Up until this point, all vantages discussed in this book have been symmetric—if instrumenting a point enables you to see traffic from A to B, it also enables you to see traffic from B to A. A multihomed host like a router has multiple interfaces that traffic can enter or exit.

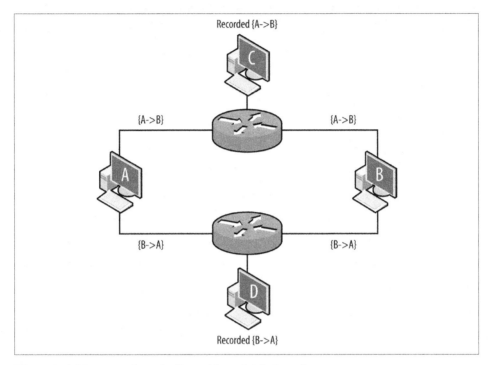

Figure 2-4. Vantage when dealing with multiple interfaces

Figure 2-4 shows an example of multiple interfaces and their potential impact on vantage at layer 3. In this example, A and B are communicating with each other: A sends the packet {A→B} to B, B sends the packet {B→A} to A. C and D are monitoring at the routers: router 1 is configured so that the shortest path from A to B is through it. Router 2 is configured so that shortest path from B to A is through it. The net effect of this configuration is that the vantages at C and D are asymmetric. C will see traffic from A to B, D will see traffic from B to A, but neither of them will see both sides of the interaction. While this example is contrived, this kind of configuration can appear due to business relationships and network instabilities. It's especially problematic when dealing with networks that have multiple interfaces to the Internet.

IP packets have a built-in expiration function: a field called the *time-to-live* (TTL) value. The TTL is decremented every time a packet crosses a router (not a layer 2 facility like a switch), until the TTL reaches zero. In most cases, the TTL should not be a problem

—most modern stacks set the TTL to at least 64, which is considerably longer than the number of hops required to cross the entire Internet. However, the TTL is manually modifiable and there exist attacks that can use the TTL for evasion purposes. Table 2-1 lists default TTLs by operating system.

Table 2-1. Default TTLs by operating system

Operating system	TTL value
Linux (2.4, 2.6)	64
FreeBSD	64
Mac OS X	64
Windows XP	128
Windows 7, Vista	128
Solaris	255

Figure 2-5 shows how the TTL operates. Assume that hosts C and D are operating on monitoring ports and the packet is going from A to B. Furthermore, the TTL of the packet is set to 2 initially. The first router receives the packet and passes it to the second router. The second router drops the packet; otherwise, it would decrement the TTL to zero. TTL does not directly impact vantage, but instead introduces an erratic type of blind spot—packets can be seen by one sensor, but not by another several routers later as the TTL decrements.

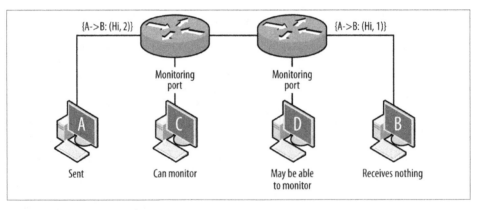

Figure 2-5. Hopping and router vantage

The net result of this is that the packet is observed by C, never received by B, and *possibly* (depending on the router configuration) observed at D.

Physical Taps

Instead of configuring the networking hardware to report data on a dedicated interface, you can monitor the cables themselves. This is done using network taps, which are objects that physically connect to the cables and duplicate traffic for monitoring purposes. Network taps have the advantage of moving the process of collecting and copying data off the network hardware, but only have the vantage of the cables to which they connect.

Network Layers and Addressing

Entities on a network will have multiple addresses that can be used to reach them. For example, the host *www.mysite.com* may have the IP address 196.168.1.1 and the Ethernet Address 0F:2A:32:AA:2B:14. These addresses are used to resolve the identity of a host at different abstraction layers of the network. In most networks, a host will have a MAC (Ethernet) address and an IPv4 or IPv6 address.

These addresses are dynamically moderated through various protocols, and various types of networking hardware will modify the relationships between addresses. The most common examples of these are DNS modifications, which associate a single name with multiple addresses and vice versa; this is discussed in more depth in Chapter 8. The following addresses are commonly used on networks:

MAC address
> A 48-byte identifier used by the majority of layer 2 protocols, including Ethernet, FDDI, Token Ring, Bluetooth, and ATM. MAC addresses are usually recorded as a set of six hexadecimal pairs (e.g., 12:34:56:78:9A:BC). MAC addresses are assigned to the hardware by the original manufacturer, and the first 24 bits of the interface are reserved as a manufacturer ID. As layer 2 addresses, MAC addresses don't route; when a frame is transferred across a router, the addressing information is replaced with the addressing information of the router's interface. IPv4 and IPv6 addresses are related to MAC addresses using *Address Resolution Protocol* (ARP).

IPv4 address
> An IPv4 address is a 32-bit integer value assigned to every routable host, with exceptions made for reserved dynamic address spaces (see Chapter 8 for more information on these addresses). IPv4 addresses are most commonly represented in dotted quad format: four integers between 0 and 255 separated by periods (e.g., 128.1.11.3).

IPv6 address
> IPv6 is the steadily advancing replacement for IPv4 that fixes a number of design flaws in the original protocol, in particular the allotment of IP addresses. IPv6 uses a 128-bit address to identify a host. By default, these addresses are described as a set of 16-bit hexadecimal values separated by colons (e.g., AAAA: 2134:0918:F23A:A13F:2199:FABE:FAAF). Given their length, IPv6 addresses use a number of conventions to shorten the representation: initial zeroes are trimmed, and the longest sequence of 16-bit zero values is eliminated and replaced by double colons (e.g., 0019:0000:0000:0000:0000:0000:0000:0182 becomes 19::182).

All of these relationships are dynamic, and multiple addresses at one layer can be associated with one address at a another layer. As discussed earlier, a single DNS name can be associated with multiple IP addresses through the agency of the DNS service. Similarly, a single MAC address can support multiple IP addresses through the agency of the ARP protocol. This type of dynamism can be used constructively (like for tunneling) and destructively (like for spoofing).

Packet Data

In the context of this book, packet data really means the output of *libpcap*, either through an IDS or *tcpdump*. Originally developed by LBNL's Network Research Group, *libpcap* is the fundamental network capture tool and serves as the collector for tools such as Snort, *bro*, and *tcpdump*.

Packet capture data is a large haystack with only scattered needles of value to you. Capturing this data requires balancing between the huge amount of data that can be captured and the data that it makes sense to actually capture.

Packet and Frame Formats

On almost any modern system, *tcpdump* will be capturing IP over Ethernet, meaning that the data actually captured by *libpcap* consists of Ethernet frames containing IP packets. While IP contains over 80 unique protocols, on any operational network, the overwhelming majority of traffic will originate from three protocols: TCP (protocol 6), UDP (protocl 17), and ICMP (protocol 1).

While TCP, UDP, and ICMP make up the overwhelming majority of IP traffic, a number of other protocols may appear in networks, in particular if VPNs are used. IANA has a complete list (*http://bit.ly/protocol-numbers*) of IP suite protocols. Some notable ones to expect include IPv6 (protocol number 41), GRE (protocol number 47), and ESP (protocol number 50). GRE and ESP are used in VPN traffic.

Full *pcap* capture is often impractical. The sheer size and redundancy of the data means that it's difficult to keep any meaningful fraction of network traffic for a reasonable time. There are three major mechanisms for filtering or limiting packet capture data: the use of rolling buffers to keep a timed subsample, manipulating the snap length to capture only a fixed size packet (such as headers), and filtering traffic using BPF or other filtering rules. Each approach is an analytic trade-off that provides different benefits and disadvantages.

Rolling Buffers

A *rolling buffer* is a location in memory where data is dumped cyclically: information is dropped linearly, and when the buffer is filled up, data is dumped at the beginning of the buffer, and the process repeats. Example 2-1 gives an example of using a rolling buffer with *tcpdump*. In this example, the process writes approximately 128 MB to disk, and then rotates to a new file. After 32 files are filled (specified by the -W switch), the process restarts.

Example 2-1. Implementing a rolling buffer in tcpdump

```
host$ tcpdump -i en1 -s 0 -w result -C 128 -W 32
```

Rolling buffers implement a time horizon on traffic analysis: data is available only as long as it's in the buffer. For that reason, working with smaller file sizes is recommended, because when you find something aberrant, it needs to be pulled out of the buffers quickly.

Limiting the Data Captured from Each Packet

An alternative to capturing the complete packet is to capture a limited subset of payload, controlled in *tcpdump* by the snaplen (-s) argument. Snaplen constrains packets to the frame size specified in the argument. If you specify a frame size of at least 68 bytes, you will record the TCP or UDP headers.[1] That said, this solution is a poor alternative to NetFlow, which is discussed later in this chapter.

Filtering Specific Types of Packets

An alternative to filtering at the switch is to filter after collecting the traffic at the spanning port. With *tcpdump* and other tools, this can be easily done using *Berkeley Packet Filtering* (BPF). BPF allows an operator to specify arbitrarily complex filters, and consequently your possiblities are fairly extensive. Some useful options are described in this section, along with examples. Figure 2-6 provides a breakdown of the headers for Ethernet frames, IP, UDP, ICMP, and TCP.

---

1. The snaplen is based on the Ethernet frame size, so 20 additional bytes have to be added to the size of the corresponding IP headers.

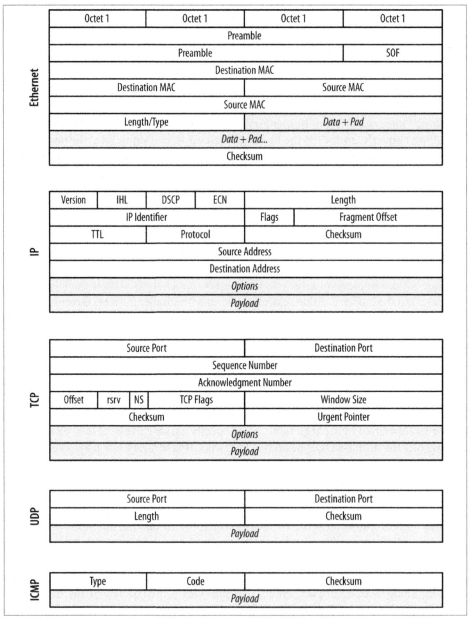

Figure 2-6. Frame and packet formats for Ethernet, IP, TCP, UDP, and ICMP

As we walk through the major fields, I identify BPF macros that describe and can be used to filter on these fields. On most Unix-style systems, the *pcap-filter* manpage provides a summary of BPF syntax. Available commands are also summarized in the FreeBSD manpage for BPF (*http://bit.ly/bsd-manpages*).

In an Ethernet frame, the most critical fields are the two MAC addresses. These 48-byte fields are used to identify the hardware addresses of the interfaces that sent and will receive the traffic. MAC addresses are restricted to a single collision domain, and will be modified as a packet traverses multiple networks (see Figure 2-5 for an example). MAC addresses are accessed using the *ether src* and *ether dst* predicates in BPF.

---

tcpdump and MAC Addresses

Most implementations of *tcpdump* require a command-line switch before showing link-level (i.e., Ethernet) information. In Mac OS X, the *-e* switch will show the MAC addresses.

Within an IP header, the fields you are usually most interested in are the IP addresses, the length, the TTL, and the protocol. The IP identifier, flags, and fragment offset are used for attacks involving packet reassembly—however, they are also largely a historical artifact from before Ethernet was a nearly universal transport protocol. You can get access to the IP addresses using src host and dst host predicates, which also allow filtering on netmasks.

Address Filtering in BPF

Addresses in BPF can be filtered using the various host and net predicates. To understand how these work, consider a simple *tcpdump* output.

```
host$ tcpdump -n -r sample.pcap  | head -5
reading from file sample.pcap, link-type EN10MB (Ethernet)
20:01:12.094915 IP 192.168.1.3.56305 > 208.78.7.2.389: Flags [S],
  seq 265488449, win 65535, options [mss 1460,nop, wscale 3,nop,
  nop,TS val 1111716334 ecr 0,sackOK,eol], length 0
20:01:12.094981 IP 192.168.1.3.56302 > 192.168.144.18.389: Flags [S],
  seq 1490713463, win 65535, options [mss 1460,nop,wscale 3,nop,
  nop,TS val 1111716334 ecr 0,sackOK,eol], length 0
20:01:12.471014 IP 192.168.1.102.7600 > 192.168.1.255.7600: UDP, length 36
20:01:12.861101 IP 192.168.1.6.17784 > 255.255.255.255.17784: UDP, length 27
20:01:12.862487 IP 192.168.1.6.51949 > 255.255.255.255.3483: UDP, length 37
```

src host or dst host will filter on exact IP addresses; filtering for traffic to or from 192.168.1.3 as shown here:

```
host$ tcpdump -n -r sample.pcap  src host 192.168.1.3 | head -1
reading from file sample.pcap, link-type EN10MB (Ethernet)
20:01:12.094915 IP 192.168.1.3.56305 > 208.78.7.2.389: Flags [S],
  seq 265488449, win 65535, options [mss 1460,nop,wscale 3,nop,
```

```
           nop,TS val 1111716334 ecr 0,sackOK,eol], length 0
host$ tcpdump -n -r sample.pcap  dst host 192.168.1.3 | head -1
reading from file sample.pcap, link-type EN10MB (Ethernet)
20:01:13.898712 IP 192.168.1.6.48991 > 192.168.1.3.9000: Flags [S],
  seq 2975851986, win 5840, options [mss 1460,sackOK,TS val 911030 ecr 0,
  nop,wscale 1], length 0
```

src net and dst net allow filtering on netblocks. The example below shows how we can progressively filter addresses in the 192.168.1 network using just the address or CIDR notation:

```
# use src net to filter just by matching octets
host$ tcpdump -n -r sample.pcap  src net 192.168.1 | head -3
reading from file sample.pcap, link-type EN10MB (Ethernet)
20:01:12.094915 IP 192.168.1.3.56305 > 208.78.7.2.389: Flags [S],
  seq 265488449, win 65535, options [mss 1460,nop,wscale 3,nop,nop,
  TS val 1111716334 ecr 0,sackOK,eol], length 0
20:01:12.094981 IP 192.168.1.3.56302 > 192.168.144.18.389: Flags [S],
  seq 1490713463, win 65535, options [mss 1460,nop,wscale 3,nop,
  nop,TS val 1111716334 ecr 0,sackOK,eol], length 0
# Match an address
host$ tcpdump -n -r sample.pcap  src net 192.168.1.5 | head -1
reading from file sample.pcap, link-type EN10MB (Ethernet)
20:01:13.244094 IP 192.168.1.5.50919 > 208.111.133.84.27017: UDP, length 84
# Match using a CIDR block
host$ tcpdump -n -r sample.pcap  src net 192.168.1.64/26 | head -1
reading from file sample.pcap, link-type EN10MB (Ethernet)
20:01:12.471014 IP 192.168.1.102.7600 > 192.168.1.255.7600: UDP, length 36
```

To filter on protocols, use the ip proto predicate. BPF also provides a variety of protocol-specific predicates, such as tcp, udp, and icmp. Packet length can be filtered using the less and greater predicates, while filtering on the TTL requires more advanced bit manipulation, which is discussed later.

The following snippet filters out all traffic except that coming within this block (hosts with the netmask /24).

```
host$ tcpdump -i en1 -s 0 -w result src net 192.168.2.0/24
```

Example 2-2 demonstrates filtering with *tcpdump*

Example 2-2. Examples of filtering using tcpdump

```
host$ # Filtering out everything but internal traffic
host$ tcpdump -i en1 -s 0 -w result src net 192.168.2.0/24 && dst net \
    192.168.0.0/16
host$ # Filtering out everything but web traffic, identified by port
host$ tcpdump -i en1 -s 0 -w result ((src port 80 || src port 443) && \
    (src net 192.168.2.0))
```

In TCP, the port number and flags are the most critical. TCP flags are used to maintain the TCP state machine, while the port numbers are used to distinguish sessions and for service identification. Port numbers can be filtered using the `src port` and `dst port` switches, as well as the `src portrange` and `dst portrange` switches, which filter across a range of port values. BPF supports a variety of predicates for TCP flags, including `tcp-fin`, `tcp-syn`, `tcp-rst`, `tcp-push`, `tcp-ack`, and `tcp-urg`.

Address Classes and CIDR Blocks

An IPv4 address is a 32-bit integer. For convenience, these integers are usually referred to using dotted quad notation like o1.o2.o3.o4, so the IP address represented by 0x000010FF is written as 0.0.16.255. Level 3 routing is almost never done to individual addresses, but instead to groups of addresses—historically, *classes*, now *netblocks*.

It used to be that a class A address (0.0.0.0–127.255.255.255) had the high order bit set to zero, the next 7 assigned to an entity, and the remaining 24 bits under the owner's control. This gave the owner 2^{24} addresses to work with. A class B address (128.0.0.0–191.255.255.255) assigned 16 bits to the owner, and class C (192.0.0.0–223.255.255.255) assigned 8 bits. This approach led rapidly to address exhaustion, and in 1993, *Classless Inter-Domain Routing* (CIDR) was developed to replace the naive class system. Under the CIDR scheme, users are assigned a netblock via an address and a netmask. The netmask indicates which bits in the address the user can manipulate, and by convention, those bits are set to zero. For example, a user who owns the addresses 192.28.3.0–192.28.3.255 will be given the block 192.28.3.0/24.

As with TCP, the UDP port numbers are most important, and are accessible using the same `port` and `portrange` switches as TCP.

Because ICMP is the Internet's error-message passing protocol, ICMP messages tend to contain extremely rich data. The ICMP type and code are the most critical because they define the syntax for whatever payload (if any) follows. BPF provides a variety of type and code specific filters, including `icmp-echoreply`, `icmp-unreach`, `icmp-tstamp`, and `icmp-redirect`.

What If It's Not Ethernet?

For the sake of brevity, this book focuses exclusively on IP over Ethernet, but you may well encounter a number of other transport and data protocols. The majority of these protocols are highly specialized and may require additional capture software besides the tools built on *libpcap*.

ATM

> *Asynchronous Transfer Mode*, the great IP slayer of the '90s, ATM is now largely used for ISDN and PSTN transport, and some legacy installations.

Fibre Channel
> Primarily used for high-speed storage, Fibre Channel is the backbone for a variety of SAN implementations.

CAN
> Stands for *controller area network*. Primarily associated with embedded systems such as vehicular networks, CAN is a bus protocol used to send messages in small isolated networks.

Any form of filtering imposes performance costs. Implementing a spanning port on a switch or a router sacrifices performance that the switch or router could be using for traffic. The more complicated a filter is, the more overhead is added by the filtering software. At nontrivial bandwidths, this will be a problem.

NetFlow

NetFlow is a traffic summarization standard developed by Cisco Systems and originally used for network services billing. While not intended for security, NetFlow is fantastically useful for that purpose because it provides a compact summary of network traffic sessions that can be rapidly accessed and contains the highest-value information that you can keep in a relatively compact format. NetFlow has been increasingly used for security analysis since the publication of the original *flow-tools* package in 1999, and a variety of tools have been developed that provide NetFlow with additional fields, such as selected snippets of payload.

The heart of NetFlow is the concept of a *flow*, which is an approximation of a TCP session. Recall that TCP sessions are assembled at the endpoint by comparing sequence numbers. Juggling all the sequence numbers involved in multiple TCP sessions is not feasible at a router, but it is possible to make a reasonable approximation using timeouts. A flow is a collection of identically addressed packets that are closely grouped in time.

NetFlow v5 Formats and Fields

NetFlow v5 is the earliest common NetFlow standard, and it's worth covering the values in NFv5's fields before discussing alternatives. NetFlow's fields (listed in Table 2-2) fall into three broad categories: fields copied straight from IP packets, fields summarizing the results of IP packets, and fields related to routing.

Table 2-2. NetFlow v5 fields

Bytes	Name	Description
0–3	srcaddr	Source IP address
4–7	dstaddr	Destination IP address
8–11	nexthop	Address of the next hop on the router

Bytes	Name	Description
12–13	input	SNMP index of the input interface
14–15	output	SNMP index of the output interface
16–19	packets	Packets in the flow
20–23	dOctets	Number of layer 3 bytes in the flow
24–27	first	sysuptime at flow start [a]
28–31	last	sysuptime at the time of receipt of the last flow's packet
32–33	srcport	TCP/UDP source port
34–35	dstport	TCP/UDP destination port, ICMP type and code
36	pad1	Padding
37	tcp_flags	Or of all TCP flags in the flow
38	prot	IP protocol
39	tos	IP type of service
40–41	src_as	ASN number of source
42–43	dst_as	ASN of destination
44	src_mask	Source address prefix mask
45	dst_mask	Destination address prefix mask
46–47	pad2	Padding bytes

[a] This value is relative to the router's system uptime.

The srcaddr, dstaddr, srcport, dstport, prot, and tos fields of a NetFlow record are copied directly from the corresponding fields in IP packets. Flows are generated for *every* protocol in the IP suite, however, and that means that the srcport and dstport fields, which strictly speaking are TCP/UDP phenomena, don't necessarily always mean something. In the case of ICMP, NetFlow records the type and code in the dstport field. In the case of other protocols, ignore the value.

The packets, dOctets, first, last, and tcp_flags fields all summarize traffic from one or more packets. packets and dOctets are simple totals, with the caveat that the dOctets value is the layer 3 total of octets, meaning that IP and protocol headers are added in (e.g., a one-packet TCP flow with no payload will be recorded as 40 bytes, and a one-packet UDP flow with no payload as 28 bytes). The first and last values are, respectively, the first and last times observed for a packet in the flow.

tcp_flags is a special case. In NetFlow v5, the tcp_flags field consists of an OR of all the flags that appear in the flow. In well-formed flows, this means that the SYN, FIN, and ACK flags will always be high.

The final set of fields—nexthop, input, output, src_as, dst_as, src_mask, and dst_mask—are all routing-related. These values can be collected only at a router.

"Flow and Stuff:" NetFlow v9 and IPFIX

Cisco developed several versions of NetFlow over its lifetime, with NetFlow v5 ending up as the workhorse implementation of the standard. But v5 is a limited and obsolete standard, focused on IPv4 and designed before flows were commonly used. Cisco's solution to this was NetFlow v9, a template-based flow reporting standard that enabled router administrators to specify what fields were included in the flow.

Template-based NetFlow has since been standardized by the IETF as IPFIX.[2] IPFIX provides several hundred potential fields for flows, which are described in RFC 5102 (*http://bit.ly/rfc-5102*).

The priority of the standard is on network monitoring and traffic analysis rather than information security. To address optional fields, IPFIX has the concept of a "vendor space." In the course of developing the SiLK toolkit, the CERT Network Situational Awareness Group at Carnegie Mellon University developed a set of security-sensitive fields that are in their IPFIX vendor space and provide a set of useful fields for security analysis.

NetFlow Generation and Collection

NetFlow records are generated directly by networking hardware appliances (e.g., a router or a switch), or by using software to convert packets into flows. Each approach has different trade-offs.

Appliance-based generation means using whatever NetFlow facility is offered by the hardware manufacturer. Different manufacturers use similar sounding but different names than Cisco, such as Jflow by Juniper Networks and NetStream by Huawei. Because NetFlow is offered by so many different manufacturers with a variety of different rules, it's impossible to provide a technical discussion about the necessary configurations in the space provided by this book. However, the following rules of thumb are worth noting:

- NetFlow generation can cause performance problems on routers, especially older models. Different companies address this problem in different ways, ranging from reducing the priority of the process (and dropping records), to offloading the Net-Flow generation task to optional (and expensive) hardware.

- Most NetFlow configurations default to some form of sampling in order to reduce the performance load. For security analysis, NetFlow should be configured to provide unsampled records.

---

2. RFC 5101 (*http://bit.ly/rfc-5101*), 5102 (*http://bit.ly/rfc-5102*), and 5103 (*http://bit.ly/rfc-5103*).

- Many NetFlow configurations offer a number of aggregation and reporting formats. You should collect raw NetFlow, not aggregations.

The alternative to router-based collection is to use an application that generates NetFlow from *pcap* data, such as the CERT's Yet Another Flowmeter (YAF) tool (*http://tools.netsa.cert.org*), softflowd (*http://bit.ly/softflowd*), or the extensive flow monitoring tools provided by QoSient's Argus (*http://bit.ly/qo-argus*) tool. These applications take *pcap* as files or directly off a network interface and aggregate the packets as flows. These sensors lack a router's vantage, but at the same time are able to devote more processing resources to analyzing the packets and can produce richer NetFlow output, incorporating features such as deep packet inspection.

Further Reading

1. Richard Bejtlich, *The Tao of Network Security Monitoring: Beyond Intrusion Detection* (Addison–Wesley, 2004).

2. Kevin Fall and Richard Stevens, *TCP/IP Illustrated, Volume 1: The Protocols (2nd Edition)* (Addison–Wesley, 2011).

3. Michael Lucas, *Network Flow Analysis* (No Starch Press, 2010).

4. Radia Perlman, *Interconnections: Bridges, Routers, Switches, and Internetworking Protocols (2nd Edition)* (Addison–Wesley, 1999).

5. Chris Sanders, *Practical Packet Analysis: Using Wireshark to Solve Real-World Problems* (No Starch Press, 2011).

## CHAPTER 3

Host and Service Sensors: Logging Traffic at the Source

In this chapter, we consider sensors operating in the host or service domain. Host sensors include system logs as well as host-based security tools such as antivirus (AV) software and tools like McAfee's Host Intrusion Prevention System (HIPS). Host sensors monitor the state of a host and its operating system, tracking features such as local disk usage and peripheral access. Service sensors, including HTTP server logs and mail transfer logs, describe the activity of a particular service: who sent mail to whom, what URLs were accessed in the last five minutes, activity that's moderated through a particular service. For the sake of clarity, I will use "log" to refer to either host or service logs throughout the remainder of the chapter.

Where available, logs are often preferable to network data because they are generated by the affected process, removing the process of interpretation and guesswork often needed with network data. Host and service logs provide concrete information about events that, viewed from the network perspective, are hard to reconstruct.

Logs have a number of problems, the most important one being a management headache —in order to use one, you have to know it exists and get access to it. In addition, host-based logs come in a large number of formats, many of them poorly documented. At the risk of a sweeping generalization, the overwhelming majority of logs are designed for debugging and troubleshooting individual hosts, not to evaluate security across networks. Where possible, you'll often need to reconfigure them to include more security-relevant information, possibly needing to write your own aggregation programs. Finally, logs are a target; attackers will modify or disable logging if possible.

Logs complement network data. Network data is good at finding blind spots, confirming the results of logs and identifying things that the logs won't pick up. An effective security system combines both: network logs for a broad scope, logs for fine detail.

The remainder of this chapter is focused on data from a number of host logs, including system logfiles. We begin by discussing several varieties of log data and preferable message formats. We then discuss specific host and service logs: Unix system logs, HTTP server log formats, and email log formats.

Accessing and Manipulating Logfiles

Operating systems have dozens of processes generating log data at any time. In Unix systems, these logfiles are usually stored as text files in the */var/log* directory. Example 3-1 shows this directory for Mac OS X (the ellipses indicate where lines were removed for clarity).

Example 3-1. A /var/log directory from a Mac OS X system

```
drwxr-xr-x   2 _uucp          wheel      68 Jun 20  2012 uucp
...
drwxr-xr-x   2 root           wheel      68 Dec  9  2012 apache2
drwxr-xr-x   2 root           wheel      68 Jan  7 01:47 ppp
drwxr-xr-x   3 root           wheel     102 Mar 12 12:43 performance
...
-rw-r--r--   1 root           wheel     332 Jun  1 05:30 monthly.out
-rw-r-----   1 root           admin    6957 Jun  5 00:30 system.log.7.bz2
-rw-r-----   1 root           admin    5959 Jun  6 00:30 system.log.6.bz2
-rw-r-----   1 root           admin    5757 Jun  7 00:30 system.log.5.bz2
-rw-r-----   1 root           admin    5059 Jun  8 00:30 system.log.4.bz2
-rw-r--r--   1 root           wheel     870 Jun  8 03:15 weekly.out
-rw-r-----   1 root           admin   10539 Jun  9 00:30 system.log.3.bz2
-rw-r-----   1 root           admin    8476 Jun 10 00:30 system.log.2.bz2
-rw-r-----   1 root           admin    5345 Jun 11 00:31 system.log.1.bz2
-rw-r--r--   1 root           wheel  131984 Jun 11 18:57 vnetlib
drwxrwx---  33 root           admin    1122 Jun 12 00:23 DiagnosticMessages
-rw-r-----   1 root           admin    8546 Jun 12 00:30 system.log.0.bz2
-rw-r--r--   1 root           wheel  108840 Jun 12 03:15 daily.out
-rw-r--r--   1 root           wheel   22289 Jun 12 04:51 fsck_hfs.log
-rw-r-----   1 root           admin  899464 Jun 12 20:11 install.log
```

Note several features of this directory. The *system.log* files are started daily at 0030 and are differentiated numerically. There are a number of subdirectories for handling various services. Check the configuration of each individual service you want to acquire logfiles for, but it's not uncommon for Unix systems to dump them to a subdirectory of */var/log* by default.

Unix logfiles are almost always plain text. For example, a brief snippet of a system log reads as follows:

```
$ cat system.log
Jun 19 07:24:49 local-imac.home loginwindow[58]: in pam_sm_setcred(): Done
    getpwnam()
Jun 19 07:24:49 local-imac.home loginwindow[58]: in pam_sm_setcred(): Done
```

```
            setegid() & seteuid()
Jun 19 07:24:49 local-imac.home loginwindow[58]: in pam_sm_setcred():
            pam_sm_setcred: krb5 user admin doesn't have a principal
Jun 19 07:24:49 local-imac.home loginwindow[58]: in pam_sm_setcred(): Done
            cleanup3
```

The majority of Unix system logs are text messages created by filling in templates with specific event information. This kind of *templated text* is easy to read, but doesn't scale very well.

As of Vista, Windows has extensively revamped their logging structure. Windows recognizes two classes of logfiles: Windows logs and application/service logs. Windows logs are further subdivided into five classes:

Application log
  The application log contains messages from individual applications. Note that services such as IIS may use auxiliary logs to contain additional information.

Security log
  Contains security events, such as logon attempts and audit policy changes.

System log
  Messages about system status, such as driver failures.

Forwardedevents log
  Stores events from remote hosts.

These logs are recorded in *%SystemRoot%\System32\Config* by default on most Windows installs; however, the more effective mechanism for accessing and reading the files is to use the Windows Event Viewer, as seen in Figure 3-1.

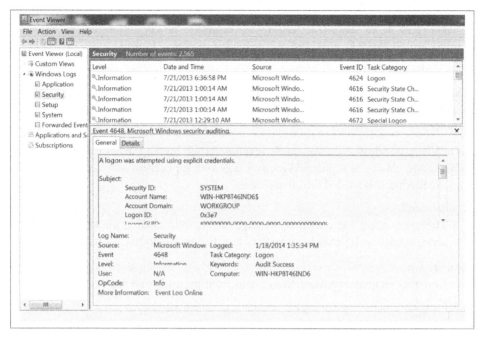

Figure 3-1. The Windows event log

Note the use of the Event ID in Figure 3-1; as with Unix systems, the Windows event messages are templated text, though Windows explicitly identifies the type of event using a unique numeric code. These messages are accessible from Microsoft's website.

Application logfiles are much less consistently located. As seen in the */var/log* directory, administrative structure may be set up to record a logfile in a fixed location, but almost every application has the ability to move around logfiles as necessary. When working with a particular application, consult its documentation to find out where it drops logs.

The Contents of Logfiles

Logs are usually designed to provide debugging and troubleshooting information for an administrator on the host. Because of this, you will often find that host-based logs require both some degree of parsing and some degree of reorganization to make them satisfactory security logs. In this section, we discuss mechanisms for interpreting, troubleshooting, and converting host log data.

The Characteristics of a Good Log Message

Before discussing how to convert a log message, and before complaining about how bad most log messages are, it behooves us to describe what a good security message should look like. A good security log should be *descriptive*, it should be *relatable* to other data, and it should be *complete*.

A descriptive message is one that contains enough information for an analyst to identify all necessary accessible resources for the event described by the message. For example, if a host log records that a user attempted to illegally access a file, it should contain the user's ID and the file accessed. A host log recording a change in group permissions for a user needs to record the user and the group. A log recording a failed remote login attempt should include the ID that attempted the login and the address that attempted the login.

For example, consider a log message about a failed login attempt on host 192.168.2.2, local name *myhost*. A nondescriptive message would look like this:

```
Mar 29 11:22:45.221 myhost sshd[213]: Failed login attempt
```

This message doesn't tell me anything about why the failure occurred and doesn't provide any information to differentiate between this and any other failed login attempts. I have no information on the target of the attack; is it against the *admin* account or some user? Analysts with only this information will have to reconstruct the attempt solely from timing data, and they can't even be sure what host was contacted because the name of the host is nondescriptive and there is no addressing information.

A more descriptive message would look like this:

```
Mar 29 11:22:45.221 myhost (192.168.2.2) sshd[213]: Failed
    login attempt from host 192.168.3.1 as 'admin',
    incorrect password
```

A good mental exercise for building a descriptive message is to fall back to the "five Ws and one H" approach from investigation and journalism: who, what, when, where, why, and how. The nondescriptive log message answers what (failed login) and when, and provides a partial answer where (*myhost*). The descriptive log message answers who (192.168.3.1 as *admin*), why and how (incorrect password), and provides a better where.

A relatable message is one where the event is easily related to information from other sources. For host-based events, this requires IP address and timing information including whether an event was remote or physically local, if the event was remote, the IP address and port of the remote event, and the IP address and port of the host. Relatability is a particular headache when dealing with service logs, as these types of logs often introduce additional addressing schemes on top of IP. For example, here's an unrelatable mail log message:

```
Mar 29 11:22:45.221 myhost (192.168.2.2) myspamapp[213]:
    Message <21394.283845@spam.com> title 'Herbal Remedies and Tiny Cars'
    from 'spammer@spam.com' rejected due to unsolicited commercial content
```

The message has a lot of information, but it has no way to relate the message sent back to a particular IP address that sent the message. When looking at log messages, consider how you will relate this information to other sources, *particularly* network traffic. A more relatable message would be as follows:

```
Mar 29 11:22:45.221 myhost (192.168.2.2) myspamapp[213]:
    Message <21394.283845@spam.com> title 'Herbal Remedies and Tiny Cars'
    from 'spammer@spam.com' at SMTP host 192.168.3.1:2034 rejected due
    to unsolicited commercial content
```

This example includes client port and addressing information, so I can now relate it to network traffic.

A complete log message is one that contains all the information about a particular event within that single log message. Completeness reduces the number of records an analyst has to search through and provides the analyst with a clear indicator that there is no further information to acquire from this process. Incomplete messages are usually a function of complicated process. For example, an antispam tool might run several different filters on a message, with each filter and the final decision being a separate log line. For example:

```
Mar 29 11:22:45.221 myhost (192.168.2.2) myspamapp[213]:
    Received Message <21394.283845@spam.com> title
    'Herbal Remedies and Tiny Cars' from 'spammer@spam.com' at
    SMTP host 192.168.3.1:2034
Mar 29 11:22:45.321 myhost (192.168.2.2) myspamapp[213]:
    Message <21394.283845@spam.com> passed reputation filter
Mar 29 11:22:45.421 myhost (192.168.2.2) myspamapp[213]:
    Message <21394.283845@spam.com> FAILED Bayesian filter
Mar 29 11:22:45.521 myhost (192.168.2.2) myspamapp[213]:
    Message <21394.283845@spam.com> Dropped
```

With incomplete messages, you have to track state across multiple messages, each of which gives a snippet of information and which you're going to have to group together to do any useful analysis. Consequently, I prefer the message to be aggregated at the start, like this:

```
Mar 29 11:22:45.521 myhost (192.168.2.2) myspamapp[213]:
    Received Message <21394.283845@spam.com> title
    'Herbal Remedies and Tiny Cars' from 'spammer@spam.com' at
    SMTP host 192.168.3.1:2034 reputation=pass Bayesian=FAIL decision=DROP
```

Log messages are often only minimally modifiable directly. Instead, to build an effective message you might have to write some kind of logging shim. For example, if the log system outputs syslog messages, you can receive and parse those messages, convert them to a friendlier format, and then forward them on. When considering converting logfiles, in addition to the rules above, consider the following:

Convert time to epoch time

Almost all record correlation involves identifying the same phenomenon from different sensors, meaning that you need to look for records that are close in time. Converting all time values to epoch time reduces parsing complexity, throws out the nightmare of time zones and daylight saving time, and ensures a consistent treatment for a consistent value.

Make sure sensors are synchronized
A corrollary to the first note; make sure that when sensors report the same event, they are reporting the same time. Trying to correct for this after the fact is terribly difficult, so make sure that all the sensors are coordinated, that they all report the same time, and that the clocks are corrected and resynchronized regularly.

Include addressing information
Wherever possible, include the flow five-tuple (source IP, destination IP, source port, destination port, protocol). If some of the values can be inferred from the record (e.g., HTTP servers are running TCP), they can be dropped.

Ensure that delimiters are understood by the logger
On several occasions, I have encountered helpful administrators reconfiguring HTTP logs to use pipes rather than spaces as delimiters. A worthy sentiment, except when the logging module doesn't know to escape the pipe when it occurs in text. If the logger can change its delimiter and understands that the change requires escaping the character, let the logger do it.

Use error codes rather than text if possible
Text doesn't scale well—it's bulky, difficult to parse, and often repetitive. Logging systems that generate template messages can also include an error code of some kind as a compact representation of the message. Use this rather than text to save space.

Existing Logfiles and How to Manipulate Them

We can break logfiles into three major categories: *columnar*, *templated*, or *annotative*. Columnar logs record records in discrete columns that are distinguishable by delimiters or fixed text width. Templated logfiles look like English text, but the text comes from a set of document templates and is enumerable. Annotative logfiles use multiple text records to describe a single event.

Columnar data, such as HTTP's CLF format, records one message per event. This message is a summary of the entire event, and consists of a fixed set of fields in columnar format. Columnar logs are relatively easy to deal with as the fields are cleanly delineated and the format is rigid; every message has the same columns and the same information.

When dealing with columnar data, keep in mind the following:

- Is the data delimited or fixed-width? If it's fixed-width, are there fields that could conceivably exceed that width, and if so, are the results truncated or is the column expanded?

- If the data is delimited, is the delimiter escaped when used in the fields? Customizable formats (such as HTTP logs) may use a default delimiter and automatically escape it; if you decide to use your own delimiter, it probably won't be automatically escaped.

- Is there a maximum record length? If there is a maximum record length, you may encounter truncated messages with missing fields.

ELF and CLF logfiles, discussed later in this chapter, are good examples of columnar formats.

Templated text messages record one message per event, but the events are recorded as unformatted English text. The messages are *templated* in the sense that they come from a fixed and enumerable set of templates. Where possible, it's best to convert templated text messages into some kind of indexed numeric format. In the best case, this is at least partly done. For example, the Windows Event Log shown in Figure 3-1 has an Event ID that describes the type of event and can be used to determine the other arguments that will be provided.

When dealing with templated text, keep in mind the following:

- Can you get a complete list of the log messages? As an example, consider the Windows logfile in Figure 3-1. Each of these messages is text, but it has a unique integer ID for the message. Check the documentation for a list of all potential log messages.

Converting Text to Columns

Templated text can be parsed; the messages belong to an enumerable set and can conceivably be converted into a columnar format. Creating such a system, however, requires developing an intermediary application that can read the text, parse each individual message, and deposit the result in a schema. Doing so is a nontrivial development task (and will have to be updated when new messages are developed), but it also can reduce the amount of space required and increase the readability of the data.

1. From whatever documentation you can find on the text format, identify and select the messages most relevant to security. Any conversion script is going to consist of a bunch of regular expressions, and the fewer expressions you have to maintain, the happier you'll be.

2. For each message, identify the parameters it contains. As an example, consider the following made-up templated messages: "Antispam tool SPAMKILLER identifies email <*12938@yahoo.com*> as Spam," "Antispam tool SPAMKILLER identifies email <*12938@yahoo.com*> as Commercial," "Antispam tool SPAMKILLER identifies email <*12938@yahoo.com*> as Legitimate." There are three potential parameters

---

here: the name of the antispam tool (enumerable), the message ID (a string), and the output (enumerable).

3. Once you've identified parameters for each potential message, merge the parameters to create a superset. The goal of this stage is to create a schema representation of all the parameters that a message may potentially have; a particular message may not have all of them.

4. Try to generate at least one event record for every templated message. Documentation can be inaccurate.

In annotative logs, a single event is split across multiple messages unified through a common ID. Event logs, system logs, and antispam may all potentially use this format. Annotative logs spread an event across multiple messages, and effectively parsing them requires identifying the common identifier, pulling all of those messages, and dealing with the potential for missing messages.

Representative Logfile Formats

In this section, we discuss several common log formats, including ELF and CLF, the standard log formats for HTML messages. The formats discussed here are customizable, and we provide guidelines for improving the log messages in order to provide more security-relevant information.

HTTP: CLF and ELF

HTTP is the modern Internet's reason for existence, and since its development in 1991, it has metamorphosed from a simple library protocol into the Internet's glue. Applications for which, 10 years ago, a developer would have implemented a new protocol are now routinely offloaded to HTTP and web servers.

HTTP is a challenging protocol to nail down. The core protocol is incredibly simple, but any modern web browsing session involves combining HTTP, HTML, and JavaScript to create ad hoc clients of intense complexity. In this section, we briefly discuss the core components of HTTP with a focus on the analytical aspects.

HTTP is fundamentally a very simple file access protocol. To understand how simple it is today, try the exercise in Example 3-2 using *netcat*. *netcat* (which can also be invoked as *nc*, perhaps because administrators find it so useful that they want to make it easy to invoke) is a flexible network port access tool that can be used to directly send information to ports. It is handy for scripting and capable of a variety of tasks with minimum automation.

Example 3-2. Accessing an HTTP server using the command line

```
host$ echo 'GET /' | nc www.oreilly.com 80 > oreilly.html
host$ kill %1
```

Executing the command in the previous example should produce a valid HTML file. In its simplest, most unadorned form, HTTP sessions consist of opening up a connection, passing a method and a URI, and receiving a file in return.

HTTP is simple enough to be run at the command line by hand if need be—however, that also means that an enormous amount of functionality is handed over to optional headers. When dealing with HTTP logs, the primary challenge is deciding which headers to include and which to ignore.

HTTP Headers Worth Noting

There are well over a hundred unique HTTP headers, tracked in RFC 4229 (*http://bit.ly/ rfc-4229*). Of these, a limited number are particularly critical to track. These include:

Cookie

The Cookie header describes the contents of HTTP cookies sent by the client to the server.

Host

The Host header defines the name of the host that the client is contacting. This is critical when dealing with virtually hosted HTTP servers—that is, multiple servers at the same IP address differentiated by their domain name.

Referer

The *Referer* (sic) header includes the URL of the web page containing the link that initiated this request.

User-Agent

The User-Agent header provides information on the HTTP client, generally the type of client and the build.

There are two standards for HTTP log data: common log format (CLF) and extended log format (ELF). Most HTTP log generators (such as Apache's *mod_log*) provide extensive configuration options.

CLF is a single-line logging format developed by NCSA for the original HTTP server; the W3C provides a minimal definition of the standard (*http://bit.ly/CLF-format*). A CLF event is defined as a seven-value single-line record in the following format:

```
remotehost rfc931 authuser [date] "request" status bytes
```

Where remotehost is the IP name or address of the remote host, rfc931 is the remote login account name of the user, authuser is the user's authenticated name, date is the date and time of the request, request is the request, status is the HTTP status code, and bytes is the number of bytes.

Pure CLF has several eccentricities that can make parsing problematic. The rfc931 and authuser fields are effectively artifacts; in the vast majority of the CLF records, the fields will be set to "–". The actual format of the date value is unspecified and can vary between different HTTP server implementations.

A common modification of CLF is *Combined Log Format*. The Combined Log Format adds two additional fields to CLF: the HTTP referer field and the user-agent string.

ELF is an expandable columnar format that has largely been confined to IIS, although tools such as Bluecoat also use it for logging. As with CLF, the W3C maintains the standard on their website (*http://bit.ly/log-file-format*).

An ELF file consists of a sequence of directives followed by a sequence of entries. Directives are used to define attributes common to the entries, such as the date of all entries (the Date directive), and the fields in the entry (the Fields directive). Each entry in ELF is a single HTTP request, and the fields that are defined by the directive are included in that entry.

ELF fields come in one of three forms: *identifier, prefix-identifier*, or *prefix(header)*. The prefix is a one or two character string that defines the direction the information took (c for client, s for server, r for remote). The identifier describes the contents of the field, and the *prefix(header)* value includes the corresponding HTTP header. For example, cs-method is in the *prefix-identifier* format and describes the method sent from client to server, while time is a plain *identifier* denoting the time at which the session ended.

Example 3-3 shows simple outputs from CLF, Combined Log Format, and ELF. As the example shows, each event is a single line.

Example 3-3. Examples of CLF and ELF

```
#CLF
192.168.1.1 - - [2012/Oct/11 12:03:45 -0700] "GET /index.html" 200
1294

# Combined Log Format
192.168.1.1 - - [2012/Oct/11 12:03:45 -0700] "GET /index.html" 200 1294
"http://www.example.com/link.html" "Mozilla/4.08 [en] (Win98; I ;Nav)"

#ELF
#Version: 1.0
#Date: 2012/Oct/11 00:00:00
#Fields: time c-ip cs-method cs-uri
12:03:45 192.168.1.1 GET /index.html
```

Most HTTP logs are some form of CLF output. Although ELF is an expandable format, I find the need to carry the header around problematic in that I don't expect to change formats that much, and would rather that individual log records be interpretable without this information. Based on principles I discussed earlier, here is how I modify CLF records:

1. Remove the rfc931 and authuser fields. These fields are artifacts and waste space.

2. Convert the date to epoch time and represent it as a numeric string, In addition to my general disdain for text over numeric representations, time representations have never been standardized in HTTP logfiles. You're better off moving to a numeric format to ignore the whims of the server.

3. Incorporate the server IP address, the source port, and the destination port. I expect to move the logfiles to a central location for analysis, so I need the server address to differentiate them. This gets me closer to a five-tuple that I can correlate with other data.

4. Add the duration of the event, again to help with timing correlation.

5. Add the host header. In case I'm dealing with virtual hosts, this also helps me identify systems that contact the server *without* using DNS as a moderator.

Cookbook: Creating Logfiles

Log configuration in Apache is handled via the *mod_log_config* module, which provides the ability to express logs using a sequence of string macros. For example, to express the default CLF format, you specify it as:

```
LogFormat "%h %l %u %t \"%r\" %>s %b"
```

Combined Log Format is expressed as:

```
LogFormat "%h %l %u %t \"%r\" %>s %b \"%{Referer}i\" \"%{User-agent}i\""
```

While my extended format contains the hostname, local IP address, server port, epoch time, request string, request status, response size, response time, referer, user-agent string, and host from the request:

```
LogFormat "%h %A %p %{msec}t \"%r\" %>s %b %T \"%{Referer}i\"
    \"${User-Agent}i\" \"${Host}i\""
```

Logging in *nginx* is controlled with HttpLogModule, which uses a similar log_format directive. To configure CLF, specify it with:

```
log_format clf $remote_addr - $remote_user [$time_local] "$request"
    $status $body_bytes_sent;
```

Combined Log Format is defined as follows:

```
log_format combined $remote_addr - $remote_user [$time_local] "$request"
    $status $body_bytes_sent "$http_referer" "$http_user_agent";
```

My extended format is defined as:

```
log_format extended $server_addr $remote_addr $remote_port $msec
    "$request$" $status $body_bytes_sent $request_time $http_referer
    $http_user_agent $http_host
```

SMTP

SMTP log messages vary by the MTA used and are highly configurable. In this section, we discuss two log formats that are representative of the major Unix and Windows families: *sendmail* and Microsoft Exchange.

In this section, we focus on logging the transfer of email messages. The logging tools for these applications provide an enormous amount of information about the server's internal status, connection attempts, and other data that, while enormously valuable, requires a book of its own.

Sendmail moderates mail exchange through *syslog*, and consequently is capable of sending an enormous number of informational messages besides the actual email transaction. For our purposes, we are concerned with two classes of log messages: messages describing connections to and from the mail server, and messages describing actual mail delivery.

By default, *sendmail* will send messages to */var/maillog*, although the logging information it sends is controlled by *sendmail*'s internal logging level. *Sendmail* uses its own internal logging level ranging from 1 to 96; a log level of *n* logs all messages of severity 1 to *n*. Notable log levels include 9 (all message deliveries logged), 10 (inbound connections logged), 12 (outbound connections logged), and 14 (connection refusals logged). Of note is that anything above log level 8 is considered an informational log in *syslog*, and anything above 11 a debug log message.

A *sendmail* log line consists of five fixed values, followed by a list of one or more *equates*:

```
<date> <host> sendmail[<pid>]: <qid>: <equates>
```

Where <date> is the date, <host> is the name of the host, sendmail is a literal string, <pid> is the sendmail process ID, and the <qid> is an internal queue ID used to uniquely identify messages. Sendmail sends at least two log messages when sending an email message, and the only way to group those messages together is through the qid. Equates are descriptive parameters given in the form <key>=<value>. *Sendmail* can send a number of potential equates, listed in Table 3-1 for messages.

For every email message received, *sendmail* generates at least two log lines. The first line is the *receiver* line, and describes the message's point of origin. The final line, the *sender* line, describes the disposition of the mail: sent, quarantined, and where it was delivered to.

Table 3-1. Relevant sendmail equates

Equate	Description
arg1	Current *sendmail* implementations enable internal filtering using rule sets; arg1 is the argument passed to the ruleset.
from	The from address of the envelope.
msgid	The message ID of the email.
quarantine	If *sendmail* quarantines a mail, this is the reason it was held.
reject	If *sendmail* rejects a mail, this is the reason for rejection.
relay	This is the name and address of the host that sent the message; in recipient lines, it's the host that sent it, in sender lines, the host that received it.
ruleset	This is the ruleset that processed the message, and provides the justification for rejecting, quarantining, or sending the message.
stat	The status of a message's delivery.
to	The email address of a target; multiple to equates can appear in the same line.

Sendmail will take one of four basic actions with a message: reject it, quarantine it, bounce it, or send it. Rejection is implemented by message filtering and is used for spam filtering; a rejected message is dropped. Quarantined messages are moved off the queue to a separate area for further review. A bounce means the mail was not sent to the target, and results in a nondelivery report being sent back to the origin.

Managing Email Rules and Filtering

Email traffic analysis is complicated, largely because email is attacked constantly (via spam), and there's a constantly escalating war between spammers and defenders. Even in a relatively small enterprise, it's easy to build a complex defensive infrastructure with relatively little work. In addition to the spam and defensive issues, email operates in its own little world—the IP addresses logged by email infrastructure are pretty much exclusively used by the email infrastructure.

As usual, the first step in email instrumentation is figuring out how email is routed. Is there some kind of dedicated antispam hardware at the gateway, such as a Barracude or an IronPort box? How many SMTP servers are there, and how do they connect to the actual email servers (POP, IMAP, Eudora, Exchange)? Figure out where a mail message will be sent if it's correctly routed, quarantined, rejected, or bounced. If webmail is available, figure out where it actually is; where is the webmail server, what's the route to SMTP, etc.

Once you've identified the hardware, figure out what blocking is going on. Blocking techniques include black-box sources (such as AV or IronPort's reputation service), public blacklists such as SpamHaus's SBL, and internal rules. Each requires a little different treatment.

Since black-box detection systems are basically opaque, it's important to track what version of the system's knowledge base is being used and when the system is updated; verifying updates with network monitoring is a good idea. If you have multiple instances of the same detector, make sure that their updates are coordinated.

Most blacklist services are publically accessible. Knowing which organization runs the blacklist, the frequency of its updates, and the delivery mechanisms are all good things. As with AV, verifying communications (particularly if its a DNSBL) is also a good thing.

Internal monitoring should be identified, audited, and kept under version control. Because these are the rules that you have the most control over, it's also a good idea to compare them to the rest of your blocking infrastructure and see what can be pushed out of the email system. If you're blocking a particular address, for example, you might be better off blocking at the router or the firewall.

Email works within its own universe, and the overwhelming majority of IP addresses recorded in email logs are the addresses of other email servers. To that end, while SMTP tracking is important, it's often the case that to fully figure out what happened with a message, you also need to track the IMAP or POP3 servers.

Microsoft Exchange: Message Tracking Logs

Exchange has one master log format for handling messages, the Message Tracking Log (MTL).

Table 3-2. MTL fields

Field name	Description
date-time	ISO 8601 representation of the date and time format.
client-ip	The IP address of the host that submitted the message to the server.
client-hostname	The client_ip's FQDN.
server-ip	The IP address of the server.
server-hostname	The server_ip's FQDN.
source-context	This is optional information about the source, such as an identifier for the transport agent.
connector-id	The name of the connector.
source	Exchange enumerates a number of source identities for defining the origin of a message, such as an inbox rule, a transport agent, or DNS. The source field will contain this identity.
event-id	The event type. This is also an enumerable quantity, and includes a number of status messages about how the message was handled.

Field name	Description
internal-message-id	This is an internal integer identifier used by Exchange to differentiate messages. The ID is not shared between Exchange servers, so if a message is passed around, this value will change.
message-id	This is the standard SMTP message ID. Exchange will create one if the message does not already have one.
network-message-id	This is a message ID like _internal-message-id+ except that it is shared across copies of the message and created when a message is cloned or duplicated, such as when it's sent to a distribution list.
recipient-address	The addresses of the recipients; this is a semicolon-delimited list of names.
recipient-status	This is a *per-recipient* status code indicating how each recipient was handled
total-bytes	The total size of the message in bytes.
recipient-count	The size of recipient-address in terms of number of recipients.
related-recipient-address	Certain Exchange events (such as redirection) will result in additional recipients being added to the list; those addresses are added here.
reference	This is message-specific information; the contents are a function of the type of message (defined in event-id).
message-subject	The subject found in the Subject: header.
sender-address	The sender, as specified in the Sender: header; if Sender: is absent, From: is used instead.
return-path	The return email address, as specified in Mail From:.
message-info	Event-type dependent message information.
directionality	The direction of the message; an enumerable quantity.
tenant-id	No longer used.
original-client-ip	The IP address of the client.
original-server-ip	The IP address of the server.
custom-data	Additional data dependent on the type of event.

Logfile Transport: Transfers, Syslog, and Message Queues

Host logs can be transferred off their hosts in a number of ways depending on how the logs are generated and on the capabilities of the operating system. The most common approaches involve using regular file transfers or the *syslog* protocol. A newer approach uses *message queues* to transport log information.

Transfer and Logfile Rotation

Most logging applications write to a rotating logfile (see, for example, the rotated system logs in "Accessing and Manipulating Logfiles" on page 36). In these cases, the logfile will be closed and archived after a fixed period and a new file started. Once the file is closed, it can be copied over to a different location to support analytics.

File transfer is simple. It can be implemented using *ssh* or any other copying protocol. The major headache is ensuring that the files are actually complete when copied; the rotation period for the file effectively dictates your response time. For example, if a file is rotated every 24 hours, then you will, on average, have to wait a day to get a hold of the latest events.

Syslog

The grandfather of systematic system logging utilities is *syslog*, a standard approach to logging originally developed for Unix systems that now comprises a standard, a protocol, and a general framework for discussing logging messages. Syslog defines a fixed message format and the ability to send that message to logger daemons that might reside on the host or be remotely located.

All syslog messages contain a time, a *facility*, a *severity*, and a text message. Table 3-3 and Table 3-4 describe the facilities and priorities encoded in the syslog protocol. As Table 3-3 shows, the facilities referred to by syslog comprise a variety of fundamental systems (some of them largely obsolete). Of more concern is what facilities are *not* covered—DNS and HTTP, for example. The priorities (in Table 3-4) are generally more germane, as the vocabulary for their severity has entered into common parlance.

Table 3-3. syslog facilities

Value	Meaning
0	Kernel
1	User-level
2	Mail
3	System daemons
4	Security/Authorization
5	Syslogd
6	Line printer
7	Network news
8	UUCP
9	Clock daemon
10	Security/Authorization
11	ftpd

Value	Meaning
12	ntpd
13	Log audit
14	Log alert
15	Clock daemon
16-23	Reserved for local use

Table 3-4. syslog priorities

Value	Meaning
0	Emergency: system is unusable
1	Alert: action must be taken immediately
2	Critical: critical conditions
3	Error: error conditions
4	Warning: warning conditions
5	Notice: normal but significant condition
6	Informational: informational messages
7	Debug: debugging information

Syslog's reference implementations are UDP-based, and the UDP standard results in several constraints. Most important, UDP datagram length is constrained by the MTU of the layer 2 protocol carrying the datagram, effectively imposing a hard limit of about 1,450 characters on any syslog message. The syslog protocol itself specifies that messages should be less than 1,024 characters, but this is rarely observed while the UDP cutoff *will* affect long messages. In addition, syslog runs on top of UDP, which means that when messages are dropped, they are lost forever.

The easiest way to solve this problem is to use TCP-based syslog, which is implemented in the open source domain with tools such as syslog-ng (*http://bit.ly/syslog-ng*) and rsyslog (*http://www.rsyslog.com*). Both of these tools provide TCP transport, as well as a number of other capabilities such as database interfaces, the ability to rewrite messages *en route*, and selective transport of syslog messages to different receivers. Windows does not support syslog natively, but there exist a number of commercial applications that provide similar functionality.

CEF: The Common Event Format

Syslog is a transport protocol—it doesn't specify anything about the actual contents of a message. A number of different organizations have attempted to develop interoperability standards for security applications, such as Common Intrusion Detection Framework (CIDF) and Intrusion Detection Message Exchange Format (IDMEF). None of them have achieved serious industry acceptance.

What *has* been accepted widely is CEF. Originally developed by ArcSight (now part of Hewlett-Packard) to provide sensor developers with a standard format in which to send messages to their SIEM. CEF is a record format that specifies events using a numeric header and a set of key/value pairs. For example, a CEF message for an attack from host 192.168.1.1 might look like this:

```
CEF:0|My Attack Detector|Test|1.0|1000|Attack|5|src=192.168.1.1
```

CEF is transport-agnostic, but the majority of CEF implementations use syslog as their transport of choice. The actual specification and key/value assignments are available from HP.

Further Reading

1. Richard Bejtlich, *The Practice of Network Security Monitoring: Understanding Incident Detection and Response* (No Starch Press, 2013).

2. Anton Chuvakin, *Logging and Log Management: The Authoritative Guide to Dealing with Syslog, Audit Logs, Alerts, and other IT 'Noise'* (Syngress, 2012).

## CHAPTER 4

Data Storage for Analysis: Relational Databases, Big Data, and Other Options

This chapter focuses on the mechanics of storing data for traffic analysis. Data storage points to the basic problem in information security analysis: information security events are scattered in a vast number of innocuous logfiles, and effective security analysis requires the ability to process large volumes of data quickly.

There are a number of different approaches available for facilitating rapid data access, the major choices being flat files, traditional databases, and the emergent NoSQL paradigm. Each of these designs offers different strengths and weaknesses based on the structure of the data stored and the skills of the analysts involved.

Flat file systems record data on disk and are accessed directly by analysts, usually using simple parsing tools. Most log systems create flat file data by default: after producing some fixed number of records, they close a file and open up a new file. Flat files are simple to read and analyze, but lack any particular tools for providing optimized access.

Database systems such as Oracle and Postgres are the bedrock of enterprise computing. They use well-defined interface languages, you can find system administrators and maintainers with ease, and they can be configured to provide extremely stable and scalable solutions. At the same time, they are *not* designed to deal with log data; the data we discuss in this book has a number of features that ensure that much of the power of a relational database will go unused.

Finally, there are the emerging technologies loosely grouped under "NoSQL" and "big data." These include distributed platforms such as Hadoop, databases like MongoDB and Monet, and specialized tools like Redis and Apache SOLR. These tools are capable, with the right hardware infrastructure, of providing extremely powerful and reliable distributed query tools. However, they require heavy duty programming and system administration skills as well as a significant hardware commitment.

Analysis involves returning to the well multiple times—when working on a problem, analysts will go back to the main data repository and pull related data. The data they choose will be a function of the data they've already chosen as patterns become apparent and questions start taking shape (see Chapter 10 for this workflow in more depth). For this reason, efficient data access is a critical engineering effort; the time to access data directly impacts the number of queries an analyst can make, and that concretely impacts the type of analyses they will do.

Choosing the right data system is a function of the volume of data stored, the type of data stored, and the population that's going to analyze it. There is no single right choice, and depending on the combination of queries expected and data stored, each of these strategies can be the best.

Log Data and the CRUD Paradigm

The CRUD (create, read, update, and delete) paradigm describes the basic operations expected of a persistent storage system. Relational database management systems (RDBMS), the most prevalent form of persistent storage, expect that users will regularly and asynchronously update existing contents. Relational databases are primarily designed for data integrity, not performance.

Ensuring data integrity requires a significant amount of the system's resources. Databases use a number of different mechanisms to enforce integrity, including additional processing and metadata on each row. These features are necessary for the type of data that RDBMSes were designed for. That data is not log data.

This difference is shown in Figure 4-1. In RDBMSes, users add and query data from a system constantly, and the system spends resources on tracking these interactions. Log data does not change, however; once an event has occurred, it is never updated. This changes the data flow as shown in the figure on the right. In log collection systems, the only things that write to disk are the sensors; users only *read* from disk.

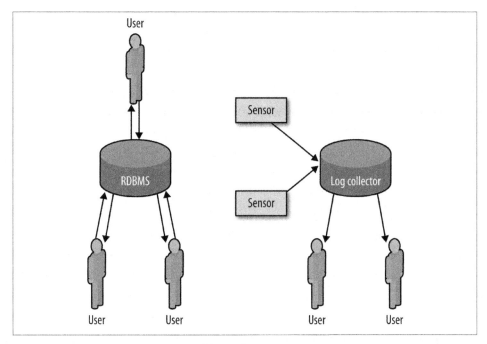

Figure 4-1. Comparing RDBMS and log collection systems

This separation of duties between users and sensors means that, when working with log data, the integrity mechanisms used by databases are wasted. For log data, a properly designed flat file collection system will often be just as fast as a relational database.

Creating a Well-Organized Flat File System: Lessons from SiLK

In Chapter 5, we discuss SiLK, the analysis system CERT developed to handle large Netflows. SiLK was a very early big data system. While it doesn't use current big data technologies, it was designed around similar principles, and understanding how those principles work can inform the development of more current systems.

Log analysis is primarily I/O bound, meaning that the primary constraint on performance is the number of records read, as opposed to the complexity of the algorithms run on the records. For example, in the original design of SiLK, we found that it was considerably faster to keep compressed files on disk—the performance hit from reading the records off of disk was much higher than the performance hit of decompressing a file in memory.

Because performance is I/O bound, a good query system will read the minimum number of relevant records possible. In log collection systems, the most effective way to reduce the records read is to index them by time and *always* require a user to specify the time queried. In SiLK, log records are stored in hourly files in a daily hierarchy, for exam-

ple: */data/2013/03/14/sensor1_20130314.00* to */data/2013/03/14/sensor1_20130314.23*.
SiLK commands include a globbing function that hides the actual filenames from the
user; queries specify a start date and an end date, which in turn is used to derive the
files.

This partitioning process does not have to stop with time. Because network traffic (and
log data) is usually dominated by a couple of major protocols, those individual protocols
can be split off into their own files. In SiLK installations, it's not unusual to split web
traffic from all other traffic because web traffic makes up 40–80% of the traffic on most
networks.

As with most data partitioning schemes, there's more art than science in deciding when
to stop subdividing the data. As a rule of thumb, having no more than three to five
further partitions after time is acceptable because as you add additional partitions, you
increase complexity for users and developers. In addition, determining the exact partitioning scheme usually requires some knowledge of the traffic on the network, so you
can't do it until *after* you've acquired a better understanding of the network's structure,
composition, and the type of data it encounters.

Data Formats and Data Optimization

You decide to store data in flat files and create a system that accepts a billion records a
day. You decide to use ASCII text, and are recording zero-packed source and destination
IP addresses. This means that your IPv4 addresses will take 15 bytes of storage each,
compared to the 4-byte binary representation. This means that every day, you will sac-
rifice 22 GB of space for that text representation. If you have a single GigE interface to
transfer that data on, you will use three minutes just to transfer the wasted space.

Once you start working in large volume datasets, spatial dependencies become issues
on disks (affecting query time and storage duration), as well as on the network (affecting
query time and performance). Because your operations are I/O bound, converting representations to a binary format will save space, increase performance, and, far too often,
actually make a design implementable.

The problem of actually developing a compact binary representation of data has largely
been addressed through a number of different representation schemes developed by
Google and other companies. These tools all work in roughly the same way: you specify
a schema using an interface definition language (IDL), and then run a tool on the schema
to create a linkable library that can read and write data in a compact format. There is a
loose similarity to XML and JSON, but with an emphasis on a highly compact, binary
representation.

Google developed the first of these systems in the form of Protocol Buffers. Multiple
tools are available now, including but not limited to:

Protocol Buffers (http://bit.ly/protocolbuff)
> Google describes these as a "smaller, faster, simpler" version of XML. Language bindings are available in Java, C++, and Python. Protocol Buffers (PB) are the oldest implementation and, while less feature-rich than other implementations, are very stable.

Thrift (http://thrift.apache.org)
> Originally from Facebook and now maintained by the Apache foundation. In addition to providing serialization and deserialization capabilities, Thrift includes data transport and RPC mechanisms.

Avro (http://bit.ly/avro-doc)
> Developed in tandem with Hadoop, and more dynamic than either PB or Thrift. Avro specifies schemas using Javascript Object Notation (JSON), and transfers the schema as part of the messsage contents. Avro is consequently more flexible to schema changes.

Other serialization standards exist, including MessagePack (*http://www.msgpack.org*), ICE (*http://www.zeroc.com*), and Etch (*http://etch.apache.org*). As of the publication of this book, however, PB, Thrift, and Avro are considered the big three.

Taking a record and converting it into an all-ASCII string binary format is a waste of space. The goal of any conversion process should be to reduce the amount of gratuitous data in the record; read the section "The Characteristics of a Good Log Message" on page 38 in Chapter 3 for further discussion on how to reduce record sizes.

A Brief Introduction to NoSQL Systems

The major advance in big data in the past decade has been the popularization of NoSQL big data systems, particularly the MapReduce paradigm introduced by Google. MapReduce is based around two concepts from functional programming: mapping, which is the independent application of a function to all elements in a list, and reducing, which is the combination of consecutive elements in a list into a single element. Example 4-1 clearly shows how these elements work.

Example 4-1. Map and reduce functions in Python

```
>>> # Map works by applying a function to every element in an array, for example, we
... # create a sample array of 1 to 10
>>> sample = range(1,11)
>>> # We now define a doubling function
...
>>> def double(x):
...     return x * 2
...
>>> # We now apply the doubling function to the sample data
... # This results in a list whose elements are double the
... # original's
```

```
...
>>> map(double, sample)
[2, 4, 6, 8, 10, 12, 14, 16, 18, 20]
>>> # Now we create a 2-parameter function which adds two elements
...
>>> def add(a, b):
...     return a + b
...
>>> # We now run reduce with add and the sample, add is applied
... # to every element in turn, so we get add(1,2) which produces
... # 3, the list now looks like [3,3,...] as opposed to
... # [1,2,3....], and the process is repeated, 3 is added to 3
... # and the list now looks like [6,4,...] until everything is
... # added
...
>>> reduce(add, sample)
55
```

MapReduce is a convenient paradigm for parallelization. Map operations are implicitly parallel because the mapped function is applied to list element individually, and reduction provides a clear description of how the results are combined. This easy parallelization enables the implementation of any of a number of big data approaches.

For our purposes, a big data system is a distributed data storage architecture that relies on massive parallelization. Recall the discussion above about how flat file systems can enhance performance by intelligently indexing data. But now instead of simply storing the hourly file on disk, split it across multiple hosts and run the same query on those hosts in parallel. The finer details depend on the type of storage, for which we can define three major categories:

Key stores

Including MongoDB, Accumulo, Cassandra, Hypertable, and LevelDB. These systems effectively operate as a giant hashtable in that a complete document or data structure is associated with a key for future retrieval. Unlike the other two options, key store systems don't use schemas; structure and interpretation are dependent on the implementor.

Columnar databases

Including MonetDB, Sensage, and Paraccel. Columnar databases split each record across multiple column files with the same index.

Relational databases

Including MySQL, Postgres, Oracle, and Microsoft's SQL Server. RDBMSes store complete records as individually distinguishable rows.

Figure 4-2 explains these relations graphically. In a key store, the record is stored by its key while the relationship of the recorded data and any schema is left to the user. In a columnar database, rows are decomposed into their individual fields and then stored, one field per file, in individual column files. In an RDBMS, each row is a unique and distinguishable entity. The schema defines the contents of each row, and rows are stored sequentially in a file.

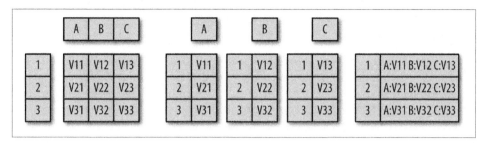

Figure 4-2. Comparing data storage systems

Key stores are a good choice when you have no idea what the structure of the data is, you have to implement your own low level queries (e.g., image processing and anything not easily expressed in SQL), or even if the data has structure. This reflects their original purpose of supporting unstructured text searches across web pages. Key stores will work well with web pages, *tcpdump* records containing payload, images, and other datasets where the individual records are relatively large (on the order of 60 kb or more, around the size of the HTML on a modern web page). However, if the data possesses some structure, such as the ability to be divided into columns, or extensive and repeated references to the same data, then a columnar or relational model may be preferable.

Columnar databases are preferable when the data is easily divided into individual log records that don't need to cross-reference each other, and when the contents are relatively small, such as the CLF and ELF record formats discussed in Chapter 3. Columnar databases can optimize queries by picking out and processing data from a subset of the columns in each record; their performance improves when they query on fewer columns or return fewer columns. If your schema has a limited number of columns (for example, an image database containing a small date field, a small ID field, and a large image field), then the columnar approach will not provide a performance boost.

RDBMSes were originally designed for information that's frequently replicated across multiple records, such as a billing database where a single person may have multiple bills. RDBMSes work best with data that can be subdivided across multiple tables. In security environments, they're usually best suited to maintaining personnel records, event reports, and other knowledge—things that are produced after processing data or that reflect an organization's structure. RDBMSes are good at maintaining integrity and concurrency; if you need to update a row, they're the default choice. The RDBMS approach is probably unwarranted if your data doesn't change after creating it, individual records don't have cross-references, or your schemas store large blobs.

Other Miscellaneous Storage Tools

In addition to the three major storage systems discussed earlier, there are a couple of other tools and techniques for improving access speed. These storage systems are less prevalent than the big three, but are generally optimized for specific data or query types.

Graph databases include Neo4j, ArangoDB, and Titan. Graph databases provide scalable, highly efficient queries when working with graph data (see Chapter 13). Traditional database systems, including the three mentioned earlier, are notoriously poor at managing graphs, as any representation involves making multiple queries to generate the graph over time. Graph databases provide queries and tools for analyzing graph structures.

The Lucene library and its companion search engine, Solr, make up an open source text search engine tool.

Redis is a memory-based key value storage system. If you need to rapidly access data which can fit in memory (for example, lookup tables), Redis is a very good choice for handling the lookup and modifications.

Finally, if your wallet is big enough, you should consider the advantages of solid state storage (SSD). SSD solutions can be expensive, but they have the enormous advantage of being functionally transparent as part of the filesystem. At the high end, companies like Violin memory, Fusion-IO, and STEC provide multi-TB rack mounted units that can be configured to receive and process data at wire speeds.

What Storage Approach to Use

When choosing a storage architecture, consider the type of data you will collect and the type of reporting you will do with it. Do you expect that you will mostly generate fixed reports, or do you expect that your analysts will conduct a large number of exploratory queries?

Table 4-1 provides a summary of the types of decisions that go into choosing a storage approach. The decisions are listed in order of preference: 1 is best, 3 is worst, X means don't bother at all. We will discuss each option in detail in order to explain how they impact storage choices.

Table 4-1. Making decisions about data systems

Situation	Relational	Columnar	Key-store
Have access to multiple disks and hosts	2	1	1
Have access to a single host	1	X	X
Data is less than a terabyte	1	2	3
Data is multiterabyte	2	1	1
Expect to update rows	1	X	X
Never update rows	2	1	1
Data is unstructured text	2	3	1
Data has structure	2	1	3
Individual records are small	2	1	3
Individual records are large	3	2	1
Analysts have some development skills	1	1	1
Analysts have no development skills	1	1	2

The first decision is really a hardware decision. Big data systems such as columnar databases and key stores will *only* provide you with a performance advantage if you can run parallel nodes, and the more the better. If you have a single host, or even less than four hosts available, you are probably better off sticking with more traditional database architectures in order to exploit their more mature administrative and development facilities.

The next pair of questions is really associated with that hardware question: is your data really that big? I use a terabyte as an arbitrary cutoff point for big data because I can realistically buy a 1 TB SSD. If your data isn't that big, again default to relational databases or an in-memory storage system like Redis.

The next question is associated with data flow and the CRUD paradigm. If you expect to regularly update the contents of a row, then the best choice is a relational database. Columnar and other distributed architectures are designed around the idea that their contents are relatively static. It's possible to update data in them, but it usually involves some kind of batch process where the original data is removed and replacements are put in place.

Streaming Analytics Versus Storing in One Place

The classic analytical system is a centralized repository. Data from multiple sensors is fed into a huge database, and then analysts pull data out of the huge database. This is not the only approach, and a hot alternative uses streaming analytics. At the time of writing this book, distributed streaming analytic systems such as Storm (*http://storm-project.net*) and IBM's Websphere (*http://ibm.co/ibm-websphere*) are taking off.

Streaming approaches enable sophisticated real-time analysis by processing the data as a stream of information. In a stream, the data is touched once by a process, and minimal past state is maintained.

Streaming processing is extremely useful in areas where the process is well-defined and there is a need for real-time analysis. As such, it is not particularly useful for exploratory analysis (see Chapter 10). However, when working with well-defined alarms and processes, streaming analytics will reduce the overhead of data required at a central repository, and in large data systems, which can be quite valuable.

After dealing with the question of updates, the next set of questions deal with the structure and size of the data. Columnar and relational databases are preferable when you are dealing with well-structured, small records (such as optimized logfiles). These approaches can take advantage of the schema—for example, if a columnar database is only using two columns, it can return only those for further processing whereas the key store has to return the whole record. If records are small or structured, columnar databases are preferable, followed by relational databases. If records are large or unstructured, then the key-value approach is more flexible.

The final question on the list is arguably more social than technical, but also important when considering the design of an analysis system. If you are going to allow analysts relatively open, unstructured analysis to the data, then you need to have some well-defined and safe framework for letting them do so. If your analysts are capable of writing MapReduce functions, then you can use any system without much difficulty. However, if you expect that analysts will have minimal skills then you may find columnar or relational systems, which have SQL interfaces, to be preferable. There are relatively recent efforts to develop SQL-like interfaces for key stores, notably the Hive and Pig projects from Apache.

Where possible, it's preferable to limit analysts' direct access to the data store, instead allowing them to extract samples that can be processed in EDA tools such as SiLK or R.

Storage Hierarchy, Query Times, and Aging

Any collection system will have to deal with a continuous influx of new data, forcing older data to move into slower, less expensive storage systems over time. For the purposes of an analytic system, we can break the storage hierarchy we have for data into four tiers:

- RAM
- SSDs and flash storage
- Hard drives and magnetic storage

- Tape drives and long-term archives

By setting up a flow monitoring system, you can estimate the volume of incoming traffic and use that data to calculate initial storage requirements. The key question is how much data the analysts need.

A good rule of thumb in a business environment is that analysts need fast access to approximately a week's worth of data, reasonable access to 90 days' worth of data, and further data can be deposited in a tape archive. The 90-day rule means that analysts can pull back data to at least the previous quarter. Obviously, if your budget allows it, more data on disk is better, but 90 days is a good minimal requirement. Make sure that if you do archive to tape, that the tape data is reasonably accessible—bots last on most networks for around a year if not longer, and tracing their full activity will involve looking at that archive.

A number of external constraints also have an impact on data storage, notably the data retention requirements for your domain and industry. For example, the EU's data retention directive (directive 2006/24/EC) establishes retention requirements for telecommunications providers.

As data moves down on the hierarchy, it also often helps to reformat it into a more summarization- or storage-friendly format. For example, for rapid response I might want to keep a rolling archive of packets in high-speed storage in order to facilitate rapid response. As the data moves onto slower sources (from RAM to SSD, from SSD to disk, from disk to tape), I will start relying more on summaries such as NetFlow.

In addition to simple summarization such as NetFlow, long-term storage can be facilitated by identifying and summarizing the most obvious behaviors. For example, scanning and backscatter (see Chapter 11 for more information) take up an enormous amount of disk space on large networks; traffic has no payload, and there's little value in storing the full packet. Identifying, summarizing, and then compressing or removing scans reduces the footprint of the raw data, especially on larger networks where this type of background traffic can take up a disproprtionate number of records.

Data fusion—removing idential records or fusing them—is another viable technique. When collecting data from multiple sources, combining the records that describe the same phenomenon (by checking IP addresses, ports, and time) can reduce the payload of these separate records.

PART II
Tools

This section is about a number of tools for use in data analysis. The primary focus of this section is on two particular tools: SiLK and R. The System for Internet-Level Knowledge (SiLK) is a NetFlow analysis toolkit developed by the CERT at Carnegie Mellon University, which enables analysts to develop sophisticated flow analysis systems quickly and efficiently. R, a statistical analysis package developed at the University of Auckland, enables exploratory data analysis and visualization.

At this time, there is no killer app for network analysis. Analysis requires using many tools, often in ways they weren't really designed for. The tools covered in this section form what I believe to be a basic functional toolkit for an analyst. Combining them with a light scripting language such as Python empowers analysts to explore data and develop operationally useful products.

The remainder of this section is divided into five chapters. Chapter 5 describes the SiLK suite, Chapter 6 describes R. Chapter 7 discusses IDS; while IDSes were briefly discussed in Part I, this chapter discusses the construction and maintenance of these tools—analysts will often produce ad hoc IDSes to identify or deal with attacks. Chapter 8 discusses tools to identify the ways in which hosts are connected to the Internet, including reverse DNS lookups, looking glasses, and tools such as *traceroute* and *ping*. Finally, Chapter 9 discusses additional tools that are useful for particular analytic tasks.

## CHAPTER 5

The SiLK Suite

SiLK, the System for Internet-Level Knowledge, is a toolkit originally developed by Carnegie Mellon's CERT to conduct large-scale netflow analysis. SiLK is now used extensively by the Department of Defense, academic institutions, and industry as a basic analytical toolkit.

This chapter focuses primarily on using SiLK as an analytical tool. The CERT Network Situational Awareness team has published extensive references (*http:// tools.netsa.cert.org/*) on using SiLK, installing collectors, and setting up the suite.

What Is SiLK and How Does It Work?

SiLK is a suite of tools for querying and analyzing NetFlow data. The SiLK suite enables an analyst to rapidly and efficiently query very large volumes of network traffic in order to identify complex aggregate phenomena or extract individual events.

SiLK is effectively a database at the command line. Each tool performs a specific query, manipulation, or aggregation of data, and commands are chained together to produce results. By chaining together multiple records along pipes, SiLK enables the analyst to create complex commands that field data along multiple channels simultaneously. For example, the following sequence of SiLK queries pull HTTP (port 80) traffic from flow data, producing a time series and a list of activity by busiest address. See Example 5-1 for the basics of SiLK operation: commands are passed through a series of pipes, which can be stdin, stdout, or fifos (named pipes).

Example 5-1. Some overly complicated rwfilter voodoo

```
$ mkfifo out2
$ rwfilter --proto=6 --aport=80 data.rwf --pass=stdout |
        rwfilter --input=stdin --proto=6 --pass=stdout
        --all=out2 | rwstats --top --count=10 --fields=1 &
        rwcount out2 --bin-size=300
```

Data is maintained in an efficient binary representation up until the last moment, until commands that produce text (or some optional outputs) are called to produce output.

SiLK is very much an old-school Unix application suite: a family of tools tied together with pipes and using a lot of optional arguments. By using this approach, it's possible to create powerful analytic scripts with SiLK, because the tools have well-defined interfaces that will efficiently handle binary data. Effectively using SiLK involves connecting the appropriate tools together in order to process binary data and produce text only at the very end of the process.

This chapter also uses some basic Unix shell commands such as ls, cat, and head. I don't require you to know the shell on an expert level.

Acquiring and Installing SiLK

The SiLK homepage is maintained at the CERT NetSA Security Suite web page. The SiLK package is available free for download, and can be installed on most Unix systems without much difficulty. The CERT also provides a live CD image that can be used on its own.

The SiLK live CD comes with a training dataset called LBNL-05, anonymized header traces from Lawrence Berkeley National Labs in 2005. If you install the live CD, the data will be immediately accessible. If not, you can fetch the data from The LBNL-05 reference data page (*http://bit.ly/lbnl-ref*).[1]

In addition to the live CD, SiLK is available in several package managers, including homebrew.

The Datafiles

The LBNL datafiles are stored in a file hierarchy; Example 5-2 shows the results of downloading and unarchiving them.

Example 5-2. Downloading the SiLK archives

```
$ gunzip -c SiLK-LBNL-05-noscan.tar
$ gunzip -c SiLK-LBNL-05-scanners.tar
$ cd SiLK-LBNL-05
$ ls
README-S0.txt   in              out             silk.conf
README-S1.txt   inweb                           outweb
$ ls in/2005/01/07/*.01
in/2005/01/07/in-S0_20050107.01 in/2005/01/07/in-S1_20050107.01
```

---

1. You'll notice that there are two datasets, one with scans and one without. To understand why, read Pang *et al.*, "The Devil and Packet Trace Anonymization," ACM CCR 36(1), January 2006.

When collecting data, SiLK partitions the data into subdirectories that divide traffic by the type of traffic and the time the event occurred. This provides scalability and speeds up analysis. However, it's also generally a black box, and one we're breaking right now simply to have some files to work with. For the purposes of demonstration and education, we're going to work with four specific files:

- *inweb/2005/01/06/iw-S0_20050106.20*
- *inweb/2005/01/06/iw-S0_20050106.21*
- *in/2005/01/07/in-S0_20050107.01*
- *in/2005/01/07/in-S1_20050107.01*

These files are not special in any way. I chose them just to provide examples of scan and nonscan traffic. The following data discusses how to partition data and what the filenames mean.

Choosing and Formatting Output Field Manipulation: rwcut

SiLK records are stored in a compact binary format. They can't be read directly, and are instead accessed using the rwcut tool (see Example 5-3). In the following example, and any other examples with an output greater than 80 characters, the lines are manually broken for clarity.

Example 5-3. Simple file access with rwcut

```
$ rwcut inweb/2005/01/06/iw-S0_20050106.20 | more
            sIP|             dIP|sPort|dPort|pro|    packets|       bytes|\
    flags|              sTime|   dur|            eTime|sen|
  148.19.251.179|    128.3.148.48| 2497|   80|  6|         16|        2631|\
FS PA   |2005/01/06T20:01:54.119| 0.246|2005/01/06T20:01:54.365|   ?|
  148.19.251.179|    128.3.148.48| 2498|   80|  6|         14|        2159|\
 S PA   |2005/01/06T20:01:54.160| 0.260|2005/01/06T20:01:54.420|   ?|
...
```

In its default invocation, rwcut outputs 12 fields: source and destination IP addresses and ports, protocol, number of packets, number of bytes, TCP flags, start time, duration, end time, and sensor of a flow. These values have been discussed previously in Chapter 2, except for the sensor field. SiLK can be configured to identify individual sensors, which is useful when you're trying to figure out where traffic came from or where it's going. The sensor field is whatever ID is assigned during configuration. In the default data there are no sensors, so the value is set to a question mark (?).

All SiLK commands have built-in documentation. Typing **rwcut --help** brings up an enormous help page. We will cover the basic options. A fuller description of options can be found in the SiLK documentation for rwcut (*http://bit.ly/silk-rwcut*).

The most commonly used rwcut commands select the fields displayed during invocation. rwcut can actually print 29 different fields, in arbitrary order. A list of these fields is in Table 5-1.

rwcut fields are specified using the --fields= option, which takes the numeric values in Table 5-1 or the string values, and prints the requested fields in the order specified, as in Example 5-4.

Table 5-1. rwcut fields

Field	Numeric ID	Description
sIP	1	Source IP address
dIP	2	Destination IP address
sPort	3	Source port
dPort	4	Destination Port: if ICMP, the ICMP type and code is encoded here also
protocol	5	Layer 3 protocol
packets	6	Packets in the flow
bytes	7	Bytes in the flow
flags	8	OR of TCP flags
sTime	9	Start time in seconds
eTime	10	End time in seconds
dur	11	Duration (eTime–sTime)
sensor	12	Sensor ID
in	13	SNMP ID of the incoming interface on the router
out	14	SNMP ID of the outgoing interface on the router
nhIP	15	Next hop address
sType	16	Classification of the source address (internal, external)
dType	17	Classification of the destination address (internal, external)
scc	18	Country code of the source IP
dcc	19	Country code of the destination IP
class	20	Class of the flow
type	21	Type of the flow
sTime +msec	22	sTime in milliseconds
eTime +msec	23	eTime in milliseconds
dur +msec	24	duration msecs
icmpTypeCode	25	ICMP type and code

Field	Numeric ID	Description
initialFlags	26	Flags in the first TCP packet
sessionFlags	27	Flags in all packets *except* the first
attributes	28	Attributes of the flow observed by the generator
application	29	Guess as to the application in the flow

Example 5-4. Some examples of field ordering

```
$# Show a limited set of fields
$ rwcut --field=1-5 inweb/2005/01/06/iw-S0_20050106.20 | head -2
           sIP|              dIP|sPort|dPort|pro|
 148.19.251.179|    128.3.148.48| 2497|   80|  6|
$#Note the -, now explicitly enumerate
$ rwcut --field=1,2,3,4,5 inweb/2005/01/06/iw-S0_20050106.20 | head -2
           sIP|              dIP|sPort|dPort|pro|
 148.19.251.179|    128.3.148.48| 2497|   80|  6|
$#Field order is based on what you enter in --field
$ rwcut --field=5,1,2,3,4 inweb/2005/01/06/iw-S0_20050106.20 | head -2
pro|            sIP|              dIP|sPort|dPort|
  6| 148.19.251.179|    128.3.148.48| 2497|   80|
$#We can use text instead of numbers
$ rwcut --field=sIP,dIP,proto inweb/2005/01/06/iw-S0_20050106.20 |head -2
           sIP|              dIP|pro|
 148.19.251.179|    128.3.148.48|  6|
```

rwcut supports a number of other output formatting and manipulation tools. Some particularly useful ones, which let you control the lines that appear in the output, include:

--no-title

>   Commonly used with SiLK commands that produce tabular output. Drops the title from the output table.

--num-recs

>   Outputs a specific number of records, eliminating the need for the head pipe in the previous example. The default value is zero, which makes rwcut dump the entire contents of whatever file it's reading.

--start-rec-num *and* --end-rec-num

>   Can be used to fetch a range of records in the file.

Example 5-5 shows a few ways to manipulate record numbers and headers.

Example 5-5. Manipulating record numbers and headers

```
$# Drop the title
$ rwcut --field=1-9 --no-title inweb/2005/01/06/iw-S0_20050106.20 | head -5
 148.19.251.179|    128.3.148.48| 2497|   80|  6|        16|      2631|FS PA
  |2005/01/06T20:01:54.119|
```

```
 148.19.251.179|    128.3.148.48| 2498|   80|  6|        14|      2159| S PA
          |2005/01/06T20:01:54.160|
 148.19.251.179|    128.3.148.48| 2498|   80|  6|         2|        80|F   A
          |2005/01/06T20:07:07.845|
  56.71.233.157|    128.3.148.48|48906|   80|  6|         5|       300| S
          |2005/01/06T20:01:50.011|
   56.96.13.225|    128.3.148.48|50722|   80|  6|         6|       360| S
          |2005/01/06T20:02:57.132|
$# Drop the head statement
$ rwcut --field=1-9 inweb/2005/01/06/iw-S0_20050106.20 --num-recs=5
             sIP|              dIP|sPort|dPort|pro|   packets|     bytes|    flags
|              sTime|
 148.19.251.179|    128.3.148.48| 2497|   80|  6|        16|      2631|FS PA
|2005/01/06T20:01:54.119|
 148.19.251.179|    128.3.148.48| 2498|   80|  6|        14|      2159| S PA
|2005/01/06T20:01:54.160|
 148.19.251.179|    128.3.148.48| 2498|   80|  6|         2|        80|F   A
|2005/01/06T20:07:07.845|
  56.71.233.157|    128.3.148.48|48906|   80|  6|         5|       300| S
|2005/01/06T20:01:50.011|
   56.96.13.225|    128.3.148.48|50722|   80|  6|         6|       360| S
|2005/01/06T20:02:57.132|
$# Print only the third through fifth record
$ rwcut --field=1-9 inweb/2005/01/06/iw-S0_20050106.20 --start-rec-num=3
   --end-rec-num=5
             sIP|              dIP|sPort|dPort|pro|   packets|     bytes|    flags
|              sTime|
 148.19.251.179|    128.3.148.48| 2498|   80|  6|         2|        80|F   A
|2005/01/06T20:07:07.845|
  56.71.233.157|    128.3.148.48|48906|   80|  6|         5|       300| S
|2005/01/06T20:01:50.011|
   56.96.13.225|    128.3.148.48|50722|   80|  6|         6|       360| S
|2005/01/06T20:02:57.132|
```

A number of options manipulate output format. Tabulation is controllable with the --column-separator, --no-final-column, and --no-columns switches. --column-seperator will change the character used to distinguish columns, while --no-final-column drops the delimiter at the end of the line. --no-columns removes any space padding between columns. The --delimited switch combines all three: it takes a character as an argument, uses that character as a column separator, removes all padding in the columns, and drops the final column separator.

In addition, there are a variety of switches for changing column content:

--integer-ips

Converts IP addresses to integers rather than dotted quads. This switch is deprecated as of SiLK v3, and users should now use --ip-format=decimal.

--ip-format

> The updated version of --integer-ips, --ip-format specifies how addresses are rendered. Options include canonical (dotted quad for IPv4, canonical IPv6 for IPv6), zero-padded (canonical, except zeroes are expanded to the maximal value for each format, so 127.0.0.1 is 127.000.000.001), decimal (print as the corresponding 32-bit or 128-bit integer), hexadecimal (print the integer in hexadeximal format), and force-ipv6 (prints all addresses in canonical IPv6 format, including IPv4 addresses mapped to the ::ffff:0:0/96 netblock).

--epoch-time

> Prints timestamps as epoch values with floating-point millisecond precision.

--integer-tcp-flags

> Converts TCP flags to their integer equivalents.

--zero-pad-ips

> Pads the dotted quad IP address format with zeros, so that 128.2.11.12 is printed as 128.002.011.012. Deprecated in favor of --ip-format in SiLK v3.

--icmp-type-and-code

> Places the ICMP type in the source port and the ICMP code in the destination port.

--pager

> Specifies the program to use for paging output.

Example 5-6 shows some of the preceding options.

Example 5-6. Other formatting examples

```
$# Change from fixed with columns to delims
$ rwcut --field=1-5 inweb/2005/01/06/iw-S0_20050106.20 --no-columns --num-recs=2
sIP|dIP|sPort|dPort|protocol|
148.19.251.179|128.3.148.48|2497|80|6|
148.19.251.179|128.3.148.48|2498|80|6|
$# Change the column separator
$ rwcut --field=1-5 inweb/2005/01/06/iw-S0_20050106.20 --column-sep=:
  --num-recs=2
            sIP:            dIP:sPort:dPort:pro:
 148.19.251.179:   128.3.148.48: 2497:   80:  6:
 148.19.251.179:   128.3.148.48: 2498:   80:  6:
$# Use --delim to change everything at once
$ rwcut --field=1-5 inweb/2005/01/06/iw-S0_20050106.20 --delim=: --num-recs=2
sIP:dIP:sPort:dPort:protocol
148.19.251.179:128.3.148.48:2497:80:6
148.19.251.179:128.3.148.48:2498:80:6
$# Convert IP addresses to integers
$ rwcut --field=1-5 inweb/2005/01/06/iw-S0_20050106.20 --integer-ip --num-recs=2
      sIP|        dIP|sPort|dPort|pro|
2484337587|2147718192| 2497|   80|  6|
2484337587|2147718192| 2498|   80|  6|
```

```
$# Use epoch time
$ rwcut --field=1-5,9 inweb/2005/01/06/iw-S0_20050106.20 --epoch --num-recs=2
            sIP|            dIP|sPort|dPort|pro|       sTime|
 148.19.251.179|    128.3.148.48| 2497|   80|  6|1105041714.119|
 148.19.251.179|    128.3.148.48| 2498|   80|  6|1105041714.160|
$# Zero pad IP addresses
$ rwcut --field=1-5,9 inweb/2005/01/06/iw-S0_20050106.20 --zero-pad --num-recs=2
            sIP|            dIP|sPort|dPort|pro|               sTime|
148.019.251.179|128.003.148.048| 2497|   80|  6|2005/01/06T20:01:54.119|
148.019.251.179|128.003.148.048| 2498|   80|  6|2005/01/06T20:01:54.160|
```

You will note that, as the command lines get more complex, I have truncated the longer options. SiLK uses GNU-style long options universally, so the only requirement for specifying an option is to type enough characters to make the name unambiguous. Expect more and more truncation as we build more and more complex commands.

Basic Field Manipulation: rwfilter

The most basic SiLK command with analytical values is rwcut paired with rwfilter through a pipe. Example 5-7 shows a simple rwfilter command.

Example 5-7. A simple rwfilter command

```
$ rwfilter --dport=80 inweb/2005/01/06/iw-S0_20050106.20 --pass=stdout
  | rwcut --field=1-9 --num-recs=5
            sIP|            dIP|sPort|dPort|pro|    packets|    bytes|   flags
  |           sTime|
 148.19.251.179|    128.3.148.48| 2497|   80|  6|       16|     2631|FS PA
  |2005/01/06T20:01:54.119|
 148.19.251.179|    128.3.148.48| 2498|   80|  6|       14|     2159| S PA
  |2005/01/06T20:01:54.160|
 148.19.251.179|    128.3.148.48| 2498|   80|  6|        2|       80|F   A
  |2005/01/06T20:07:07.845|
  56.71.233.157|    128.3.148.48|48906|   80|  6|        5|      300| S
  |2005/01/06T20:01:50.011|
  56.96.13.225|    128.3.148.48|50722|   80|  6|        6|      360| S
  |2005/01/06T20:02:57.132|
```

rwfilter with a single filter (the --dport option in this case), and a single redirect (the --pass=stdout) is about as simple as you can get. rwfilter is the workhorse of the SiLK suite: it reads input (directly from a file, using a set of globbing specifications, or through a pipe), applies one or more filters to each record in the data, and then redirects the records based on whether a record matches the filters (passes) or doesn't match (fails).

SiLK's rwfilter documentation (*http://bit.ly/rwfilter-doc*) is humongous, but primarily consists of repetitively describing the filter specifications for every field, so don't be intimidated. `rwfilter` options basically do one of three things: they specify how to filter data, how to read data, or how to direct the result of those filters.

Ports and Protocols

The easiest filters to start with are `--sport`, `--dport`, and `--protocol`. As the names imply, they filter on the source port, destination port, and protocol, respectively (see Example 5-8). These values can filter on a specific value (e.g., `--sport=80` will pass any traffic where the source port is 80), or a range specified with a dash or commas (so `--sport=79-83` will pass anything where the source port is between 79 and 83 inclusive, and could be expressed as `--sport=79,80,81,82,83`).

Example 5-8. Example filtering on sport

```
$ rwfilter --dport=4350-4360  inweb/2005/01/06/iw-S0_20050106.20
  --pass=stdout | rwcut --field=1-9 --num-recs=5
          sIP|            dIP|sPort|dPort|pro|    packets|      bytes|    flags
  |                  sTime|
 218.131.115.42| 131.243.105.35|   80| 4360|  6|          2|         80|F   A
  |2005/01/06T20:24:21.879|
   148.19.96.160|131.243.107.239|   80| 4350|  6|         27|      35445|FS PA
  |2005/01/06T20:59:42.451|
   148.19.96.160|131.243.107.239|   80| 4352|  6|          4|        709|FS PA
  |2005/01/06T20:59:42.507|
   148.19.96.160|131.243.107.239|   80| 4351|  6|         15|      16938|FS PA
  |2005/01/06T20:59:42.501|
   148.19.96.160|131.243.107.239|   80| 4353|  6|          4|        704|FS PA
  |2005/01/06T20:59:42.544|
$ rwfilter --sport=4000-  inweb/2005/01/06/iw-S0_20050106.20
  --pass=stdout | rwcut --field=1-9 --num-recs=5
          sIP|            dIP|sPort|dPort|pro|    packets|      bytes|    flags
  |              sTime|
 56.71.233.157|    128.3.148.48|48906|   80|  6|          5|        300| S
  |2005/01/06T20:01:50.011|
   56.96.13.225|    128.3.148.48|50722|   80|  6|          6|        360| S
  |2005/01/06T20:02:57.132|
   56.96.13.225|    128.3.148.48|50726|   80|  6|          6|        360| S
  |2005/01/06T20:02:57.432|
 58.236.56.129|    128.3.148.48|32621|   80|  6|          3|        144| S
  |2005/01/06T20:12:10.747|
   56.96.13.225|    128.3.148.48|54497|  443|  6|          6|        360| S
  |2005/01/06T20:09:30.124|
$ rwfilter --dport=4350,4352  inweb/2005/01/06/iw-S0_20050106.20
  --pass=stdout | rwcut --field=1-9 --num-recs=5
          sIP|            dIP|sPort|dPort|pro|    packets|      bytes|    flags
  |                  sTime|
   148.19.96.160|131.243.107.239|   80| 4350|  6|         27|      35445|FS PA
  |2005/01/06T20:59:42.451|
   148.19.96.160|131.243.107.239|   80| 4352|  6|          4|        709|FS PA
  |2005/01/06T20:59:42.507|
```

```
   148.19.96.160|131.243.107.239|  80| 4352|  6|         1|        40|    A
   |2005/01/06T20:59:42.516|
$ rwfilter --proto=1 in/2005/01/07/in-S0_20050107.01 --pass=stdout
 | rwcut --field=1-6 --num-recs=2
          sIP|            dIP|sPort|dPort|pro|    packets|
   35.223.112.236|     128.3.23.93|   0| 2048|  1|          1|
   62.198.182.170|     128.3.23.81|   0| 2048|  1|          1|
$ rwfilter --proto=1,6,17 in/2005/01/07/in-S0_20050107.01 --pass=stdout
 | rwcut --num-recs=2 --fields=1-6
          sIP|            dIP|sPort|dPort|pro|    packets|
   116.66.41.147|131.243.163.201| 4283| 1026| 17|          1|
   116.66.41.147|131.243.163.201| 3131| 1027| 17|          1|
$ rwfilter --proto=1,6,17 in/2005/01/07/in-S0_20050107.01 --fail=stdout
 | rwcut --num-recs=2   --fields=1-6
          sIP|            dIP|sPort|dPort|pro|    packets|
   57.120.186.177|     128.3.26.171|   0|   0| 50|         70|
   57.120.186.177|     128.3.26.171|   0|   0| 50|         81|
```

Note the use of `--fail` in the last example. Because there are 255 potential protocols, specifying "everything but TCP, ICMP, and UDP" could be expressed in two ways: either by specifying everything you want (`--proto=0,2-5,7-16,18-`), or by using the `--fail` option. I'll discuss more advanced manipulation of `--pass` and `--fail` in the next chapter.

Size

Volume (size) options (bytes and packets) are similar to the protocol and port options in that you express them numerically. Unlike the enumerations (ports and protocol), these numeric values can be expressed only as single digits or ranges, *not* as comma-separated values. So, `--packets=70-81` is acceptable, but `--bytes=1,2,3,4` is not.

IP Addresses

The simplest form of IP address filtering simply expresses the IP address directly (see Example 5-9). The following examples show strict filtering on the source (`--saddress`) and destination (`--daddress`) address, and the `--any-address` option. `--any-address` will match *either* source or destination addresses.

Example 5-9. Filtering on IP addresses

```
$ rwfilter --saddress=197.142.156.83 --pass=stdout
   in/2005/01/07/in-S0_20050107.01 | rwcut --num-recs=2
          sIP|            dIP|sPort|dPort|pro|    packets|     bytes|   flags|
            sTime|       dur|                eTime|sen|
   197.142.156.83|   224.2.127.254|44510| 9875| 17|         12|      7163|        |
2005/01/07T01:24:44.359|    16.756|2005/01/07T01:25:01.115|   ?|
   197.142.156.83|   224.2.127.254|44512| 9875| 17|          4|      2590|        |
2005/01/07T01:25:02.375|     5.742|2005/01/07T01:25:08.117|   ?|
$ rwfilter --daddress=128.3.26.249 --pass=stdout
```

```
   in/2005/01/07/in-S0_20050107.01 | rwcut --num-recs=2
            sIP|          dIP|sPort|dPort|pro|   packets|    bytes|   flags|
                 sTime|      dur|              eTime|sen|
211.210.215.142|   128.3.26.249| 4068|   25|  6|        7|      388|FS PA   |
   2005/01/07T01:27:06.789|     5.052|2005/01/07T01:27:11.841|   ?|
   203.126.20.182|   128.3.26.249|51981| 4587|  6|       56|     2240|F   A   |
   2005/01/07T01:27:04.812|    18.530|2005/01/07T01:27:23.342|   ?|
$ rwfilter --any-address=128.3.26.249
   --pass=stdout in/2005/01/07/in-S0_20050107.01 | rwcut --num-recs=2
            sIP|          dIP|sPort|dPort|pro|   packets|    bytes|   flags|
                 sTime|      dur|              eTime|sen|
211.210.215.142|   128.3.26.249| 4068|   25|  6|        7|      388|FS PA   |
   2005/01/07T01:27:06.789|     5.052|2005/01/07T01:27:11.841|   ?|
   203.126.20.182|   128.3.26.249|51981| 4587|  6|       56|     2240|F   A   |
   2005/01/07T01:27:04.812|    18.530|2005/01/07T01:27:23.342|   ?|
```

Address options accept a variety of range descriptors. Each quad in an IP address can be expressed using the same comma-dash format that protocols and ports use. IP addresses will also accept the character *x* to mean *0-255*. This expression can be used within each quad; SiLK will match each quad separately. In addition to this comma-dash format, SiLK can match on CIDR blocks.

SiLK supports IPv6 by using IPv6's colon-based notation. The following are all examples of valid IPv6 filters in SiLK, and Example 5-10 shows how to filter them:

```
::ffff:x
::ffff:0:aaaa,0-5
::ffff:0.0.5-130,1,255.x
```

Example 5-10. Filtering IP ranges

```
$#Filtering on the last quad
$ rwfilter --daddress=131.243.104.x inweb/2005/01/06/iw-S0_20050106.20
   --pass=stdout | rwcut --field=1-5 --num-recs=5
            sIP|          dIP|sPort|dPort|pro|
 150.52.105.212|131.243.104.181|   80| 1262|  6|
 150.52.105.212|131.243.104.181|   80| 1263|  6|
   59.100.39.174| 131.243.104.27|   80| 3188|  6|
   59.100.39.174| 131.243.104.27|   80| 3191|  6|
   59.100.39.174| 131.243.104.27|   80| 3193|  6|
# Filtering a range of specific values in the third quad
$ rwfilter --daddress=131.243.104,107,219.x inweb/2005/01/06/iw-S0_20050106.20
   --pass=stdout | rwcut --field=1-5 --num-recs=5
            sIP|          dIP|sPort|dPort|pro|
 208.122.23.36|131.243.219.201|   80| 2473|  6|
205.233.167.250|131.243.219.201|   80| 2471|  6|
   58.68.205.40| 131.243.219.37|   80| 3433|  6|
208.233.181.122| 131.243.219.37|   80| 3434|  6|
   58.68.205.40| 131.243.219.37|   80| 3435|  6|
# Using CIDR blocks
$ rwfilter --saddress=56.81.0.0/16 inweb/2005/01/06/iw-S0_20050106.20
   --pass=stdout | rwcut --field=1-5 --num-recs=5
```

```
         sIP|              dIP|sPort|dPort|pro|
  56.81.19.218|131.243.219.201|   80| 2480|  6|
   56.81.16.73|131.243.219.201|   80| 2484|  6|
   56.81.16.73|131.243.219.201|   80| 2486|  6|
   56.81.30.48|131.243.219.201|  443| 2490|  6|
  56.81.31.159|131.243.219.201|  443| 2489|  6|
```

Time

There are three time options: `--stime`, `--etime`, and `--active-time`. These fields require a time range, which in SiLK is written in the format:

YYYY/MM/DDTHH:MM:SS-YYYY/MM/DDTHH:MM:SS

Note the T separating the day and hour. The `--stime` and `--etime` fields filter exactly what it says on the can, which can be a bit counterintuitive; specifying `--stime=2012/11/08T00:00:00-2012/11/08T00:02:00` filters any record whose *start time* is between midnight and two minutes after midnight on November 8, 2012. Records that started *before* midnight and are still being transmitted during that range will not pass. To find records that occurred within a particular period, use the `--active-time` filter.

TCP Options

Flows are aggregates of packets, and in the majority of cases, this aggregation is relatively easy to understand. For example, the number of bytes in a flow is the sum of the number of bytes of all the packets that comprise the flow. TCP flags, however, are a bit more problematic. In NetFlow v5, a flow's flags are the bitwise OR of the flags in its constituent packets—meaning that a flow indicates that a flag was present or absent in the *entire* flow, but not *where*. A flow could conceivably consist of a gibberish sequence of flags such as a FIN, then an ACK and SYN. Monitoring software such as YAF expands Net-Flow to include additional flag fields, which SiLK can take advantage of.

The core flag filtering switches are `--flags-initial`, `--flags-all`, and `--flags-session`. These options accept flags in the form *high flags/mask flags*. If a flag is listed in the mask, SiLK always parses it. If a flag is listed in the high flags, SiLK passes it *only* if the value is high. The flags themselves are expressed using the characters in Table 5-2.

Table 5-2. Expressing TCP flags in rwfilter

Character	Flag
F	FIN
S	SYN
R	RST
P	PSH
A	ACK

Character	Flag
U	URG
E	ECE
C	CWR

The combination of high flags and mask flags tends to confuse people, so let's review some examples. Remember that the basic rule is that in order to evaluate a flag, it *must* be in the mask. A flag specified as high but not specified in the mask will be ignored.

- Setting the value to S/S will pass any record where the SYN flag is high.
- Setting the value to S/SA will pass any record where the SYN flag is high *and* the ACK flag is low.
- Setting the value to SA/SA will pass any record where *both* SYN and ACK flags are high.
- A combination like SAF/SAFR will return any record where the SYN, ACK, FIN flags are high *and* the RST flag is low, which would be expected of a normal TCP connection.

In addition to these options, SiLK provides a set of flag-specific options in the form of `--syn-flag`, `--fin-flag`, and so on for each potential flag. These options take a 1 or 0 as an argument: setting the value to 1 will pass records where the flag is high, 0 will pass records where the flag is low, and not including the option will pass all records.

What Should TCP Flags Look Like?

The combination of TCP flags in any particular flow can be a useful indicator of the flow's behavior, and there are certain flag combinations that raise suspicion.

Almost all TCP flows should pass *either* SAF/SAFR or SAR/SAFR, *without* passing SAFR/SAFR. This is because most sessions will end in a FIN, with aberrations ending in a RST. If both FIN and RST are seen, that's suspicious.

A TCP session without an ACK flag is curious, *especially* if that session has four or more packets. Stacks are usually hardcoded to give up after *n* packets, where *n* tends to be in the neighborhood of three.

For a client, the initial flag should be a SYN, while a server should have a SYN+ACK. You should never see a SYN after the initial flag. Resynchronization would mean a new session started using the same ephemeral port, which is weird for TCP.

The PSH and URG flags are, in my mind, the universal indicator of boring sessions. If I see a session *without* PSH, especially if the session is long, it strikes me as curious. In my mind, a "normal" TCP session will have FSPA high. A flow with just PA high is usually a keep-alive and an indication of a broken flow—look in the repository for the same address combination and you'll probably find a SAP flow occurring before it.

Backscatter/response messages include A, SA, and RA flows. A good number of RA packets will arrive on any large network due to backscatter from spoofed DDoS attacks. There isn't really anything you can do about these packets; they're not even directly aimed at your network.

Helper Options

If you compare `rwfilter`'s option-based filtering against `tcpdump`'s BPF filtering, it's immediately obvious that `rwfilter`'s approach is much more primitive. This was an intentional decision: rwfilter is focused on processing large volumes as quickly as possible, and the overhead involved in processing some kind of parseable language was deemed too expensive.

The place where this usually trips people up is the lack of obvious `not` and `or` operators. For example, if you want to filter out all web sessions, you may try to filter traffic where one port is 80, and the other is ephemeral. The initial attempt might be:

```
rwfilter --sport=80,1024-65535 --dport=80,1024-65535 --pass=stdout
```

The problem is that this will also pass any flows where the source and destination port are both 80, and flows where the source and destination port are both ephemeral. To deal with problems like this, `rwfilter` has a collection of helper functions, which combined with the `--fail` option and multiple filters should be able to address any of these problems.

In the case of ports, the `--aport` option refers to either the source *or* the destination port. Using `--aport` and two filters, you can identify the appropriate sessions as follows:

```
rwfilter --aport=80 --pass=stdout | rwfilter --input-pipe=stdin
        --aport=1024-65535 --pass=stdout
```

The first filter identifies anything engaged in port 80 traffic, and the second takes that set and identifies anything that also used an ephemeral port.

A number of IP address helper options are available. `--anyaddress` filters across source and destination addresses simultaneously. `--not-saddress` and `--not-daddress` pass records with addresses that *don't* match the option specification.

Miscellaneous Filtering Options and Some Hacks

`rwfilter` has a couple of direct text output options: `--print-stat` (see Example 5-11) and `--print-volume-stat`. These can be used to print a summary of the traffic without having to resort to cut, count, or other display tools. They also will print volumes of records that did *not* pass a filter.

Example 5-11. Using --print-stat

```
$ rwfilter --print-volume-stat in/2005/01/07/in-S0_20050107.01 --proto=0-255
           |         Recs|        Packets|          Bytes|      Files|
Total|          2019|        2730488|      402105501|          1|
 Pass|          2019|        2730488|      402105501|           |
 Fail|             0|              0|              0|           |
$ rwfilter --print-stat in/2005/01/07/in-S0_20050107.01 --proto=0-255
Files    1.  Read     2019.  Pass     2019. Fail      0.
```

Note in Example 5-11 the use of the `--proto=0-255` option. In almost all invocations, rwfilter expects *some* form of filtering applied to it, so when you need a filter that passes everything, the easiest approach is just to specify all the protocols. `--print-stat` and `--print-volume-stat` output to stderr, so you can still use stdout for pass, fail, and all channels.

Like rwcut, rwfilter has a record limit command. `--max-pass-records` and `--max-fail-records` can be used to limit the number of records passed through a pass or fail channel.

rwfileinfo and Provenance

SiLK filter files contain a fair amount of metadata, which can be accessed using the rwfileinfo command (see Example 5-12). rwfileinfo can work with files, as seen in the examples below, or directly on stdin by using stdin or - as an argument.

Example 5-12. Using rwfileinfo

```
$ rwfileinfo in/2005/01/07/in-S0_20050107.01
in/2005/01/07/in-S0_20050107.01:
  format(id)          FT_RWAUGMENTED(0x14)
  version             2
  byte-order          littleEndian
  compression(id)     none(0)
  header-length       28
  record-length       28
  record-version      2
  silk-version        0
  count-records       2019
  file-size           56560
  packed-file-info    2005/01/07T01:00:00 ? ?
$ rwfilter --print-stat in/2005/01/07/in-S0_20050107.01 --proto=6
  --pass=example.rwf
Files    1.  Read     2019.  Pass     1353. Fail    666.
$ rwfileinfo example.rwf
example.rwf:
  format(id)          FT_RWGENERIC(0x16)
  version             16
  byte-order          littleEndian
```

```
  compression(id)      none(0)
  header-length        156
  record-length        52
  record-version       5
  silk-version         2.1.0
  count-records        1353
  file-size            70512
  command-lines
                  1  rwfilter --print-stat --proto=6 --pass=example.rwf
     in/2005/01/07/in-S0_20050107.01
$ rwfilter --aport=25 example.rwf --pass=example2.rwf --fail=example2_fail.rwf
$ rwfileinfo example2.rwf
example2.rwf:
  format(id)           FT_RWGENERIC(0x16)
  version              16
  byte-order           littleEndian
  compression(id)      none(0)
  header-length        208
  record-length        52
  record-version       5
  silk-version         2.1.0
  count-records        95
  file-size            5148
  command-lines
                  1  rwfilter --print-stat --proto=6 --pass=example.rwf
     in/2005/01/07/in-S0_20050107.01
                  2  rwfilter --aport=25 --pass=example2.rwf
     --fail=example2_fail.rwf example.rwf
```

The fields reported by `rwfileinfo` are as follows:

`example2.rwf`

> The first line of every `rwfileinfo` dump is the name of the file.

`format(id)`

> SiLK files are maintained in a number of different optimized formats; the `format` value is a C macro describing the type of the file, followed by the hexadecimal ID of that type.

`version`

> The version of the file format.

`byte-order`

> The order in which bytes are stored on disk; SiLK maintains distinct little- and big-endian formats for faster reading.

`compression(id)`

> Whether the file is natively compressed, again for faster reading.

header-length
> The size of the file header; a SiLK file with no records will be just the size of the header-length.

record-length
> The size of individual file records. This value will be 1 if records are variable length.

record-version
> The version of the records (note that record versions are distinct from file versions and SiLK versions).

silk-version
> The version of the SiLK suite used to create the file.

count-records
> The number of records in the file.

file-size
> The total size of the file; if the file is uncompressed, this value should be equivalent to the header length added to the product of the record length and record count.

command-lines
> A record of the SiLK commands used to create the file.

Example 5-13 shows how to use the --note-add command.

Example 5-13. Using --note-add

```
$ rwfilter --aport=22 example.rwf --note-add='Filtering ssh' --pass=ex2.rwf
$ rwfileinfo ex2.rwf
ex2.rwf:
  format(id)         FT_RWGENERIC(0x16)
  version            16
  byte-order         littleEndian
  compression(id)    none(0)
  header-length      260
  record-length      52
  record-version     5
  silk-version       2.1.0
  count-records      10
  file-size          780
  command-lines
               1  rwfilter --print-stat --proto=6 --pass=example.rwf
in/2005/01/07/in-S0_20050107.01
               2  rwfilter --aport=22 --note-add=Filtering ssh
--pass=ex2.rwf example.rwf
  annotations
               1  Filtering ssh
```

Combining Information Flows: rwcount

rwcount can produce time series data from the output of an rwfilter command. It works by placing counts of bytes, packets, and flow records into fixed-duration *bins*, which are equally sized time periods specified by the user. rwcount is a relatively straightforward application. Most of its complexity comes from relating the flows, which themselves have a duration, to the bins.

The simplest invocation of rwcount is shown in Example 5-14. The first thing to notice is the use of the --bin-size option. In this example, the bins are half an hour, or 1,800 seconds. If --bin-size isn't specified, rwcount will default to 30-second bins. Bin sizes don't have to be integers; floating-point specifications with a resolution down to the millisecond are acceptable for people who like *lots* of bins in their output.

Example 5-14. Simple rwcount invocation

```
$ rwfilter in/2005/01/07/in-S0_20050107.01 --all=stdout |
    rwcount --bin-size=1800
               Date|    Records|           Bytes|         Packets|
2005/01/07T01:00:00|     257.58|     42827381.72|       248724.14|
2005/01/07T01:30:00|    1589.61|    211453506.60|      1438751.93|
2005/01/07T02:00:00|     171.81|    147824612.67|      1043011.93|
```

As Example 5-14 shows, rwcount outputs four columns: a date column in SiLK's standard date format (YYYY/MM/DDTHH:MM:SS), followed by record, byte, and packet columns. The floating-point values are a function of rwcount interpolating how much traffic should be in each bin; rwcount calls this a *load scheme*.

The load scheme is an attempt by rwcount to approximate how much of a flow took place over the period specified by the bins. In the default load scheme, rwcount splits each flow proportionally across all the bins during which the flow was taking place. For example, if a flow takes place from 00:04:00 to 00:11:00, and bins are five minutes long, 1/7 of the flow will be added to the first (00:00:00-00:04:59) bin, 5/7 to the second bin (00:05:00-00:09:59), and 1/7 to the third (00:10:00-00:14:59) bin. rwcount takes an integer parameter in the --load-scheme option, with the following results:

0 Split the traffic evenly across all bins covered. In the previous example, the flow would be split into thirds, and a third added to each bin.

1 Add the entire flow to the first bin covered by the flow. In the previous example, 00:00:00-00:04:59.

2 Add the entire flow to the last bin covered by the flow. In the previous example, 00:10:00-00:14:59.

3 Add the entire flow to the middle bin covered by the flow. In the previous example, 00:05:00-00:09:59.

4 The default load scheme.

rwcount uses the flow data provided to guess which time bins are required, but sometimes you have to explicitly specify the time, especially when coordinating multiple files. This can be done using the --start-epoch and --end-epoch options to specify starting and ending bin times. Note that these parameters can use the epoch time or yyyy/mm/dd:HH:MM:SS format. rwcount also has an option to print dates using epoch time: the --epoch-slots option.

The --skip-zero option (see Example 5-15) is one of a number of output format options. Normally, rwcount prints every empty bin it has allocated, but --skip-zero causes empty bins to be omitted from the output. In addition, rwcount supports many of the output options mentioned for rwcut: --no-titles, --no-columns, --column-separator, --no-final-delimter, and --delimited.

Example 5-15. Using epoch slots and the --skip-zero option

```
rwfilter in/2005/01/07/in-S0_20050107.01 --all=stdout |
    rwcount --bin-size=1800.00 --epoch
            Date|      Records|           Bytes|         Packets|
      1105059600|      257.58|     42827381.72|      248724.14|
      1105061400|     1589.61|    211453506.60|     1438751.93|
      1105063200|      171.81|    147824612.67|     1043011.93|
$ rwfilter in/2005/01/07/in-S0_20050107.01 --all=stdout |
    rwcount --bin-size=1800.00
            --epoch --start-epoch=1105057800
            Date|      Records|           Bytes|         Packets|
      1105057800|        0.00|            0.00|            0.00|
      1105059600|      257.58|     42827381.72|      248724.14|
      1105061400|     1589.61|    211453506.60|     1438751.93|
      1105063200|      171.81|    147824612.67|     1043011.93|
$ rwfilter in/2005/01/07/in-S0_20050107.01 --all=stdout |
    rwcount --bin-size=1800.00
            --epoch --start-epoch=1105056000
            Date|      Records|           Bytes|         Packets|
      1105056000|        0.00|            0.00|            0.00|
      1105057800|        0.00|            0.00|            0.00|
      1105059600|      257.58|     42827381.72|      248724.14|
      1105061400|     1589.61|    211453506.60|     1438751.93|
      1105063200|      171.81|    147824612.67|     1043011.93|
$ rwfilter in/2005/01/07/in-S0_20050107.01 --all=stdout |
    rwcount --bin-size=1800.00
            --epoch --start-epoch=1105056000 --skip-zero
            Date|      Records|           Bytes|         Packets|
      1105059600|      257.58|     42827381.72|      248724.14|
```

```
            1105061400|         1589.61|       211453506.60|        1438751.93|
            1105063200|          171.81|       147824612.67|        1043011.93|
```

rwset and IP Sets

IP sets are SiLK's most powerful capability, and something that distinguishes the toolkit from most other analytical tools. An IP set is a binary representation of an arbitrary collection of IP addresses. IP sets can be created from text files, from SiLK data, or by using other binary SiLK structures.

The easiest way to start with IP sets is to create one, as in Example 5-16.

Example 5-16. Creating IP sets with rwset

```
$ rwfilter in/2005/01/07/in-S0_20050107.01 --all=stdout |
  rwset --sip-file=sip.set --dip-file=dip.set
$ ls -l *.set
-rw-r--r-- 1 mcollins  staff     580 Jan 10 01:06 dip.set
-rw-r--r-- 1 mcollins  staff   15088 Jan 10 01:06 sip.set
$ rwsetcat sip.set | head -5
0.0.0.0
32.16.40.178
32.24.41.181
32.24.215.49
32.30.13.177
$ rwfileinfo sip.set
sip.set:
  format(id)          FT_IPSET(0x1d)
  version             16
  byte-order          littleEndian
  compression(id)     none(0)
  header-length       76
  record-length       1
  record-version      2
  silk-version        2.1.0
  count-records       15012
  file-size           15088
  command-lines
                1  rwset --sip-file=sip.set --dip-file=dip.set
```

rwset takes flow records and produces up to four output files. The file specified with --sip-file will contain source IP addresses from the flow, --dip-file will contain destination addresses, --any-file will contain source and destination IP addresses, and nhip-file will contain next hop addresses. The output is binary and read with rwset cat, and as with all SiLK files, the file can be examined using rwfileinfo.

The power of IP sets comes when they're combined with rwfilter. rwfilter has eight commands that accept IP sets (--sipset, --dipset, --nhipset, --anyset, and their

---

negations). Sets are explicitly designed so `rwfilter` can rapidly query using them, enabling a variety of useful queries, as seen in Example 5-17.

Example 5-17. Set manipulation and response

```
$ # First, we create IP sets; I use aport=123 (NTP on UDP) to filter down
$ # to a reasonable set of addresses.  NTP clients and servers use the same
$ # port.
$ rwfilter in/2005/01/07/in-S0_20050107.01 --pass=stdout --aport=123 |
    rwset --sip-file=sip.set --dip-file=dip.set
$ # Now, let's see how many IP addresses are created
$ rwsetcat --count-ip sip.set
15
$ # Generating output using rwfilter; note the use of the --dipset file as the
$ # sip set; this means that I'm now looking for messages that responded to
$ # these addresses.  This means that I've seen ntp going to and from the
$ # address, meaning it's likely to be a legitimate speaker, as opposed to a
$ # scan on port 123.
$ rwfilter out/2005/01/07/out-S0_20050107.01 --dipset=sip.set --pass=stdout
    --aport=123 | rwcut | head -5
            sIP|           dIP|sPort|dPort|pro|   packets|     bytes|  \
flags|           sTime|       dur|                      eTime|sen|
   128.3.23.152|    56.7.90.229|  123|  123| 17|        1|       76|  \
     |  2005/01/07T01:10:00.520|     0.083|2005/01/07T01:10:00.603|   ?|
   128.3.23.152|  192.41.221.11|  123|  123| 17|        1|       76|  \
     |  2005/01/07T01:10:15.519|     0.000|2005/01/07T01:10:15.519|   ?|
   128.3.23.231|  87.221.134.185| 123|  123| 17|        1|       76|  \
     |  2005/01/07T01:24:46.251|     0.005|2005/01/07T01:24:46.256|   ?|
   128.3.26.152|  58.243.214.183| 123|10123| 17|        1|       76|  \
     |  2005/01/07T01:27:08.854|     0.000|2005/01/07T01:27:08.854|   ?|
$ # Let's look at statistics; using the same file, I look at the hosts
$ # that responded
$ rwfilter out/2005/01/07/out-S0_20050107.01 --dipset=sip.set  --aport=123
    --print-stat
Files     1.  Read      12393.  Pass      21.  Fail      12372.
$ # Now I look at everyone else; not-dipset means that I'm looking at everything
$ # on port 123 that doesn't go to these addresses.
$ rwfilter out/2005/01/07/out-S0_20050107.01 --not-dipset=sip.set  --aport=123
    --print-stat
Files     1.  Read      12393.  Pass     337.  Fail      12056.
```

Sets can also be generated by hand using `rwsetbuild`, which takes text input and produces a set file as the output. The `rwsetbuild` specification takes any of the IP address specifications used by the `--saddress` option in `rwfilter`: literal addresses, integers, ranges within dotted quads, and netmasks. Example 5-18 demonstrates this.

Example 5-18. Building a set using rwsetbuild

```
$ cat > setsample.txt
# Comments in set files are prefaced with a hashmark
# Literal address
255.230.1.1
```

```
# Note that I'm putting addresses in some semi-random order; the output
# will be ordered.
111.2.3-4.1-2
# Netmask
22.11.1.128/30
^D
$ rwsetbuild setsample.txt setsample.set
$ rwsetcat --print-ip setsample.set
22.11.1.128
22.11.1.129
22.11.1.130
22.11.1.132
111.2.3.1
111.2.3.2
111.2.4.1
111.2.4.2
255.230.1.1
```

Sets can also be manipulated using the rwsettool command, which provides a variety of mechanisms for adding and removing sets. rwsettool supports four manipulations:

--union

> Creates a set that includes any address that appears in any of the sets.

--intersect

> Creates a set that includes only addresses that appear in all the sets specified.

--difference

> Removes addresses in the latter sets from the first set.

--sample

> Randomly samples a set to produce a subset.

rwsettool is generally invoked using an output path (--output=_file_), but if nothing is specified, it will dump to stdout. As with rwfilter, rwsettool output is binary, so a pure terminal dump triggers an error. Example 5-19 shows a manipulation with rwsettool.

Example 5-19. Set manipulation with rwsettool

```
$ rm setsample2.set
$ cat > setsample2.txt
# Build a set that covers our original setsample file to
# see what happens with various functions
22.11.1.128/29
$ rwsetbuild setsample2.txt setsample2.set
$ rwsettool --union setsample.set setsample2.set | rwsetcat
22.11.1.128
22.11.1.129
22.11.1.130
22.11.1.131
```

```
22.11.1.132
22.11.1.133
22.11.1.134
22.11.1.135
111.2.3.1
111.2.3.2
111.2.4.1
111.2.4.2
255.230.1.1
$ rwsettool --intersect setsample.set setsample2.set | rwsetcat
22.11.1.128
22.11.1.129
22.11.1.130
22.11.1.131
$ rwsettool --difference setsample.set setsample2.set | rwsetcat
111.2.3.1
111.2.3.2
111.2.4.1
111.2.4.2
255.230.1.1
```

rwuniq

rwuniq is the utility knife of counting tools. It allows an analyst to specify a key containing one or more fields, and will then count a number of different values, including total number of bytes, packets, flow records, or unique IP addresses matching the key.

rwuniq's default configuration counts the number of flows that occurred for a particular key. The key itself must be specified using the --field option, which accepts the field specifiers in Table 5-1. rwuniq can accept multiple fields, and the key will be generated in the order specified in the command line. Example 5-20 demonstrates the key features of the --field option. As it shows, field order in the option affects field ordering in the output.

Example 5-20. Various field specifiers using rwuniq

```
$ rwfilter out/2005/01/07/out-S0_20050107.01 --all=stdout |
  rwuniq --field=sip,proto | head -4
            sIP|pro|   Records|
 131.243.142.85| 17|         1|
131.243.141.187| 17|         6|
    128.3.23.41| 17|         4|
$ rwfilter out/2005/01/07/out-S0_20050107.01 --all=stdout |
  rwuniq --field=1,2 | head -4
           sIP|            dIP|   Records|
  128.3.174.158|    128.3.23.44|         2|
    128.3.191.1|239.255.255.253|         8|
   128.3.161.98|131.243.163.206|         1|
$ rwfilter out/2005/01/07/out-S0_20050107.01 --all=stdout |
  rwuniq --field=sip,sport | head -4
```

```
          sIP|sPort|   Records|
  131.243.63.143|53504|       1|
  131.243.219.52|61506|       1|
 131.243.163.206| 1032|       1|
$ rwfilter out/2005/01/07/out-S0_20050107.01 --all=stdout |
  rwuniq --field=sport,sip | head -4
sPort|           sIP|   Records|
55876|   131.243.61.70|       1|
51864|131.243.103.106|       1|
50955| 131.243.103.13|       1|
```

Also, note that when fields' orders are changed, the order in which records are output also changes. rwuniq does *not* guarantee record ordering by default; sorting can be ordered by using the --sort-output option.

rwuniq provides a number of count switches that instruct it to count additional values (see Example 5-21). The counting switches are --bytes, --packets, --flows, --sip-distinct, and --dip-distinct. Each of these fields can be used on their own, or by specifying a threshold (e.g., --bytes, --bytes=10, or --bytes=10-100). A single-value threshold (--bytes=10) provides a minimum, while a two-value threshold (--bytes=10-100) provides a range with a minimum and maximum. If you don't specify an argument, then the switch returns all values.

Example 5-21. Field spec with rwuniq

```
$ rwfilter out/2005/01/07/out-S0_20050107.01 --all=stdout |
  rwuniq --field=sport,sip --bytes --packets | head -5
sPort|           sIP|         Bytes|   Packets|
55876|   131.243.61.70|          308|         4|
51864|131.243.103.106|          308|         4|
50955| 131.243.103.13|          308|         4|
56568|   128.3.212.145|          360|         5|
$ rwfilter out/2005/01/07/out-S0_20050107.01 --all=stdout |
  rwuniq --field=sport,sip --bytes --packets=8 | head -5
sPort|           sIP|         Bytes|   Packets|
    0| 131.243.30.224|         2520|        30|
  959|   128.3.215.60|          876|        19|
 2315|131.243.124.237|          608|         8|
56838| 131.243.61.187|          616|         8|
$ rwfilter out/2005/01/07/out-S0_20050107.01 --all=stdout |
  rwuniq --field=sport,sip --bytes --packets=8-20 | head -5
sPort|           sIP|         Bytes|   Packets|
  959|   128.3.215.60|          876|        19|
 2315|131.243.124.237|          608|         8|
56838| 131.243.61.187|          616|         8|
  514|   128.3.97.166|         2233|        20|
```

rwbag

The last set of tools to discuss in this chapter are *bag tools*. A *bag* is a form of storage structure. It contains a key (which can be an IP address, a port, the protocol, or an interface index), and a count of values for that key. Bags can be created from scratch or from flow data using the rwbag command (see Example 5-22).

Example 5-22. An rwbag call, creating an IP address bag

```
$rwfilter out/2005/01/07/out-S0_20050107.01 --all=stdout |
  rwbag --sip-bytes=sip_bytes.bag
$rwbagcat sip_bytes.bag | head -5
     128.3.2.16|        10026403|
     128.3.2.46|           27946|
     128.3.2.96|          218605|
     128.3.2.98|             636|
    128.3.2.102|            1568|
```

Like sets, bags are a second-order binary structure for SiLK, meaning that they have their own toolkit (rwbagcat, rwbagtool, and rwbagbuild), the data is binary (so it can't be read with *cat* or a text editor), and they can be derived from flow data or built from a datafile.

The basic bag generation tool is rwbag, which as seen in Example 5-22, takes flow data and produces a bag file from it. rwbag can generate 27 types of bags, simultaneously if you're so inclined. These 27 types comprise three types of counting (bytes, packets, and flows), and nine types of key (sip, dip, sport, dport, proto, sensor, input, output, nhip). Combine the key and the counting type, and you have a switch that will create a bag. For example, to count all packets from source and destination IP addresses, call rwbag --sip-packets=b1.bag --dip-packets=b2.bag.

Advanced SiLK Facilities

In this section, we discuss more advanced SiLK facilities, in particular, the use of PMAPs and the collection and conversion of SiLK data.

pmaps

A SiLK *prefix map* (PMAP) is a binary file that associates specific subnetworks (prefixes) with tags. PMAPs are used to record various mappings of a network, such as whether a network belongs to a particular organization or ASN, or country code lookup. Using a source such as GeoIP (*http://www.maxmind.com*), you can build a PMAP that associates IP addresses with their country of origin.

The SiLK tool suite expects some basic PMAPs:

address_types.pmap

> Describes an address's type, conventionally indicating whether the address is inside or outside of the network you are monitoring. Specify the default filesystem location for this PMAP using the SILK_ADDRESS_TYPES environmental variable.

country_codes.pmap

> This PMAP describes the country code for an address. Specify the default location for this PMAP using the SILK_COUNTRY_CODES environmental variable.

PMAPs, like set files, can be created from text. Example 5-23 shows a simple PMAP file. Note the following attributes:

- The set of labels at the beginning. PMAPs do not store strings, but enumerable types identified by an integer. This enumeration is defined using the labels. You can see that the PMAP in Example 5-23, for instance, stores a 3 to mark normal traffic.

- The default key. Any value that doesn't match one of the network blocks listed in the map is given the default value.

- The actual declarations. Each declaration consists of a network specification, such 192.168.0.0/16, followed by a label.

Example 5-23. PMAP Input

```
# This is a simple PMAP file that tracks some of the standard RFC 1918
# reserved addresses
#
# First we create some labels
label 0 1918-reserved
label 1 multicast
label 2 future
label 3 normal
#
# Specify the mode; this must be either ip or proto-port. ip in this case
# refers to v4 addresses
#
mode ip
#
# Everything otherwise not specified is normal
default normal
# Now the maps
192.168.0.0/16     1918-reserved
10.0.0.0/8         1918-reserved
172.16.0.0/12      1918-reserved
224.0.0.0/4        multicast
240.0.0.0/4        future
```

Once you've created a text representations of the PMAP, you can compile the binary PMAP file using the rwpmapbuild command. rwpmapbuild has two mandatory arguments: an input filename, with the file in the text format described above, and a name for the output file. As with most SiLK commands, `rwpmapbuild` will not overwrite an existing output file. For example:

```
$ rwpmapbuild -i reserve.txt -o reserve.pmap
$ ls -l reserve.*
-rw-r--r-- 1 mcollins staff 406 May 27 17:16 reserve.pmap
-rw-r--r-- 1 mcollins staff 526 May 27 17:00 reserve.txt
```

Once a PMAP file is created, it can be added to `rwfilter` and `rwcut` using the `pmap-file` argument. Specifying the use of a PMAP file effectively creates a new set of fields in the filter and cut commands; since PMAP files are explicitly related to IP addresses, these new fields are bound to IP addresses.

Consider Example 5-24, which uses `rwcut`. In this example, the `--pmap-file` argument is colon-delimited; the value before the colon (`reserve` in the example) is a label, and the value after is a filename. `rwcut` binds the term reserve to the pmaps for the source and destination IP address, creating two new fields: `src-reserve` (for the mapping of the source address to the PMAP) and `dst-reserve` (for the mapping of the destination address) to the PMAP.

Example 5-24. Creating the src-reserve and dst-reserve fields

```
$ rwcut --pmap-file=reserve:reserve.pmap --fields=1-4,src-reserve,dst-reserve
  traceroute.rwf | head -5
         sIP|          dIP|sPort|dPort|    src-reserve|    dst-reserve|
 192.168.1.12|  192.168.1.1|65428|   53| 1918-reserved| 1918-reserved|
 192.168.1.12|  192.168.1.1|56126|   53| 1918-reserved| 1918-reserved|
 192.168.1.12|  192.168.1.1|52055|   53| 1918-reserved| 1918-reserved|
  192.168.1.1|  92.168.1.12|   53|56126| 1918-reserved| 1918-reserved|


$ # Using the pmap in filter; note that rwcut is not using the pmap
$ rwfilter --pmap-file=reserve:reserve.pmap --pass=stdout traceroute.rwf
  --pmap-src-reserve=1918-reserved  | rwcut --field=1-5
  | head -5
sIP| dIP|sPort|dPort|pro|
192.168.1.12| 192.168.1.1|65428| 53| 17|
192.168.1.12| 192.168.1.1|56126| 53| 17|
192.168.1.12| 192.168.1.1|52055| 53| 17|
192.168.1.1| 192.168.1.12| 53|56126| 17|
```

Collecting SiLK Data

There are a number of different tools for collecting data and pushing it into SiLK. The major ones are YAF, which is a flow collector, and `rwptoflow` and `rwtuc`, which convert other data into SiLK format.

YAF

Yet Another Flowmeter (YAF) is the reference implementation for the IETF IPFIX standard, and is the standard flow collection software for the SiLK toolkit. YAF can read *pcap* data from files or capture packets directly, which it then assembles into flow records and exports to disk. It has online documentation (*http://bit.ly/yaf-docu*). The tool itself can be entirely configured using command-line options, but the number of options is fairly daunting. At its simplest, a YAF command looks like this:

```
$ sudo yaf -i en1 --live=pcap -out /tmp/yaf/yaf
```

This reads data from interface en1 and drops it to the file in the temporary directory. Additional options control how data is read and how it is converted into flow and output format

yaf output is specified via the --out switch in tandem with the --ipfix and --rotate switches. By default, --out outputs to a file; in the example above, the file is */tmp/yaf/yaf*, but any valid filename will do (if --out is set to -, then yaf will output to stdout).

When --out is specified with --rotate, yaf writes the output to files that are rotated by a delay specified by the --rotate switch (e.g., --rotate 3600 will update files every hour). In this mode, yaf uses the name specified by --out as a base filename, and attaches a suffix specified in YYYYMMDDhhmmss format, along with a decimal serial number and then a *.yaf* file extension.

When yaf is specified with the --ipfix switch, it communicates IPFIX data to a daemon located elsewhere on the network. In this case (the most complicated option), --ipfix takes a transport protocol as an argument, while --out takes the IP address of the host. The additional --ipfix-port switch takes a port number when needed. Consult the documentation for more information.

The most important options are:

--live
Specifies the type of data being read; possible values formats are pcap, dag, or napatech. dag and napatech refer to proprietary packet capture systems, so unless you have that hardware, just set --live to pcap.

--filter
Applies a BPF filter to the *pcap* data.

--out
The output specifier, discussed above. The output specifier will be a file, a file prefix, or an IP address depending on whatever other switches are used.

--ipfix

Takes a transport protocol (tcp, udp, sctp, or spread) as an argument, and specifies that output is IPFIX transported over the network. Consult the yaf documentation for more information.

--ipfix-port

Used only if --ipfix is specified. It specifies the port that the IPFIX data is sent to.

--rotate

Used only with files. If present, the filename in --out is used as a prefix, and files are written with a timestamp appended to them. The --rotate option takes an argument and the number of seconds before moving to a new file.

--silk

Specifies output that can be parsed by SiLK's rwflowpack tools.

--idle-timeout

Specifies the idle timeout for flows in seconds. If a flow is present in the flow cache and isn't active, it's flushed as soon as it's been inactive for the duration of the idle timeout. Defaults to 300 seconds (five minutes).

--active-timeout

Specifies the active timeout for flows; the active timeout is the maximum amount of time an active flow will be stored in cache before being flushed. Defaults to 30 minutes (1,800 seconds). Note that the active timeout determines the maximum observed duration of collected flows.

YAF has many more options, but these are the basic ones to consider when configuring flows. Consult the YAF manpage for more details.

Cookbook: YAF

YAF has a ton of options, and how they operate together can be a bit confusing. Here are some examples of YAF invocations:

Read yaf from an interface (en1) and write to a file on disk:

```
$sudo yaf -i en1 --live=pcap -o /tmp/yaf/yaf
```

Rotate the files every five minutes:

```
$sudo yaf -i en1 --rotate 300 --live=pcap -o /tmp/yaf/yaf
```

Read a file from disk and convert it:

```
$yaf <example.pcap >yafout
```

Run a BPF filter on the data, in this case for TCP data only

```
$ sudo yaf -i en1 --rotate 300 --live=pcap -o /tmp/yaf/yaf --filter="tcp"
```

Export the YAF data over IPFIX to address 128.2.14.11:3059

```
$ sudo yaf --live pcap --in eth1 --out 128.2.14.11 --ipfix-port=3059
  --ipfix tcp
```

rwptoflow

SiLK uses its own compact binary formats to represent NetFlow data that tools such as rwcut and rwcount present in a human-readable form. There are times when an analyst needs to convert other data into SiLK format, such as taking packet captures from IDS alerts and converting it into a format where IP set filtering can be done on the data.

The go-to tool for this task is rwptoflow. rwptoflow is a packet data to flow conversion tool. It does *not* aggregate flows; instead, each flow generated by rwptoflow is converted into a one-packet flow record. The resulting file can then be manipulated by the SiLK suite as any other flow file.

rwptoflow is invoked relatively simply with an input filename as its argument. In Example 5-25, the *pcap* data from a traceroute is converted into flow data using rwpto flow. The resulting raw file is then read using rwcut and you can see the correspondence between the traceroute records and the resulting flow records.

Example 5-25. Converting pcap data with rwptoflow

```
$ tcpdump -v -n -r traceroute.pcap  | head -6
reading from file traceroute.pcap, link-type EN10MB (Ethernet)
21:06:50.559146 IP (tos 0x0, ttl 255, id 8010, offset 0, flags [none],
             proto UDP (17), length 64)
   192.168.1.12.65428 > 192.168.1.1.53: 63077+ A? jaws.oscar.aol.com. (36)
21:06:50.559157 IP (tos 0x0, ttl 255, id 37467, offset 0, flags [none],
             proto UDP (17), length 86)
   192.168.1.12.56126 > 192.168.1.1.53: 30980+ PTR?
   dr._dns-sd._udp.0.1.168.192.in-addr.arpa. (58)
21:06:50.559158 IP (tos 0x0, ttl 255, id 2942, offset 0, flags [none],
             proto UDP (17), length 66)
   192.168.1.12.52055 > 192.168.1.1.53: 990+ PTR? db._dns-sd._udp.home. (38)
$ rwptoflow traceroute.pcap > traceroute.rwf
$ rwcut --num-recs=3 --fields=1-5 traceroute.rwf
   sIP|    dIP|sPort|dPort|pro|
 192.168.1.12|   192.168.1.1|65428|   53|  17|
 192.168.1.12|   192.168.1.1|56126|   53|  17|
 192.168.1.12|   192.168.1.1|52055|   53|  17|
```

rwtuc

When correlating data between different sources, you will occasionally want to convert it into SiLK's format. rwtuc is the default tool for converting data into SiLK representation, as it works with columnar text files. Using rwtuc, you can convert IDS alerts and other data into SiLK data for further manipulations.

The easiest way to invoke rwtuc is to use it as an inverse of rwcut. Create a file with columnar entries and make sure that the titles match those used by rwcut:

```
$cat rwtuc_sample.txt
sIP        |dIP       |proto
128.2.11.4 | 29.3.11.4 | 6
11.8.3.15  | 9.12.1.4  | 17
$ rwtuc < rwtuc_sample.txt > rwtuc_sample.rwf
$ rwcut rwtuc_sample.rwf --field=1-6
 sIP| dIP|sPort|dPort|pro|   packets|
 128.2.11.4|  29.3.11.4|    0|    0|  6|         1|
  11.8.3.15|   9.12.1.4|    0|    0| 17|         1|
```

As the following fragment shows, rwtuc will read the columns, use the headers to determine column content, and stuff any unspecified fields with a default value if no column is provided. rwtuc can also take column specifications at the command line using the --fields and --column-separator switches, as so:

```
$cat rwtuc_sample2.txt
128.2.11.4  x 29.3.11.4 x 6 x 5
7.3.1.1     x  128.2.11.4 x 17 x 3
$ rwtuc --fields=sip,dip,proto,packets --column-sep=x < rwtuc_sample2.txt
  > rwtuc_sample2.rwf
$ rwcut --fields=1-7 rwtuc_sample2.rwf
  sIP|  dIP|sPort|dPort|pro|   packets|    bytes|
128.2.11.4|  29.3.11.4|    0|    0|  6|         5|         5|
    7.3.1.1| 128.2.11.4|    0|    0| 17|         3|         3|
```

SiLK's binary format requires values for every field, which means that rwtuc makes a best guess for field values that it doesn't have. For instance, the previous example specifies packets as a field but not bytes, so rwtuc just defines the packet value to be identical to the byte value.

If there exists a common default value (e.g., all traffic has the same protocol), this value can be defined using one of a number of field-stuffing options in rwtuc. These options are identical to the field filtering options in rwfilter, except they only take single values. For example, --proto=17 sets the protocol of every entry to 17.

In the fragment below, we use the field stuffing command --bytes=300 to set a value of 300 bytes for every entry in *rwtuc_sample2.txt*:

```
$ rwtuc --fields=sip,dip,proto,packets --column-sep=x --bytes=300 <
  rwtuc_sample2.txt > rwtuc_sample2.rwf
$ rwcut --fields=1-7 rwtuc_sample2.rwf
  sIP|  dIP|sPort|dPort|pro|   packets|    bytes|
128.2.11.4|  29.3.11.4|    0|    0|  6|         5|       300|
    7.3.1.1| 128.2.11.4|    0|    0| 17|         3|       300|
```

The resulting RWF file will contain a value of 300 bytes, even though the byte value is not in the original text file. The packet values, which are specified in the file, are set to whatever was specified there.

Further Reading

1. Time Shimeall, Sid Faber, Markus DeShon, and Drew Kompanek, "Using SiLK for Network Traffic Analysis," Software Engineering Institute.

## CHAPTER 6

An Introduction to R for Security Analysts

R is an open source statistical analysis package developed initially by Ross Ihaka and Robert Gentleman of the University of Auckland. R was designed primarily by statisticians and data analysts, and is related to commercial statistical packages such as S and SPSS. R is a toolkit for exploratory data analysis; it provides statistical modeling and data manipulation capabilities, visualization, and a full-featured programming language.

R fulfills a particular utility knife-like role for analysis. Analytic work requires some tool for creating and manipulating small ad hoc databases that summarize raw data. For example, hour summaries of traffic volume from a particular host broken down by services. These tables are more complex than the raw data but are not intended for final publication—they still require more analysis. Historically, Microsoft Excel has been the workhorse application for this type of analysis. It provides numeric analysis, graphing, and a simple columnar view of data that can be filtered, sorted, and ordered. I've seen analysts trade Excel files around like they were scraps of paper.

I switched from Excel to R because I found it to be a superior product for large-scale numerical analysis. The graphical nature of Excel makes it clunky when you deal with significantly sized datasets. I find R's table manipulation capabilities to be superior, it provides provenance in the form of saveable and sharable workspaces, the visualization capabilities are powerful, and the presence of a full-featured scripting language enables rapid automation. Much of what is discussed in this chapter can be done in Excel, but if you can invest the time to learn R, I believe you'll find it well spent.

The first half of this chapter focus on accessing and manipulating data using R's programming environment. The second half focuses on the process of statistical testing using R.

Installation and Setup

R is a well-maintained open source project. The Comprehensive R Archive Network (CRAN) (*http://cran.r-project.org*) maintains current binaries for Windows, Mac OS X, and Linux systems, an R package repository, and extensive documentation.

The easiest way to install R is to grab the appropriate binary (at the top of the home page). R is also available for every major package manager. For the rest of this chapter, I am going to assume you're using R within its own graphical interface.

There are a number of other tools available for working with R, depending on the tools and environments you're comfortable with. RStudio (*http://www.rstudio.com*) is an integrated development environment providing data, project, and task management tools in a more traditional IDE framework. For Emacs users, Emacs Speaks Statistics or ESS-mode (*http://ess.r-project.org*) provides an interactive environment.

Basics of the Language

This section is a crash course in R's language. R is a rich language with a surface I'm barely scratching. However, at the end of this section, you'll be able to write a simple R program, run it at the command line, and save it as a library.

The R Prompt

Starting R will present you with a window and command prompt. An example R console is shown in Figure 6-1. As this figure shows, the console is dominated by a large text window and a series of buttons at the top that provide supplemental functions. Note the two text fields under the button row. The first shows the current working directory and the second is the help function. R is very well documented, so get used to using that box.

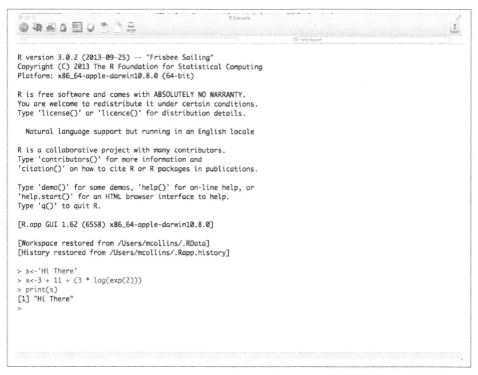

```
R version 3.0.2 (2013-09-25) -- "Frisbee Sailing"
Copyright (C) 2013 The R Foundation for Statistical Computing
Platform: x86_64-apple-darwin10.8.0 (64-bit)

R is free software and comes with ABSOLUTELY NO WARRANTY.
You are welcome to redistribute it under certain conditions.
Type 'license()' or 'licence()' for distribution details.

  Natural language support but running in an English locale

R is a collaborative project with many contributors.
Type 'contributors()' for more information and
'citation()' on how to cite R or R packages in publications.

Type 'demo()' for some demos, 'help()' for on-line help, or
'help.start()' for an HTML browser interface to help.
Type 'q()' to quit R.

[R.app GUI 1.62 (6558) x86_64-apple-darwin10.8.0]

[Workspace restored from /Users/mcollins/.RData]
[History restored from /Users/mcollins/.Rapp.history]

> s<-'Hi There'
> x<-3 + 11 + (3 * log(exp(2)))
> print(s)
[1] "Hi There"
>
```

Figure 6-1. The R console

In Figure 6-1, I've typed a couple of simple commands, recreated here:

```
> s<-'Hi There'
> x<- 3 + 11 + (3 * log(exp(2)))
> print(s)
[1] "Hi There"
> print(x)
[1] 20
```

The command line prompt for R is >; after that, you can enter commands by hand. If a command is partly completed (for example, by opening but not closing parentheses), the next prompt will be a sign, and continue until closure.

```
> s<- 3 * (
+ 5 + 11
+ + 2
+ )
> s
[1] 54
```

Note that when R returns a value (for example, the output of s in the previous example), it prints a [1] in square brackets. The value in brackets is an array index; if an array spreads over several lines, the relevant index will be printed at the beginning of each line.

```
> s<-seq(1,20)
> s
 [1]  1  2  3  4  5  6  7  8  9 10 11 12
[13] 13 14 15 16 17 18 19 20
```

Help can be accessed by using `help(term)` or `?term`. Search through help via `help.search()` or `??`.

To quit R, use the switch icon or the appropriate quit command (Command-Q or Ctrl-Q) for the operating system. If you're using pure command-line R (i.e., without the graphical interface), you can end the session using Ctrl-D or typing *q()* at the prompt.

When R terminates, it asks whether you want to save the workspace. Workspace files can be reloaded after a session to continue whatever work that was being done at the time of termination.

R Variables

R supports a number of different data types, including scalar integers, character data (strings), Booleans and floating-point values, vectors, matrices, and lists. The scalar types, as shown in the following example, can be assigned using the ← ("gets"), =, and → operators. R overloads some complicated scoping into its assignment operators, and for our purposes (and almost all R programming), R style guides recommend using the ← operator instead of the = sign.

```
> # Assign some value directly
> a<-1
> b<-1.0
> c<-'A String'
> d<-T
> # We'll assign e to d
> e<-d
> e
[1] TRUE
> d
[1] TRUE
> # Now we we reassign d, and we see d changes but e remains the same.
> d<-2
> d
[1] 2
> e
[1] TRUE
```

An R *vector* is an ordered set of one or more values of the same type: character, logical, or string. Vectors can be created using the c function or any of a number of other functions. Vectors are the most commonly used element in R: the scalar values we used earlier were technically vectors of length 1.[1]

```
> # An example of an integer vector
> int.vec<-c(1,2,3,4,5)
> int.vec
[1] 1 2 3 4 5
> # Floating point numbers will be cast to integer, or integers to floats
> # as needed
> float.vec<-c(1,2.0,3)
> float.vec
[1] 1 2 3
> float.vec<-c(1,2.45,3)
> float.vec
[1] 1.00 2.45 3.00
> # Vectors can also be logical
> logical.vec<-c(T,F,F,T)
> logical.vec
[1]  TRUE FALSE FALSE  TRUE
> # They will be cast to integers if put into a numeric vector
> mixed.vec<-c(1,2,FALSE,TRUE)
> mixed.vec
[1] 1 2 0 1
> # Character vectors consist of one or more strings; note that a
> #string is a single element
> char.vec <- c("One","Two","Three")
> char.vec
[1] "One"   "Two"   "Three"
> # Length gives vector lengths
> length(int.vec)
[1] 5
> # Note that the character vector's length is the length of the total
> # number of strings, not the individual characters
> length(char.vec)
[1] 3
```

Note the length of the character vector: in R, strings are treated as a single element regardless of the number of characters. There are functions for accessing strings—nchar to get the length, and substr and strsplit to extract elements from a string—but individual character strings are not as directly accessible as they are in Python.

R provides a number of functions for vector arithmetic. A vector can be added to or multiplied by another vector; if they're equally sized, the result will be calculated on an element-by-element basis. If one vector is smaller, it will be repeated to make a vector of equal size. (A vector whose length is not a factor of the other vector will raise an error.) This applies to single-element vectors as well: add a single element to a longer

---

1. Note the use of periods rather than underscores; R's predecessors (S and S-Plus) established this convention and while it's not a syntactical mistake to use an underscore, most R code will use periods the way other languages use underscores.

vector and each element in the vector will be added to; multiply and each element will be multiplied.

Vectors are indexable. Individual elements can be accessed using square brackets, so v[k] is the *k*th element of v. Vectors also support ranged slicing, such as v[a:b]. A negative index will eliminate the indexed element from the vector, like in the following code block:

```
> # We start by creating a vector out of two others
> v1 <- c(1,2,3,4,5)
> v2 <- c(6,7,8,9,10)
> v3 <- c(v1,v2)
> v3
 [1]  1  2  3  4  5  6  7  8  9 10
> # Note that there's no nesting
> # Basic arithmetic - multiplication and addition
> 2 * v1
[1]  2  4  6  8 10
> 2 * v3
 [1]  2  4  6  8 10 12 14 16 18 20
> 1 + v1
[1] 2 3 4 5 6
> v1 * v2
# Multiplication
[1]  6 14 24 36 50
# Slicing a range
> v3[1:3]
[1] 1 2 3
# This is identical to v3[1]
> v3[1:1]
[1] 1
> v3[2:4]
[1] 2 3 4
# Reverse the range to reverse the vector
> v3[3:1]
[1] 3 2 1
# Use negative numbers to cut out elements
> v3[-3]
[1]  1  2  4  5  6  7  8 .9 10
> v3[-1:-3]
[1]  4  5  6  7  8  9 10
> # You can use logical vectors as selectors; selection returns anything where
> # the index is true
> v3[c(T,F)]
[1] 1 3 5 7 9
```

R can construct matrices out of vectors using the matrix function. As with vectors, matrices can be added and multiplied (with themselves, vectors, and other matrices), and selected and sliced using a number of different approaches, like those shown here:

```
> # Matrices are constructed using the matrix commmand, as shown in the
> # basic form below. Note that columns are filled up first.
> s<-matrix(v3,nrow=2,ncol=5)
> s
     [,1] [,2] [,3] [,4] [,5]
[1,]    1    3    5    7    9
[2,]    2    4    6    8   10
> # Adding a single element
> s + 3
     [,1] [,2] [,3] [,4] [,5]
[1,]    4    6    8   10   12
[2,]    5    7    9   11   13
> # Multiplication
> s * 2
     [,1] [,2] [,3] [,4] [,5]
[1,]    2    6   10   14   18
[2,]    4    8   12   16   20
> # Multiplication by a matrix
> s * s
     [,1] [,2] [,3] [,4] [,5]
[1,]    1    9   25   49   81
[2,]    4   16   36   64  100
> # Adding a vector, note that addition goes
> # through the columns first
> s + v3
     [,1] [,2] [,3] [,4] [,5]
[1,]    2    6   10   14   18
[2,]    4    8   12   16   20
> # Adding a smaller vector, note that
> # it loops over the matrix, column-first
> s + v1
     [,1] [,2] [,3] [,4] [,5]
[1,]    2    6   10    9   13
[2,]    4    8    7   11   15
> # Slicing; the use of the comma will strike most people as weird.
> # Before the commma are the rows, after the comma are the columns.
> # The result is returned as a vector, which is why the "column" is now
> # horizontal
> s[,1]
[1] 1 2
> s[1,]
[1] 1 3 5 7 9
> # Accesssing a single element
> s[1,1]
[1] 1
> # Now I'm accessing the 1st and 2nd column elements from the
> # first row; again, get a vector back
> s[1,1:2]
[1] 1 3
> # First and second row elements from the first column
> s[1:2,1]
[1] 1 2
```

```
> # Now I get a matrix back because I pull two vectors
> s[1:2,1:2]
     [,1] [,2]
[1,]    1    3
[2,]    2    4
> # Selection using booleans, the first value is the row I pull from
> s[c(T,F)]
[1] 1 3 5 7 9
> s[c(F,T)]
[1]  2  4  6  8 10
> # If I specify another vector, it'll pull out columns
> s[c(F,T),c(T,F,T,T,F)]
[1] 2 6 8
```

An R *list* is effectively a vector of vector elements, each of which can be composed of its own lists. Lists, like matrices, are constructed with their own special command. Lists can be sliced like a vector, although individual elements are accessed using double brackets. Of more interest, lists can be *named*; individual vectors can be assigned a name and then accessed using the $ operator.

```
# Review elements of earlier vectors
> v3
 [1]  1  2  3  4  5  6  7  8  9 10
> v4
[1] "Hi"    "There" "Kids"
> # Create a list; note that we can add an arbitrary number of elements.
> # Each element added is a new index.
> list.a <- list(v3,v4,c('What','The'),11)
> # Dump the list; note the list indices in double brackets.
> list.a
[[1]]
 [1]  1  2  3  4  5  6  7  8  9 10

[[2]]
[1] "Hi"    "There" "Kids"

[[3]]
[1] "What" "The"

[[4]]
[1] 11
> # Lists do not support vector arithmetic.
> list.a + 1
Error in list.a + 1 : non-numeric argument to binary operator
> # Individual elements can be examined via indexing.  Single brackets
> # return a list.
> list.a[1]
[[1]]
 [1]  1  2  3  4  5  6  7  8  9 10
> # Double brackets return the element itself; note that the list index
> # (the [[1]]) isn't present here
> list_a[[1]]
```

```
[1]  1  2  3  4  5  6  7  8  9 10
> # The single brackets returned a list, and the double brackets then returned
> # the first element in that single-element list.
> list_a[1][[1]]
 [1]  1  2  3  4  5  6  7  8  9 10
> # Access using double brackets, then a single bracket in the vector.
> list_a[[1]][1]
[1] 1
> list_a[[2]][2]
[1] "There"
> # We can modify the results.
> list_a[[2]][2] <- 'Wow'
> # Now we'll create a named list.
> list_b <- list(values=v1,rant=v2,miscellany=c(1,2,3,4,5,9,10))
> # The parameter names become the list element names, and the arguments
> # are the actual elements of the list.
> list_b
$values
[1] 1 2 3 4 5

$rant
[1]  6  7  8  9 10

$miscellany
[1]  1  2  3  4  5  9 10

> # Named elements are accessed using the dollar sign.
> list_b$miscellany
[1]  1  2  3  4  5  9 10
> # After accessing, you can use standard slicing.
> list_b$miscellany[2]
[1] 2
> # Note that the index and the name point to the same value.
> list_b[[3]]
[1]  1  2  3  4  5  9 10
```

Understanding list syntax is important for data frames, which we discuss in more depth later.

Writing Functions

R functions are created by binding the results of the function command to a symbol, like so:

```
> add_elements <- function(a,b) a + b
> add_elements(2,3)
[1] 5
> simple_math <- function(x,y,z) {
+     t <- c(x,y)
+     z * t
+ }
```

Note the curly braces. In R, curly braces are used to hold multiple expressions, and return the final statement of those multiple expressions. Curly braces can be used without a function or anything else, as shown here:

```
> { 8 + 7
+ 9 + 2
+ c('hi','there')
+ }
[1] "hi"     "there"
```

So, in *simple_math*, the results in the braces are evaluated sequentially and the final result returned. The final result need not have any relationship to the previous statements within the block. R does have a return statement to control the termination and return of a function, but the convention is not to use it if the results are obvious.

As the examples show, function arguments are defined in the function statement. Arguments can be given a default value by using the = sign; any argument to which you assign a default value becomes optional. Argument assignment can be done through order or by explicitly using the argument name, as shown here:

```
# Create a function with an optional argument
> test<-function(x,y=10) { x + y }
# If the argument is not passed, R will use the default
> test(1)
[1] 11
> # Call both arguments and values are set positionally
> test(1,5)
[1] 6
> # The value can also be assigned using the argument name
> test(1,y=9)
[1] 10
> # For all variables
> test(x=3,y=3)
[1] 6
> # Names supercede position
> test(y=8,x=4)
[1] 12
> # A value without a default still must be assigned.
> test()
Error in x + y : 'x' is missing
```

R's functional features allow you to treat functions as objects that can be manipulated, evaluated, and applied as needed. Functions can be passed to other functions as parameters, and by using the apply and Reduce functions, can be used to support more complex evaluation.

```
> # Create a function to be called by another function
> inc.func<-function(x) { x + 1 }
> dual.func<-function(y) { y(2) }
> dual.func(inc.func)
[1] 3
```

```
> # R has a number of different apply functions based on input type
> # (matrix, list, vector) and output type.
> test.vec<-1:20
> test.vec
 [1]  1  2  3  4  5  6  7  8  9 10 11 12 13 14 15 16 17 18 19 20
> # Run sapply on an anonymous function; note that the function isn't bound
> # to an object; it exists for the duration of the run.  I could just as
> # easily call sapply(c,inc.func) to use the function inc.func defined above.
> sapply(test.vec,function(x) x+2)
 [1]  3  4  5  6  7  8  9 10 11 12 13 14 15 16 17 18 19 20 21 22
> # Where sapply is the classic map function, Reduce is the classic fold/reduce
> # function, reducing a vector a single value.  In this case, the function
> # passed adds a and b together, adding the integers 1 to 20 together yields 210
> # Note Reduce's capitalization
> Reduce(function(a,b) a+b,1:20)
[1] 210
```

A point about loops in R: R's loops (particularly the for loop) are notoriously slow. Many tasks that would be done with a for loop in Python or C are done in R using a number of functional constructs. *sapply* and *Reduce* are the frontend for this.

Conditionals and Iteration

The basic conditional statement in R is if...then...else, using else if to indicate multiple statements. The if statement is itself a function, and returns a value that can be evaluated.

```
> # A simple if/then which prints out a string
> if (a == b) print("Equivalent") else print("Not Equivalent")
[1] "Not Equivalent"
> # We could just return values directly
> if (a==b) "Equivalent" else "Not Equivalent"
[1] "Not Equivalent"
# If/then is a function, so we can plug it into another function or an if/then
> if((if (a!=b) "Equivalent" else "Not Equivalent") == \
      "Not Equivalent") print("Really not equivalent")
> a<-45
> # Chain together multiple if/then statements using else if
> if (a == 5) "Equal to five" else if (a == 20)  "Equal to twenty" \
  else if (a == 45) "Equal to forty five" else "Odd beastie"
[1] "Equal to forty five"
> a<-5
> if (a == 5) "Equal to five" else if (a == 20)  "Equal to twenty" \
 else if (a == 45) "Equal to forty five" else "Odd beastie"
[1] "Equal to five"
> a<-97
> if (a == 5) "Equal to five" else if (a == 20)  "Equal to twenty" \
 else if (a == 45) "Equal to forty five" else "Odd beastie"
[1] "Odd beastie"
```

R provides a `switch` statement as a compact alternative to multiple `if`/`then` clauses. The switch statement uses positional arguments for integer comparisons, and optional parameter assignments for text comparison.

```
> # When switch takes a number as its first parameter, it returns the
> # argument with an index that corresponds to that number, so the following
> returns the second argument, "Is"
> switch(2,"This","Is","A","Test")
[1] "Is"
> proto<-'tcp'
> # If parameters are named, those text strings are used for matching
> switch(proto,tcp=6,udp=17,icmp=1)
[1] 6
> # The last parameter is the default argument
> proto<-'unknown'
> switch(proto, tcp=6,udp=17,icmp=1, -1)
[1] -1
> # To use a switch repeatedly, bind it to a function
> proto<-function(x) { switch(x, tcp=6,udp=17,icmp=1)}
> proto('tcp')
[1] 6
> proto('udp')
[1] 17
> proto('icmp')
[1] 1
```

R has three looping constructs: `repeat`, which provides infinite loops by default; `while`, which does a conditional evaluation in each loop; and `for`, which iterates over a vector. Internal loop operations are controlled by `break` (which terminates the loop), and `next` (which skips through an iteration), as seen here:

```
> # A repeat loop; note that repeat loops run infinitely unless there's a break
> # statement in the loop.  If you don't specify a condition, it'll run forever.
> i<-0
> repeat {
+    i <- i + 1
+    print(i)
+    if (i > 4) break;
+ }
[1] 1
[1] 2
[1] 3
[1] 4
[1] 5
> # The while loop with identical functionality; this one doesn't require the
> # break statement
> i <- 1
> while( i < 6) {
+        print(i)
+        i <- i + 1
+ }
[1] 1
```

```
[1] 2
[1] 3
[1] 4
[1] 5
> # The for loop is most compact
> s<-1:5
> for(i in s) print(i)
[1] 1
[1] 2
[1] 3
[1] 4
[1] 5
```

Although R provides these looping constructs, it's generally better to avoid loops in favor of functional operations such as `sapply`. R is *not* a general purpose programming language; it was explicitly designed to provide statistical analysts with a rich toolkit of operations. R contains an enormous number of optimized functions and other tools available for manipulating data. We cover some later in this chapter, but a good R reference source is invaluable.

Using the R Workspace

R provides users with a persistent workspace, meaning that when a user exits an R session, they are provided the option to save the data and variables they have in place for future use. This is done largely transparently, as the following command-line example shows:

```
> s<-1:15
> s
 [1]  1  2  3  4  5  6  7  8  9 10 11 12 13 14 15
> t<-(s*3) - 5
> t
 [1] -2  1  4  7 10 13 16 19 22 25 28 31 34 37 40
>
Save workspace image? [y/n/c]: y
$ R --silent
> s
 [1]  1  2  3  4  5  6  7  8  9 10 11 12 13 14 15
> t
 [1] -2  1  4  7 10 13 16 19 22 25 28 31 34 37 40
```

Whenever you start R in a particular directory, it checks for a workspace file (*.RData*) and loads its contents if it exists. On exiting a session, *.RData* will be updated if requested. It can also be saved in the middle of a session using the `save.image()` command. This can be a lifesaver when trying out new analyses or long commands.

You can get a list of objects in a workspace using the `ls` function, which returns a vector of object names. They can be deleted using the `rm` function. Objects in a workspace can be saved and loaded using the `save` and `load` functions. These take a list of objects and a filename as an argument, and automatically load the results into the environment.

```
> # let's create some simple objects
> a<-1:20
> t<-rnorm(50,10,5)
> # Ls will showm to us
> ls()
[1] "a" "t"
> # Now we save them
> save(a,t,file='simple_data')
> # we delete them and look
> rm(a,t)
> ls()
character(0)
> load('simple_data')
> ls()
[1] "a" "t"
```

If you have a simple R script you want to load up, use the `source` command to load the file. The `sink` command will redirect output to a file.

Data Frames

Data frames are a structure unique to R and, arguably, the most important structure from an analyst's view. A data frame is an ad hoc data table: a tabular structure where each column represents a single variable. In other languages, data frames are implemented partially by using arrays or hashtables, but R includes data frames as a basic structure and provides facilities for selecting, filtering, and manipulating the contents of a data frame in a far more sophisticated way from the start.

Let's start by creating a simple data frame, as you can see in Example 6-1. The easiest way to construct a data frame is to use the `data.frame` operation on a set of identically sized vectors.

Example 6-1. Creating a data frame

```
> names<-c('Manny','Moe','Jack')
> ages<-c(25,35,90)
> states<-c('NJ','NE','NJ')
> summary.data <- data.frame(names, ages, states)
> summary.data
  names ages states
1 Manny   25    NJ
2   Moe   35    NE
3  Jack   90    NJ
> summary.data$names
[1] Manny Moe   Jack
Levels: Jack Manny Moe
```

Here, `data.frame` made each array into a column to form a table with three columns and three rows. We could then extract a column. Note the use of the term "Levels" when referring to the vector of names referenced by *summary.data$names*.

Factors

In the process of creating the table, R converted the strings in the data into *factors*, which are a vector of categories. Factors can be created from strings or integers, for example:

```
> services<-c("http","bittorrent","smtp","http","http","bittorrent")
> service.factors<-factor(services)
> service.factors
[1] http        bittorrent smtp      http       http       bittorrent
Levels: bittorrent http smtp
> services
[1] "http"      "bittorrent" "smtp"      "http"      "http"      "bittorrent"
```

The *levels* of the factor describe the individual categories of the factor.

R's default behavior in many functions is to convert strings to factors. This is done in `read.table` and `data.frame` and controllable via the `stringsAsFactors` argument, as well as the `stringsAsFactors` option.

The command for accessing data frames is `read.table`, which has a variety of parameters for reading different data types. In Example 6-2, options are passed to let it read rwcut output in the input file, *sample.txt*.

Example 6-2. Passing options to read.table

```
$ cat sample.txt | cut -d '|' -f 1-4
     sIP|        dIP|sPort|dPort|
  10.0.0.1|  10.0.0.2|56968|    80|
  10.0.0.1|  10.0.0.2|56969|    80|
  10.0.0.3|...
$ R --silent
> s<-read.table(file='sample.txt',header=T,sep='|',strip.white=T)
> s
     sIP              dIP sPort dPort pro packets bytes flags
1 10.0.0.1       10.0.0.2 56968    80   6       4   172 FS  A
2 10.0.0.1       10.0.0.2 56969    80   6       5   402 FS PA
3 10.0.0.3 65.164.242.247 56690    80   6       5  1247 FS PA
4 10.0.0.4  99.248.195.24 62904 19380   6       1   407 F  PA
5 10.0.0.5 216.73.87.152 56691    80   6       7   868 FS PA
6 10.0.0.3 216.73.87.152 56692    80   6       5   760 FS PA
7 10.0.0.5 138.87.124.42  2871  2304   6       7   603 F  PA
8 10.0.0.3 216.73.87.152 56694    80   6       5   750 FS PA
9 10.0.0.1 72.32.153.176 56970    80   6       6   918 FS PA
                    sTime dur                 eTime sen  X
1 2008/03/31T18:01:03.030   0 2008/03/31T18:01:03.030   0 NA
```

```
2 2008/03/31T18:01:03.040    0 2008/03/31T18:01:03.040    0 NA
3 2008/03/31T18:01:03.120    0 2008/03/31T18:01:03.120    0 NA
4 2008/03/31T18:01:03.160    0 2008/03/31T18:01:03.160    0 NA
5 2008/03/31T18:01:03.220    0 2008/03/31T18:01:03.220    0 NA
6 2008/03/31T18:01:03.220    0 2008/03/31T18:01:03.220    0 NA
7 2008/03/31T18:01:03.380    0 2008/03/31T18:01:03.380    0 NA
8 2008/03/31T18:01:03.430    0 2008/03/31T18:01:03.430    0 NA
9 2008/03/31T18:01:03.500    0 2008/03/31T18:01:03.500    0 NA
```

Note the arguments used. `file` is self explanatory. The `header` argument instructs R to treat the first line of the file as names for the columns in the resulting data frame. `sep` defines a column separator, in this case, the default | used by SiLK commands. The `strip.white` command instructs R to strip out excess whitespace from the file. The net result is that every value is read in and converted automatically into a columnar format.

Now that I have data, I can filter and manipulate it, as shown in Example 6-3.

Example 6-3. Manipulating and filtering data

```
> # I can filter records by creating boolean vectors out of them, for example:
> s$dPort == 80
[1]  TRUE  TRUE  TRUE FALSE  TRUE  TRUE FALSE  TRUE  TRUE
> # I can then use that value to filter out the rows where s$dPort == 80
> # Note the comma. If I didn't use it, I would select the columns
> # instead of the rows.
> s[s$dPort==80,]
      sIP          dIP sPort dPort pro packets bytes flags
1 10.0.0.1      10.0.0.2 56968    80   6       4   172 FS  A
2 10.0.0.1      10.0.0.2 56969    80   6       5   402 FS PA
3 10.0.0.3 65.164.242.247 56690    80   6       5  1247 FS PA
5 10.0.0.3  216.73.87.152 56691    80   6       7   868 FS PA
6 10.0.0.3  216.73.87.152 56692    80   6       5   760 FS PA
8 10.0.0.3  216.73.87.152 56694    80   6       5   750 FS PA
9 10.0.0.1  72.32.153.176 56970    80   6       6   918 FS PA
                     sTime dur                    eTime sen  X
1 2008/03/31T18:01:03.030    0 2008/03/31T18:01:03.030    0 NA
2 2008/03/31T18:01:03.040    0 2008/03/31T18:01:03.040    0 NA
3 2008/03/31T18:01:03.120    0 2008/03/31T18:01:03.120    0 NA
5 2008/03/31T18:01:03.220    0 2008/03/31T18:01:03.220    0 NA
6 2008/03/31T18:01:03.220    0 2008/03/31T18:01:03.220    0 NA
8 2008/03/31T18:01:03.430    0 2008/03/31T18:01:03.430    0 NA
9 2008/03/31T18:01:03.500    0 2008/03/31T18:01:03.500    0 NA
> # I can also combine rules, use | for or and & for and
> s[s$dPort==80 & s$sIP=='10.0.0.3',]
      sIP          dIP sPort dPort pro packets bytes flags
3 10.0.0.3 65.164.242.247 56690    80   6       5  1247 FS PA
5 10.0.0.3  216.73.87.152 56691    80   6       7   868 FS PA
6 10.0.0.3  216.73.87.152 56692    80   6       5   760 FS PA
8 10.0.0.3  216.73.87.152 56694    80   6       5   750 FS PA
                     sTime dur                    eTime sen  X
3 2008/03/31T18:01:03.120    0 2008/03/31T18:01:03.120    0 NA
5 2008/03/31T18:01:03.220    0 2008/03/31T18:01:03.220    0 NA
```

```
6 2008/03/31T18:01:03.220   0 2008/03/31T18:01:03.220   0 NA
8 2008/03/31T18:01:03.430   0 2008/03/31T18:01:03.430   0 NA
> # I can access columns using their names
> s[s$dPort==80 & s$sIP=='10.0.0.3',][c('sIP','dIP','sTime')]
      sIP           dIP                sTime
3 10.0.0.3 65.164.242.247 2008/03/31T18:01:03.120
5 10.0.0.3  216.73.87.152 2008/03/31T18:01:03.220
6 10.0.0.3  216.73.87.152 2008/03/31T18:01:03.220
8 10.0.0.3  216.73.87.152 2008/03/31T18:01:03.430
> # And I can access a single row
> s[1,]
      sIP      dIP sPort dPort pro packets bytes flags                sTime
1 10.0.0.1 10.0.0.2 56968    80   6       4   172 FS  A 2008/03/31T18:01:03.030
  dur                eTime sen  X
1   0 2008/03/31T18:01:03.030   0 NA
```

R's data frames provide us with what is effectively an ad hoc single table database. In addition to the selection of rows and columns shown in earlier examples, we can add new columns using the $ operator.

```
> # Create a new vector of payload bytes
> payload_bytes <- s$bytes - (40 * s$packets)
> s$payload_bytes <- payload_bytes
> s[0:2,][c('sIP','dIP','bytes','packets','payload_bytes')]
      sIP      dIP bytes packets payload_bytes
1 10.0.0.1 10.0.0.2   172       4            12
2 10.0.0.1 10.0.0.2   402       5           202
```

Visualization

R provides extremely powerful visualization capabilities out of the box, and many standard visualizations are available as high-level commands. In the following example, we'll produce a histogram using a sample from a normal distribution and then plot the results on screen.

Chapter 10 discusses various visualization techniques. In this section, we focus on various features of R visualization, including controlling the images, saving them, and manipulating them.

Visualization Commands

R has a number of high-level visualization commands to plot time series, histograms, and bar charts. The workhorse command of the suite is plot, which can be used to provide a number of plots derived from scatterplots: simple scatterplots, stair steps, and series. The major plot names are listed in Table 6-1 and are described in the help command.

Table 6-1. High-level visualization commands

Command	Description
barplot	Barchart
boxplot	Box plot
hist	Histogram
pairs	Paired plot
plot	Scatterplot and related plots
qqnorm	QQ plot

Parameters to Visualization

There are two major mechanisms for controlling the parameters of a visualization. First, almost all visualization commands offer a standard suite of options as parameters. The major options are shown in Table 6-2 and the results of visualizing them are shown in the companion image, Figure 6-2.

Table 6-2. Common visualization options

Option	Parameter	Description
axes	Boolean	If true, adds axes
log	Boolean	If true, plots on a logarithmic scale
main	Character	Main title
sub	Character	Subtitle for the plot
type	Character	Controls the type of graph plotted
xlab	Character	Label for the x-axis
ylab	Character	Label for the y-axis

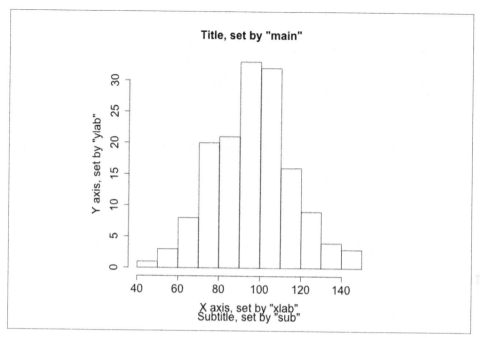

Figure 6-2. Visualizing options

Visualization options are also controlled using the par function, which provides a huge number of special options for managing axis size, point types, font choices, and the like. par takes an enormous number of options that you can read about via help(par). Table 6-3 provides some of the more important ones.

```
> # We're going to use par to draw a 3-columm, 2-row matrix, then fill in 3 cells
> # of the matrix with different plots using other par values
> par(mfcol=c(2,3))
> # Draw the default histogram
> hist(sample_rnorm,main='Sample Histogram')
> # Now we move to the 2nd row, center column
> par(mfg=c(2,2,2,3))
> # Change the size of the axes to half the default
> par(cex.axis=0.5)
> # Make the axes blue
> par(col.axis='blue')
> # Make the plot itself red
> par(col = 'red')
> # Now we plot as a scatter
> plot(sample_rnorm,main='Sample scatter')
> # After we've plotted this, it will automatically move to the
> # 3rd row, 1st column
> # Restore the axis size
> par(cex.axis=1.0)
> # Change the point type for a scatterplot. Use help(points) to get a list of
```

```
> # the numbers for PCH
> par(pch=24)
> plot(sample_rnorm,main='Sample Scatter with New Points')
```

Table 6-3. Useful par arguments

Name	Type	Description
mfcol	2-integer (row, col) vector	Breaks the canvas into a row-by-column set of cells
mfg	4-integer (row, col, nrows, ncols) vector	Specifies the specific cell in mfcol to draw in
cex [a]	Floating point	Sets the font size, defaults to 1, so specifying cex=0.5 indicates that all sizes are now half the original size
col	Character [b]	Color
lty	Number or character	Line type
pch	Number	Point type

[a] cex and col have a number of child parameters: .axis, .main, .lab, and .sub, which affect the corresponding element. cex.main is the relative size of the font for the tite, for example.

[b] Color strings can be a string like red, or a hexadecimal RGB string in the form #RRGGBB.

Annotating a Visualization

When drawing visualizations, I usually prefer to have some kind of model or annotation available to compare the visualization against. For example, if I'm comparing a visualization against a normal distribution, I want the appropriate normal distribution on the screen to compare it against the results of the histogram.

R provides a number of support functions for drawing text on a plot. These include lines, points, abline, polygon, and text. Unlike the high-level plot functions, these write directly to the screen without resetting the image. In this section, we will show how to use lines and text to annotate an image.

We'll begin by generating a histogram for a common scenario: scanning traffic plus typical user traffic on a /22 (1024 host) network. The observed parameter is the number of hosts, and we assume that under normal circumstances, that value is normally distributed with a mean of 280 hosts and a standard deviation of 30. One out of every 10 events will take place during a scan. During the scan, the count of hosts observed is always 1024, as the scanner hits everyone on the network.

```
> # First we model typical activity using a gaussian distribution via rnorm
> normal_activity <- rnorm(300,280,30)
> # We then create a vector of attacks, where every attack is 1024 hosts
> attack_activity <- rep(1024,30)
> # We concatenate the two together; because we're focusing on the number of
> # hosts and not a time dependency, we don't care about ordering
```

```
> activity_vector<-c(normal_activity, attack_activity)
> hist(activity_vector,breaks=50,xlab='Hosts observed',\
    ylab='Probability of Occurence',prob=T,main='Simulated Scan Activity')
```

Note the breaks and prob arguments in the histogram. breaks governs the number of bins in the histogram, which is particularly important when you're dealing with a long-tailed distribution like this model. prob plots the histogram as a density rather than as frequency counts.

We will now fit a curve. To do so, we create a vector of x and a vector of y values for the lines function. The x values are evenly split points on the range covered by our empirical distribution, while the y values are derived using the dnorm function:

```
> xpoints<-seq(min(activity_vector),max(activity_vector),length=50)
> # Use dnorm to calculate the corresponding y values, given a feed
> # of x values (xpoints) and a model of a normal distribution using
> # the mean and sd from the activity vector. The value will be a poor
> # fit, as the attack skews the traffic.
> ypoints<-dnorm(xpoints,mean=mean(activity_vector),sd=sd(activity_vector))
> # Plot the histogram, which wipes the canvas clean
> hist(activity_vector,breaks=50,xlab='Hosts observed',\
 ylab='Density',prob=T,main='Simulated Scan Activity')
> # Draw the fit line, using lines
> lines(xpoints,ypoints,lwd=2)
> # Draw text. The x and y value are derived from the plot.
> text(550,0.010,"This is an example of a fit")
```

Exporting Visualization

R visualizations are output on *devices*, which can be called by using a number of different functions. The default device is X11 on Unix systems, quartz on Mac OS X and win.graph on Windows. R's help for Devices (note the case) provides a list of what's available on the current platform.

To print R output, open an output device (such as png, jpeg, or pdf) and then write commands as normal. The results will be written to the device file until you deactivate it using dev.off(). At this point, you should call your default device again without parameters.

```
> # Output a histogram to the file 'histogram.png'
> png(file='histogram.png')
> hist(rnorm(200,50,20))
> dev.off()
> quartz()
```

Analysis: Statistical Hypothesis Testing

R is designed to provide a statistical analyst with a variety of tools for examining data. The programming features discussed so far in this chapter are a means to that end. The primary features we want to use R for are to support the construction of alarms by identifying statistically significant features (see Chapter 7 for more discussion of alarm construction).

Identifying attributes that are useful for alarms requires identifying "important" behavior, for various definitions of important. R provides an enormous suite of tools for exploring data and testing data statistically. Learning to use these tools requires an understanding of the common test statistics that R's tools provide. The remainder of this chapter focuses on these tasks.

Hypothesis Testing

Statistical hypothesis testing is the process of evaluating a claim about the behavior of the world based on the evidence from a particular dataset. A claim might be that the data is normally distributed, or that the attacks on our network come during the morning. Hypothesis testing begins with a hypothesis that can be compared against a model and then potentially invalidated. The language of hypothesis testing is often counterintuitive because it relies on a key attribute of the sciences—science can't prove an assertion, it can disprove that assertion or, alternatively, fail to disprove it. Consequently, hypothesis tests focus on "rejecting the null hypothesis."

Statistical testing begins with a claim referred to as the *null hypothesis* (H_0). The most basic null hypothesis is that there is no relationship between the variables in a dataset. The alternative hypothesis (H_1) states the opposite of the null—that there is evidence of a relationship. The null hypothesis is tested by comparing the likelihood of the data being generated by a process modeling the null, under the assumptions made by the null.

For example, consider the process of testing a coin to determine whether it's evenly weighted or weighted to favor one side. We test the coin by flipping it repeatedly. The null hypothesis states that the probability of landing heads is equal to the probability of landing tails: *P=0.5*. The alternative hypothesis states that the weighting is biased toward one side.

To determine whether the coin is weighted, we have to flip it multiple times. The question in constructing the test is how many times we have to flip the coin to make that determination. Figure 6-3 shows the breakdown of probabilities for coin flipping combinations[2] for one through four flips.

2. Combinations aren't ordered, so getting tails then heads is considered equivalent to getting heads then tails when calculating probabilities.

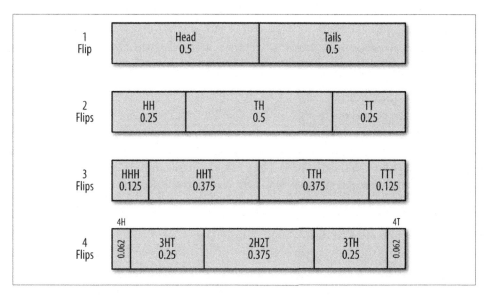

Figure 6-3. Model of coin flipping for an evenly weighted coin

The results follow the binomial distribution, which we can calculate using R's dbinom function.[3]

```
> # Use dbinom to get the probabilities of 0 to 4 heads given that
> # there are 4 coin flips and the probability of getting heads on
> # an individual flip is 0.5
> dbinom((0:4),4,p=0.5)
[1] 0.0625 0.2500 0.3750 0.2500 0.0625
> # results are in order - so 0 heads, 1 heads, 2 heads, 3 heads, 4 heads
```

In order to determine if a result is significant, we need to determine the probability of the result happening by chance. In statistical testing, this is done by using a *p-value*. The p-value is the probability that *if the null hypothesis is true*, you will get a result at least as extreme as the observed results. The lower the p-value, the lower the probability that the observed result could have occurred under the null hypothesis. Conventionally, a null hypothesis is rejected when the p-value is *below* 0.05.

To understand the concept of extremity here, consider a binomial test with no successes and four coin flips. In R:

```
> binom.test(0,4,p=0.5)

        Exact binomial test
```

---

3. A note on R convention: R provides a common family of functions for most common parametric distribu-tions. These functions are differentiated by the first letter: r for random, d for density, q for quantile, and p for probability distribution.

```
data:  0 and 4
number of successes = 0, number of trials = 4, p-value = 0.125
alternative hypothesis: true probability of success is not equal to 0.5
95 percent confidence interval:
 0.0000000 0.6023646
sample estimates:
probability of success
             0
```

That p-value of 0.125 is the sum of the probabilities that a coin flip was four heads (0.0625) AND four tails (also 0.0625). The p value is, in this context "two tailed," meaning that it accounts for both extremes. Similarly, if we account for one heads:

```
> binom.test(1,4,p=0.5)

        Exact binomial test

data:  1 and 4
number of successes = 1, number of trials = 4, p-value = 0.625
alternative hypothesis: true probability of success is not equal to 0.5
95 percent confidence interval:
 0.006309463 0.805879550
sample estimates:
probability of success
          0.25
```

The p-value is 0.625, the sum of 0.0625 + 0.25 + 0.25 + 0.0625 (everything *but* the probability of 2 heads and 2 tails).

Testing Data

One of the most common tests to do with R is to test whether or not a particular dataset matches a distribution. For information security and anomaly detection, having data that follows a distribution enables us to estimate thresholds for alarms. That said, we rarely actually encounter data that can be modeled with a distribution, as discussed in Chapter 10. Determining that a phenomenon can be satisfactorily modeled with a distribution enables you to use the distribution's characteristic functions to predict the value.

The classic example of this estimation process is the use of the mean and standard deviation to predict values of a normally distributed phenomenon. A normal distribution has a probability density function of the form:

$$\frac{1}{\sigma\sqrt{2\pi}}e^{-\frac{(x-\mu)^2}{2\sigma^2}}$$

Where μ is the mean and σ is the standard deviation of the model.

If traffic can be satisfactorily modeled with a distribution, it provides us with a mathematical toolkit for estimating the probability of an occurrence happening. The chance of actually encountering a satisfactory model, as discussed in Chapter 10, is rare—when you do, it will generally be after heavily filtering the data and applying multiple heuristics to extract something suitably well behaved.

This matters because if you use the mathematics for a model without knowing if the model *works*, then you run the risk of building a faulty sensor. There exist, and R provides, an enormous number of different statistical tests to determine whether you can use a model. For the sake of brevity, this text focuses on two tests that provide a basic toolkit. These are:

Shapiro-Wilk (shapiro.test)
> The Shapiro-Wilk test is a goodness of fit test against the normal distribution. Use this to test whether or not a sample set is normally distributed.

Kolmogorov-Smirnov (ks.test)
> A goodness of fit test to use against continuous distributions such as the normal or uniform.

All of these tests operate in a similar fashion: the test function is run against a sample set and another sample set (either provided explicitly or through a function call). A test statistic describing the quality of the fit is generated, and a p-value produced.

The Shapiro-Wilk test (*shapiro.test*) is a normality test; the null hypothesis is that the data provided is normally distributed. See Example 6-4 for an example of running the test.

Example 6-4. Running the Shapiro-Wilk test

```
># Test to see whether a random normally distributed
># function passes the shapiro test
> shapiro.test(rnorm(100,100,120))

        Shapiro-Wilk normality test

data:  rnorm(100, 100, 120)
W = 0.9863, p-value = 0.3892
> # We will explain these numbers in a moment
> # Test to see whether a uniformly distributed function passes the shapiro test
> shapiro.test(runif(100,100,120))

        Shapiro-Wilk normality test

data:  runif(100, 100, 120)
W = 0.9682, p-value = 0.01605
```

All statistical tests produce a *test statistic* (W in the Shapiro-Wilk test), which is compared against its distribution under the null hypothesis. The exact value and interpretation of the statistic is test-specific, and the p-value should be used instead as a nor-malized interpretation of the value.

The Kolmogorov-Smirnov test (*ks.test*) is a simple goodness-of-fit test that is used to determine whether or not a dataset matches a particular continuous distribution such as the normal or uniform distribution. It can be used either with a function (in which case it compares the dataset provided against the function) or with two datasets (in which case it compares them to each other). See the test in action in Example 6-5.

Example 6-5. Using the KS test

```
> # The KS test in action; let's create two random uniform distributions
> a.set <- runif(n=100, min=10, max=20)
> b.set <- runif(n=100, min=10, max=20)
> ks.test(a.set, b.set)

        Two-sample Kolmogorov-Smirnov test

data:  a.set and b.set
D = 0.07, p-value = 0.9671
alternative hypothesis: two-sided

> # Now we'll compare a set against the distribution, using the function.
> # Note that I use punif to get the distribution and pass in the same
> # parameters as I would if I were calling punif on its own
> ks.test(a.set, punif, min=10, max=20)

        One-sample Kolmogorov-Smirnov test

data:  a.set
D = 0.0862, p-value = 0.447
alternative hypothesis: two-sided
> # I need an estimate before using the test.
> # For the uniform, I can use min and max, like I'd use mean and sd for
> # the normal
> ks.test(a.set,punif,min=min(a.set),max=max(a.set))

        One-sample Kolmogorov-Smirnov test

data:  a.set
D = 0.0829, p-value = 0.4984
alternative hypothesis: two-sided
> # Now one where I reject the null; I'll treat the data as if it
> # were normally distributed and estimate again
> ks.test(a.set,pnorm,mean=mean(a.set),sd=sd(a.set))

        One-sample Kolmogorov-Smirnov test

data:  a.set
D = 0.0909, p-value = 0.3806
alternative hypothesis: two-sided
```

```
> #Hmm, p-value's high...  Because I'm not using enough samples, let's
> # do this again with 400 samples each.
> a.set<-runif(400,min=10,max=20)
> b.set<-runif(400,min=10,max=20)
> # Compare against each other
> ks.test(a.set,b.set)$p.value
[1] 0.6993742
> # Compare against the distribution
> ks.test(a.set,punif,min=min(a.set),max=max(a.set))$p.value
[1] 0.5499412
> # Compare against a different distribution
> ks.test(a.set,pnorm, mean = mean(a.set),sd=sd(a.set))$p.value
[1] 0.001640407
```

The KS test has weak *power*. The power of an experiment refers to its ability to correctly reject the null hypothesis. Tests with weak power require a larger number of samples than more powerful tests. Sample size, especially when working with security data, is a complicated issue. The majority of statistical tests come from the wet-lab world, where acquiring 60 samples can be a bit of an achievement. While it is possible for network traffic analysis to collect huge numbers of samples, the tests will start to behave wonkily with too much data; small deviations from normality will result in certain tests rejecting the data, and you can always start throwing in more data, effectively crafting the test to meet your goals.

In my experience, distribution tests are usually a poor second choice to a good visualization. Chapter 10 discusses this in more depth.

Further Reading

1. Patrick Burns, *The R Inferno* (*http://bit.ly/r-inferno*).

2. Richard Cotton, *Learning R: A Step-by-Step Function Guide to Data Analysis* (O'Reilly, 2013).

3. Russell Langley, *Practical Statistics Simply Explained* (Dover, 2012).

4. The R Project, *An Introduction to R* (*http://bit.ly/r-intro*).

5. Larry Wasserman, *All of Statistics: A Concise Course in Statistical Inference* (Springer Texts in Statistics, 2004).

## CHAPTER 7

Classification and Event Tools: IDS, AV, and SEM

This chapter focuses on the development and use of event-based sensors such as intrusion detection systems (IDSes). These systems include passive sensors such as IDSes and most AVs, as well as active systems such as firewalls. Analytically, they all behave similarly—they analyze data and create *events* in response to that data. Event construction is what differentiates an IDS from a simple reporting sensor such as NetFlow. Simple sensors report everything they observe, while an IDS or other classifying sensor is configured to report only on specific phenomena that it infers from the data it observes.

Many analytic processes will eventually result in some form of IDS. For example, you might want to develop a system detecting abusive activity on a host. Using some of the math in Part III, you build up a model of abusive activity, create some thresholds, and raise an alert whenever there's a threshold.

The problem is that these processes almost never work as intended. Operational IDS systems are *very* hard to implement properly. The problem is *not* detection; the problem is context and attribution. IDS systems are easily, and usually, configured into uselesness. Either they produce so many alarms that analysts ignore them, or they're configured to produce so few alarms that they might as well not be there. Developing effective alarms requires understanding how IDSes are used operationally, how they fail as classifiers, and the impact of those failures on analysts.

This chapter is divided into two parts. The first section breaks down IDS systems and the way they're used on floors. It discusses how IDS systems fail and how these failure modes impact analysis. The second section is focused on the construction of better detection systems, and discusses strategies to improve the efficacy of signature, and anomaly-based detection techniques.

How an IDS Works

All IDSes are expert systems of a type called a *binary classifier*. A classifier reads in data and marks it as one of two categories. Either the data is normal and requires no further action, or the data is characteristic of an attack. If it is an attack, then the system reacts as specified; event sensors generate an event, controllers block traffic, and so on.

An IDS system interprets data in a different way than passive sensors such as NetFlow. A simple sensor reports on everything it monitors, while an IDS only reports on events that it is configured to report on. IDSes differ based on the data they use to make this interpretation and the process they use to make this decision.

There are several problems with classification, which we can term the *moral*, the *statistical*, and the *behavioral*. The moral problem is that attacks can be indistinguishable from innocuous, or even permitted, user activity. For example, a DDoS attack and a flash crowd can look very similar until some time has passed. The statistical problem is that IDS systems are often configured to make hundreds or millions of tests a day—under those conditions, even low false positive rates can result in far more false positives in a day than true positives in a month. The behavioral problem is that attackers are intelligent parties interested in evading detection, and often can do so with minimal damage to their goals.

This section will discuss IDS, and often take a very pessimistic view of its capabilities. We begin with a discussion of the vocabulary of intrusion detection, then move onto the mechanics of binary classifiers, and then into the problem of engineering detection systems and the impact of classifier failures.

Basic Vocabulary

We can break IDS along two primary axes: where the IDS is placed, and how the IDS makes decisions. On the first axis, IDS is broken into *Network-Based IDS* (NIDS), and *Host-Based IDS* (HIDS). On the second axis, IDS is split between *signature-based* systems and *anomaly-based* systems.

An NIDS is effectively any IDS that begins with *pcap* data. In the open source domain, this includes systems such as Snort, Bro, and Suricata. NIDS systems operate under the constraints discussed for network sensors in Chapter 2, such as the need to receive traffic through port mirroring or direct connect to the network and an inability to read encrypted traffic.

HIDSes operate within the host domain and are usually far more varied than NIDSes. An HIDS can monitor network activity, physical access (such as whether a user is trying to use a USB device), and information from the operating system such as ACL violations or file accesses.

Figure 7-1 shows how several common IDS systems break down along these axes.

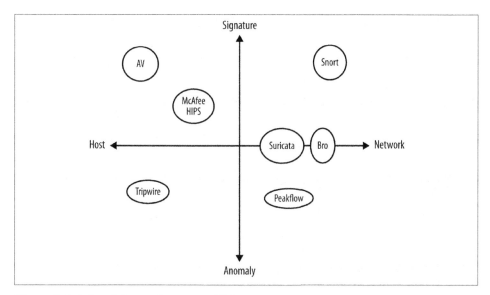

Figure 7-1. A breakdown of common IDS

Figure 7-1 shows seven examples of different IDS. These are:

Snort (http://www.snort.org)
> The most commonly used IDS. Snort is a network-based signature matching system that uses hand-crafted *Snort signatures* to identify malicious traffic. Snort provides an extensive language for describing signatures and can be manually configured to add new ones.

Bro (http://www.bro-ids.org)
> A sophisticated traffic analysis system that can be used for intrusion detection using both signatures and anomalies. Bro is less of an IDS than a traffic analysis language. Bro has recently been redesigned to work with clusters.

Suricata (http://www.openinfosecfoundation.org)
> An experimental open source IDS developed by the Open Information Security Foundation with funding from the Department of Homeland Security. Suricata is the youngest IDS listed here and is used for experimentation in new techniques in intrusion detection.

Peakflow
> A commercial traffic analysis package developed by Arbor Networks (*http:// www.arbornetworks.com*), Peakflow analyzes NetFlow traffic to identify and mitigate attacks such as DDoS.

Tripwire (http://www.tripwire.com)

A file integrity monitoring system. Tripwire monitors specific directories and raises events when it sees the contents of the directory change.

AV

Antivirus systems such as Symantec, ClamAV, or McAfee are the most common forms of a signature-based HIDS. AV systems examine host disk and memory for the binary signatures of malware and raise alerts when encountering suspicious binaries.

McAfee HIPS

McAfee's host intrusion prevention (HIPS) is one of several commercial IPS packages. HIPS systems such as this one combine binary analysis with log analysis, such as examining ACL violations or suspicious file modifications.

The vast majority of IDSes are *signature-based*. A signature-based system uses a set of rules that are derived independently from the target in order to identify malicious behavior. For example, a Snort signature written in Snort's rule language could look like this:

```
alert tcp 192.4.1.0/24 any -> $HOME_NET 22 (flow:to_server,established; \
    content:"root";)
```

This alert is raised when traffic from a suspicious network (192.4.1.0/24) attempts to contact any host on the internal network and tries to log on as root to SSH. An HIDS may offer signatures such as "raise an alert when a user tries to delete the security log." Ruleset creation and management is a significant issue for signature-based IDS, and well-crafted rules are often the secret sauce that differentiates various commercial packages.

A signature-based IDS will only raise alerts when it has a rule specifying to do so. This limitation means that signature-based IDSes usually have a high *false negative* rate, meaning that a large number of attacks go unreported by them. The most extreme version of this problem is associated with vulnerabilities. AV primarily, but also NIDS and HIDS, rely on specific binary signatures in order to identify malware (see "On Code Red and Malware Evasiveness" on page 133 for a more extensive discussion on this). These signatures require that some expert have access to an exploit; these days, exploits are commonly "zero-day," meaning that they're released and in the wild *before* anyone has the opportunity to write a signature.

Anomaly-based IDSes are built by training (or optionally configuring) the IDS on traffic data in order to create a model of normal activity. Once this model is created, deviations from the model are anomalous, suspicious, and produce events. For example, a simple anomaly-based NIDS might monitor traffic to specific hosts and generate an event when traffic suddenly spikes upward, indicating a DDoS or other suspicious event.

Anomaly-based IDSes are used far less than signature-based IDS, primarily because they have the opposite problem of a signature-based IDS—a high *false positive rate*. Anomaly-based IDSes are notorious for creating alerts incessantly, and are often dialed down to produce a minimal number of alerts rather than constantly go off.

Historically, IDS systems didn't interoperate because there wasn't anything to interoperate with; IDS reported directly to the analyst. As security systems have become more complex, there's a growing interest in *security event management* (SEM) software[1] such as ArcSight, LogRhythms, LogStash, and Splunk. An SEM is effectively a database that collects data from multiple detection systems. After it is collected, the data can be collated and compound events can be created from one or more sensors.

On Code Red and Malware Evasiveness

Sometimes there's a fine line between NIDS and AV. Read the original papers on NIDS by Paxson and Roesch and you'll see that they were thinking about hand-crafted attacks on systems that they'd be able to defend by looking for people trying to log in as root or admin. There was a functionality change around 2001, which was the beginning of a very nasty worm-heavy era in defense. Worms like Code Red and Slammer caused widespread havoc by spreading actively and destructively choking bandwidth.

The Code Red v1 and v2 worms both exploited a buffer overflow in Microsoft IIS in order to subvert IIS processes and launch an attack against the White House. The orignal Code Red worm contained a payload looking like the following:

```
GET /default.ida?NNNNNNNNNNNNNNNNNNNNNNNNNNNNNNNNNNNNNNNNNNNNNNNNNNNNNNNNNNN
NNNNNNNNNNNNNNNNNNNNNNNNNNNNNNNNNNNNNNNNNNNNNNNNNNNNNNNNNNNNNNNNNNNNNNNNNNNNN
NNNNNNNNNNNNNNNNNNNNNNNNNNNNNNNNNNNNNNNNNNNNNNNNNNNNNNNNNNNNNNNNNNNNNNNNNNNNN
NNNNNNNNNNNNNNNNNNNNNNN%u9090%u6858%ucbd3%u7801%u9090%u6858%ucbd3%u7801
%u9090%u6858%ucbd3%u7801%u9090%u9090%u8190%u00c3%u0003%u8b00%u531b%u53ff
%u0078%u0000%u00=a  HTTP/1.0
```

IDS at the time detected Code Red by looking for that specific payload, and a couple of weeks later, an updated version of the worm using the same exploit was launched. The payload for Code Red II looked like this:

```
GET /default.ida?XXXXXXXXXXXXXXXXXXXXXXXXXXXXXXXXXXXXXXXXXXXXXXXXXXXXXXXXXXX
XXXXXXXXXXXXXXXXXXXXXXXXXXXXXXXXXXXXXXXXXXXXXXXXXXXXXXXXXXXXXXXXXXXXXXXXXXXXXX
XXXXXXXXXXXXXXXXXXXXXXXXXXXXXXXXXXXXXXXXXXXXXXXXXXXXXXXXXXXXXXXXXXXXXXXXXXXXXX
XXXXXXXXXXXXXXXXXXXXXXX%u9090%u6858%ucbd3%u7801%u9090%u6858%ucbd3%u7801
%u9090%u6858%ucbd3%u7801%u9090%u9090%u8190%u00c3%u0003%u8b00%u531b%u53ff
%u0078%u0000%u00=a HTTP/1.0
```

1. A number of similar tools are associated with SEM, particularly *security information management* (SIM) and *security information and event management* (SIEM). Technically, SIM refers to the log data and information management while SEM is focused on more abstract events, but you are more likely to hear people say "SIM/SEM/SIEM" or some other aggregate.

As a buffer overflow, the Code Red worms needed to pad their contents in order to reach a specific memory location; the worms were often differentiated by the presence of an X or an N in the buffer. The thing is, the buffer contents are *irrelevant* to the execution of the worm; an attacker could change them at will without changing the functionality.

This has been a problem for IDS ever since. As originally conceived, intrusion detection systems were looking for anomalous and suspicious *user* behavior. These types of long term hacks could be detected and stopped because they'd be happening over the course of hours or days, which is enough time for analysts to examine the alert, vet it, and take a course of action. Modern attacks are largely automated, and the actual subversion and control of a host can take place instantaneously if the right conditions are met.

The problem of binary signature management has gotten significantly worse in the past decade because it's easy for attackers to modify payload without changing the functionality of the worm. If you examine threat databases such as Symantec's (see Chapter 8), you will find that there are hundreds or more variants of common worms, each of them with a different binary signature.

As for the explosive, destructive worms like Slammer, they basically calmed down for what I will best describe as evolutionary reasons. Much like it doesn't pay a physical virus to kill its host until it's had a chance to spread, modern worms are generally more restrained in their reproduction. It's better to own the Internet than to destroy it.

Classifier Failure Rates: Understanding the Base-Rate Fallacy

All IDS systems are applied exercises in *classification*, a standard problem in AI and statistics. A classifier is a process that takes in input data and classifies the data into one of at least two categories. In the case of IDS systems, the categories are usually "attack" and "normal."

Signature and anomaly-based IDSes view attacks in fundamentally different ways, and this impacts the type of errors they make. A signature-based IDS is calibrated to look for specific weird behaviors such as malware signatures or unusual login attempts. Anomaly-based IDSes are trained on normal behavior and then look for anything that steps outside the norm. Signature-based IDSes have high false negative rates, meaning that they miss a lot of attacks. Anomaly-based IDSes have high false positive rates, which means that they consider a lot of perfectly normal activity to be an attack.

IDSes are generally *binary* classifiers, meaning that they break data into two categories. Binary classifiers have two failure modes:

False positives
> Also called a *Type I error*, this occurs when something that doesn't have the property you're searching for is classified as having the property. This occurs, for instance, when email from the president of your company informing you about a promotion is classified as spam.

False negatives

Also called a *Type II error*, this occurs when something that has the property you're searching for is classified as *not* having the property. This happens, for instance, when spam mail appears in your inbox.

Sensitivity refers to the percentage of positive classifications that are correct, and *specificity* refers to the percentage of negative classifications that are correct. A perfect detection has perfect sensitivity and specificity. In the worst case, neither rate is above 50%: the same as flipping a coin.

Most systems require some degree of tradeoff; generally, increasing the sensitivity means also accepting a lower specificity. A reduction in false negatives will be accompanied by an increase in false positives, and vice versa.

To describe this tradeoff, we can use a visualization called a *receiver operating characteristic* (ROC) curve. A ROC curve plots the specificity against the false positive rates, using a third characteristic (the *operating characteristic*) as a control. Figure 7-2 shows an example of a ROC curve.

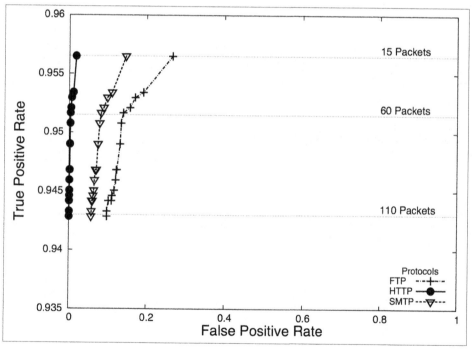

Figure 7-2. ROC curve showing packet size of messages sent for BitTorrent detection

In this case, the operating characteristic is the number of packets in a session and is shown on the horizontal lines in the plot. At this site, HTTP traffic (falling at the very left edge) has a good ratio of true to false positives, whereas SMTP is harder to classify correctly, and FTP even harder.

Now, let's ask a question. We have an ROC curve and we calibrate a detector so it has a 99% true positive rate, and a 1% false positive rate. We receive an alert. What is the probability that the alert is a true positive? It *isn't* 99%; the true positive rate is the probability that *if* an attack took place, the IDS would raise an alarm.

Let's define a *test* as the process that an IDS uses to make a judgement call about data. For example, a test might consist of collecting 30 seconds worth of network traffic and comparing it against a predicted volume, or examining the first two packets of a session for a suspicious string.

Now assume that the probability of an actual attack taking place during a test is 0.01%. This means that out of every 10,000 tests the IDS conducts, one of them will be an attack. So out of every 10,000 tests, we raise one alarm *due to an attack*—after all, we have a 99% true positive rate. However, the false positive rate is 1%, which means that 1% of the tests raise an alarm even though nothing happened. This means that for 10,000 tests, we can expect roughly 101 alarms: 100 false positives and 1 true positive, meaning that the probability that an alarm is raised *because* of an attack is 1/101 or slightly less than 1%.

This *base-rate fallacy* explains why doctors don't run every test on every person. When the probability of an actual attack is remote, the false positives will easily overwhelm the true positives. This problem is exacerbated because nobody in their right mind trusts an IDS to do the job alone.

Applying Classification

Consider the data flow in Figure 7-3, which is a simple representation of how an IDS is normally used in defense.

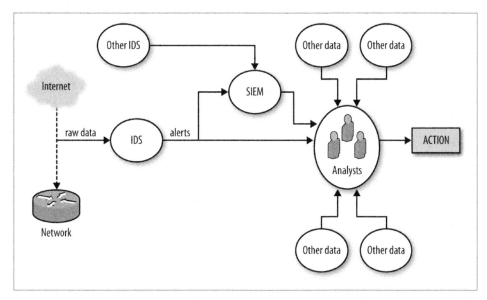

Figure 7-3. Simple detection workflow

Figure 7-3 breaks alert processing into three steps: IDS receives data, raises an alert, and that alert is then passed to analysts either directly or through a SIEM.

Once an IDS generates an alert, that alert must be forwarded to an analyst for further action. Analysts begin by examining the alert and figuring out what the alert means. This may be a relatively simple process, but often it becomes wider-ranging and may involve a number of queries. Simple queries will include looking at the geolocation, ownership, and past history of the address originating the attack (see Chapter 8), by examining the payload of the event using *tcpdump* or Wireshark. With more complex attacks, analysts will have to reach out to Google, news, blogs, and message boards to identify similar attacks or real-world events precipitating the attack.

With the exception of IPS systems, which work on very crude and obvious attacks such as DDoSes, there is always an interim analytical step between alert and action. At this point, analysts have to take the alert and determine if the alert is a threat, if the threat is relevant to them, and whether or not there's anything they can do about it. This is a nontrivial problem, consider the following scenarios:

- The IDS reports that an attacker is exploiting a particular IIS vulnerability. Are there any IIS servers on the network? Have they been patched so they're not subject to the exploit? Is there evidence from other sources that the attacker succeeded?

- The IDS reports that an attacker is scanning the network. Can we stop the scan? Should we bother given that there are another hundred scans going on right now?

- The IDS reports that a host is systematically picking through a web server and copying every file. Is the host a Google spider, and would stopping it mean that our company's primary website would no longer be visible on Google?

Note that these are not actually failures on the part of detection. The first two scenarios represent actual potential threats, but those threats may not *matter*, and that decision can only be made through a combination of context and policy decisions.

Verifying alerts takes time. An analyst might be able to seriously process approximately one alert an hour, and complex events will take days to investigate. Consider how that time is spent given the false positive rates discussed earlier.

Improving IDS Performance

There are two approaches to improving how IDSes work. The first is to improve the IDS as a classifier; that is, increase the sensitivity and specificity. The second way is to reduce the time an analyst needs to process an alert by fetching additional information, providing context, and identifying courses of action.

There are no perfect rules to this process. For example, although it's always a good (and necessary) goal to minimize false positives, analysts will take a more nuanced approach to this problem. For example, if there's a temporary risk of a nasty attack, an analyst will often tolerate a higher false positive rate in order to more effectively defend against that attack.

There's a sort of Parkinson's Law problem here. All of our detection and monitoring systems provide only partial coverage because the Internet is weird, and we don't really have a good grasp of what we're missing. As any floor improves its detection process, it will find that there are newer and nastier alerts to consider. To paraphrase Donald Rumsfeld: we do have a problem with unknown unknowns.

This problem of unknown unknowns makes false negatives a particular headache. By definition, a signature-based IDS can't alert on anything it isn't configured to alert on. That said, most signature matching systems will be configured to identify only a limited subset of all the malicious behaviors that a particular host uses. By combining signature and anomaly detecting IDSes together, you can at least begin to identify the blind spots.

Enhancing IDS Detection

Improving an IDS as a classifier involves reducing the false positive and false negative rates. This is generally best done by reducing the scope of the traffic the IDS examines. In the same way that a doctor doesn't run a test until he has a symptom to work with, we try to run the IDS only when we have an initial suspicion that something odd is going on. A number of different mechanisms are available based on whether you're using a signature- or an anomaly-based IDS.

Inconsistent Notification: A Headache with Multiple IDSes

A special category of false negative involves inconsistent IDS rulesets. Imagine that you run a network with the access points A and B, with IDS running on both. If you don't keep the ruleset on IDS A consistent with the ruleset on IDS B, you will find that A sends you alerts that B doesn't recognize and vice versa.

The easiest way to manage this problem is to treat the rulesets as any other source code. That is, put the rules in a version control system, make sure that you commit and comment them, and then install the rules from your version control system. Keeping the rules under version control's good idea anyway because if you're doing a multi-month traffic investigation, you really will want to look at those old rulesets to figure out exactly what you were blocking last April.

There is a class of IDS that makes this type of management particularly problematic, however. AV and some other detection systems are usually black-box systems. A black-box system provides ruleset updates as a subscription service, and the rulesets are usually completely inaccessible to an administrator. Inconsistent identification can be particularly problematic with black-box systems where, at the best you must keep track of what the current rulebase is and identify systems that are behind.[2]

One mechanism common to both signature and anomaly-based IDSes is using inventory to create whitelists. Pure whitelists, meaning that you implicitly trust all traffic from a host, are *always* a risk. I don't recommend simply whitelisting a host and never checking it. A better approach, and one that is going to appear in various forms throughout this discussion, is to use whitelisting as a guide for less or more extensive instrumentation.

For example, I create an inventory of all the web servers on my network. A host that is not a web server is *de facto* suspicious if I see it serving HTTP traffic. In that case, I want to capture a representative cut of traffic and figure out *why* it's now a web server. At the same time, for actual web servers, I will use my standard signatures.

In signature-based IDSes, the signature base can usually be refined so that the rule triggers only for specific protocols or in tandem with other indicators. For example, a rule to detect the payload string "herbal supplement" on port 25 will track spam emails with that title, but also internal mail such as "we're getting a lot of herbal supplement spam lately." Reducing the false positive rate in this case involves adding more constraints to the match, such as tracking only mail from outside the network (filtering on

---

2. This has the nice bonus of identifying systems that may be compromised. Malware will disable AV as a matter of course.

addresses). By refining the rule to use more selective expressions, an operator can reduce the false positive rate.

As an example, consider the following (stupid) rule to determine whether or not someone is logging on as root to an SSH server:

```
alert tcp any any -> any 22 (flow:to_server, established;)
```

A Snort rule consists of two logical sections: the header and the options. The header consists of the rule's *action* and addressing information (protocol, source address, source port, destination address, destination port). Options consist of a number of specific keywords separated by semicolons.

In the example above, the action is `alert`, indicating that Snort generates an alert and logs the packet. Alternative actions include `log` (log the packet without alerting), `pass` (ignore the packet), and `drop` (block the packet) Following the action is a string naming the protocol, `tcp` in this case, with `udp`, `icmp`, and `ip` being other options. The action is followed by source to destination information separated by the arrow (→) digraph. Source information can be expressed as an address (e.g., 128.1.11.3), a netblock (118.2.0.0/16) as above, or `any` to indicate all addresses. Snort can also define various collections of addresses with macros (e.g., `$HOME_NET` to indicate the home network for an IDS), to implement the inventory-based whitelisting discussed earlier.

This rule raises an alert when anyone successfully connects to an ssh server, which is far too vague. In order to refine the rule, I have to add additional constraints. For example, I can constrain it to only raise an alert if it comes from a specific network, and if someone tries to log on specifically as root.

```
alert tcp 118.2.0.0/16 any -> any 21 (flow:to_server,established; \
    content:"root"; pcre:"/user\s_root/i";)
```

Following the addressing information are one or more *rule options*. Options can be used to refine a rule, fine-tuning the information the rule looks for in order to reduce the false positive rate. Options can also be used to add additional information to an alert, trigger another rule, or to complete a variety of other actions.

Snort defines well over 70 options for various forms of analysis. A brief survey of the more useful rules include:

content

> `content` is Snort's bread-and-butter pattern matching rule; it does an exact match of the data passed in the content option against packet payload. `content` can use binary and text data, enclosing the binary data in pipes. For example, `content:|05 11|H|02 23|` matches the byte with contents 5, then 11, then the letter *H*, then the byte 2, then the byte 23. A number of other options directly impact content, such as `depth` (specifying where in the payload to stop searching), and `offset` (specifying where in the payload to start searching).

HTTP options

A number of HTTP options (`http_client_body`, `http_cookie`, `http_header`) will extract the relevant information from an HTTP packet for analysis by `content`.

`pcre`

The `pcre` option uses a PCRE regular expression to match against a packet. Regular expressions are expensive; make sure to use `content` to prefilter traffic and skip applying the regular expression against every packet.

`flags`

Checks to see whether or not specific TCP flags are present.

`flow`

The `flow` keyword specifies the direction traffic is flowing in, such as from a client, to a client, from a server, or to a server. The `flow` keyword also describes certain characteristics of the session, such as whether or not it was actually established.

Snort's rule language is used by several other IDSes, notably Suricata. Other systems may differentiate themselves with additional options (for example, Suricata has an `iprep` option for looking at IP address reputation).

Unlike signature-based systems, where you can't really go wrong by discussing Snort rules, anomaly-detection systems are more likely to be built by hand. Consequently, when discussing how to make an anomaly detector more effective, we have to operate at a more basic level. Throughout Part III, we discuss a number of different numerical and behavioral techniques for implementing anomaly-detection systems, as well as cases for false positives. However, this is an appropriate place to discuss general criteria for building good anomaly-detection systems.

In their simplest forms, anomaly-detection systems raise alarms via thresholds. For example, I might decide to build anomaly detection for a file server by counting the number of bytes downloaded from a server every minute. I can do so using *rwfilter* to filter the data, and *rwcount* to count it over time. I then use R, and generate a histogram showing the probability that the value is above x. The nice thing about histograms and statistical anomaly detection is that I control this nominal false positive rate. A test every minute and a 95% threshold before raising alarms means that I create three alarms an hour; a 99% threshold means one alarm every two hours.

The problem lies in picking a threshold that is actually useful. For example, if an attacker is aware that I'll raise an alarm if he's too busy, he can reduce his activity below the threshold. This type of evasiveness is really the same kind we saw with Code Red in "On Code Red and Malware Evasiveness" on page 133. The attacker in that case could change the contents of the buffer without impacting the worm's performance. When you identify phenomena for anomaly detection, you should keep in mind how it impacts the attacker's goals; detection is simply the first step.

I have four of rules of thumb I apply when evaluating phenomena for an anomaly detection system: predictability, manageable false positives, disruptibility, and impact on attacker behavior.

Predictability is the most basic quality to look for in a phenomenon. A predictable phenomenon is one whose value effectively converges over time. "Convergence" is something that I have to be a bit hand-wavy about. You may find that nine days out of ten, a threshold is x, and then on the tenth day it rises to $10x$ because of some unexplained weirdness. Expect unexplained weirdness; if you can identify and describe outliers behaviorally and whatever remains has an upper limit you can express, then you've got something predictable. False positives will happen during investigation, and true positives will happen during training!

The second rule is manageable false positives. Look at a week of traffic for any publicly available host and you will see something weird happen. Can you explain this weirdness? Is it the same address over and over again? Is it a common service, such as a crawler visiting a web server? During the initial training process for any anomaly detector, you should log how much time you spend identifying and explaining outliers, and whether you can manage those outliers through whitelisting or other behavioral filters. The less you have to explain, the lower a burden you impose on busy operational analysts.

A disruptible phenomenon is one that the attacker must affect in order to achieve his goals. The simpler, the better. For example, to download traffic from a web server, the attacker must contact the web server. He may not need to do so from the same address, and he may not need authentication, but he needs to pull down data.

Finally, there's the impact of a phenomenon on attacker behavior. The best alarms are the ones that the attacker *has* to trigger. Over time, if a detector impacts an attacker, the attacker will learn to evade or confuse it. We see this in antispam and the various tools used to trick Bayesian filtering, and we see it consistently in insider threats. When considering an alarm, consider how the attacker can evade it, such as:

By moving slower
Can an attacker impact the alarm if she reduces her activity? If so, what's the impact on the attacker's goal? If a scanner slows her probes, how long does it take to scan your network? If a file leech copies your site, how long to copy the whole site?

By moving faster
Can an attacker confuse the system if he moves faster? If he risks detection, can he move faster than your capability to block him by moving as fast as possible?

By distributing the attack
If an attacker works from multiple IP addresses, can the individual addresses slip under the threshold?

By alternating behaviors
> Can an attacker swap between suspicious and innocent behavior, and confuse the IDS that way?

Many of the techniques discussed previously imply a degree of heterogeneity in your detection system. For example, anomaly-detection systems might have to be configured individually for different hosts. I have found it useful to push that idea toward a subscription model, where analysts choose which hosts to monitor, decide on the thresholds, and provide them with whitelisting and blacklisting facilities for every host they decide to monitor. Subscriptions ensure that the analyst can treat each host individually, and eventually build up an intuition for normal behavior on that host (for example, knowing that traffic to the payroll server goes bonkers every two weeks).

The subscription model acknowledges that you can't monitor everything, and consequently the next question about any subscription-based approach is precisely *what* to monitor. Chapter 13 and Chapter 15 discuss this issue in more depth.

Enhancing IDS Response

IDS, particularly NIDS, was conceived of as a real-time detection system—there would be enough of a gap between the time the attack began and the final exploit that, armed with the IDS alerts, the defenders could stop the attack before it caused significant damage. This concept was developed in a time when attackers might use two computers, when attacks were hand-crafted by experts, and when malware was far more primitive. Now, IDS is too often a recipe for annoyance. It's not simply a case of misclassified attacks; it's a case of attackers attacking hosts that aren't there in the hopes that they'll find something to take over.

At some point, you will make an IDS as effective a detector as you can, and you'll still get false positives because there are normal behaviors that look like attacks and the only way you'll figure this out is by investigating them. Once you reach that point, you're left with the alerting problem: IDSes generate simple alerts in real time, and analysts have to puzzle them out. Reducing the workload on analysts means aggregating, grouping, and manipulating alerts so that the process of verification and response is faster and conducted more effectively.

When considering how to manipulate an alert, first ask what the response to that alert will be. Most CSIRTS have a limited set of actions they can take in response to an alert, such as modifying a firewall or IPS rules, removing a host from the network for further analysis, or issuing policy changes. These responses rarely take place in real time, and it's not uncommon for certain attacks to not merit any response at all. The classic example of the latter case is scanning: it's omnipresent, it's almost impossible to block, and there's very little chance of catching the culprit.

If a real-time response isn't necessary, it's often useful to roll up alerts, particularly by attacker IP address or exploit type. It's not uncommon for IDSes to generate multiple alerts for the same attacker. These behaviors, which are not apparent with single real-time alerts, become more obvious when the behavior is aggregated.

Prefetching Data

After receiving an alert, analysts have to validate the information and examine it. This usually involves tasks such as determining the country of origin, the targets, and any past activity by this address. Prefetching this information helps enormously to reduce the burden on analysts.

In particular with anomaly-detection sytems, it helps to present options. As we've discussed, anomaly detections are often threshold-based, raising an alert after a phenomenon exceeds a threshold. Instead of simply presenting an aberrant event, return a top-n list of the most aberrant events at a fixed interval.

Providing summary data in visualizations such as time series plots or contact graphs helps reduce the cognitive burden on the analyst. Instead of just producing a straight text dump of query information, generate relevant plots. Chapter 10 discusses this issue in more depth.

Finally, consider monitoring assets rather than simply monitoring attacks. Most detection systems are focused on attacker behavior, such as raising an alert when a specific attack signature is detected. Instead of focusing on attacker behavior, assign your analysts specific hosts on the network to watch and analyze the traffic to and from the asset for anomalies. Lower-priority targets should be protected using more restrictive techniques, such as restrictive firewalls.

Assigning analysts to assets rather than simply reacting to alerts has another advantage: analysts can develop expertise about the systems they're watching. False positives often rise out of common processes that aren't easily described to the IDS, such as a rise in activity to file servers because a project is reaching crunch time, regular requests to payroll, a service that's popular with a specific demographic. Expertise reduces the time analysts need to sift through data, and helps them throw out the trivia to focus on more significant threats.

Further Reading

1. Stefan Axelsson, "The Base-Rate Fallacy and the Difficulty of Intrusion Detection," ACM Transactions on Information and System Security, Vol. 3, Issue 3, August 2000.

2. Brian Caswell, Jay Beale, and Andrew Baker. *Snort IDS and IPS Toolkit* (Syngress, 2007).

3. Vern Paxson, "Bro: A System for Detecting Network Intruders in Real-Time," *Computer Networks: The International Journal of Computer and Telecommunications Networking*, Vol. 31, Issue 23-24, December 1999.

4. Martin Roesch, "Snort—Lightweight Intrusion Detection for Networks," Proceedings of the 1999 Large Installation Systems Administration Conference.

## CHAPTER 8

Reference and Lookup: Tools for Figuring Out Who Someone Is

Each alert or logfile line that reports an event provides some basic information about the source of the event. Just from the IP address, you can derive information about geographic location and do a reverse DNS lookup. This chapter covers tools that help you track the identity of a host.

This chapter is focused on the idea of "walking up" the OSI stack, mentioned in "Network Layering and Its Impact on Instrumentation" on page 16. I like to view the OSI layer as a sequence of lookup processes. Each layer offers a different piece of addressing information, such as the MAC address at layer 2, the IP address at 3, and the ports at 4. This information is moved between layers through the agency of various referencing systems: Address Resolution Protocol (ARP) maps IP addresses to MAC addresses, DNS maps domain names to IP addresses, and so on. Again, the abstraction isn't perfect—DNS translation doesn't move us up or down the OSI stack—but by walking up each layer, we can describe what the addresses *mean* and when they are relevant to investigation.

The remainder of this chapter is structured as follows: a section on MAC addresses, then IPv4 and IPv6, followed by Internet-layer information, then DNS, then higher-level protocols. Finally comes a discussion of other important tools that don't fit in the layering model—in particular, reputation databases and malware repositories.

It's unfortunate that some of our lookup techniques depend on poorly maintained public databases, but they can still be indispensable as long as you understand this limitation.

MAC and Hardware Addresses

Chapter 2 discusses the basics of a Media Access Controller (MAC) address. MAC addresses are defined in the network hardware to provide a locally unique address for hosts within a single layer 2 network. The majority of MAC addresses follow the 48-bit *Extended Unique Identifier* (EUI) standard: 6 bytes expressed hexadecimally (e.g., 08-21-23-41-FA-BB). More modern network hardware may use EUI-64, which adds an additional 16 bits. When a frame goes from a 48-bit system to a 64-bit system, the 48-bit address is padded to 64 bits.

Figure 8-1 shows how the EUI-48 and EUI-64 break down.

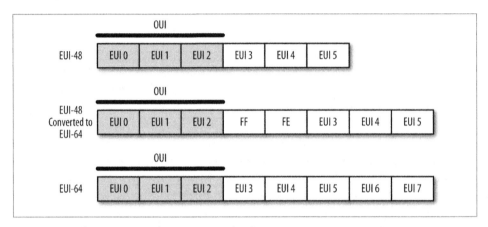

Figure 8-1. The EUI-48 and EUI-64 standards

Note two things in particular. First, if an EUI-48 is converted to an EUI-64, you can tell this by looking at bytes 3 and 4, which will be FFFE. More important is that the first 3 bytes are the *Organizationally Unique Identifier* (OUI), which is a 24-bit value assigned by the IEEE to the hardware manufacturer. OUI's are fixed serial numbers, and if you know the OUI, you can find out who manufactured the card. The IEEE maintains a list of OUI assignments (*http://bit.ly/oui-guide*), where you can use a search engine to find OUIs by company, or companies by OUI.

For example, consider the following packet from a *pcap*:

```
$ tcpdump -c 1 -e -n -r web.pcap
reading from file web.pcap, link-type EN10MB (Ethernet)
00:37:56.480768 8c:2d:aa:46:f9:71 > 00:1f:90:92:70:5a, ethertype IPv4 (0x0800),
            length 78: 192.168.1.12.50300 > 157.166.241.11.80: Flags [S],
            seq 4157917085, win 65535, options [mss 1460,nop,wscale 4,nop,
            nop,TS val 560054289 ecr 0,sackOK,eol], length 0
```

The communication goes from 8c:2d:aa:46:f9:71 to 00:1f:90:92:70:5a. Looking these up tells us that 8c:2d:aa belongs to Apple, and 00-1f-90 belongs to Actiontec Electronics, who make Verizon's FIOS routers.

There's Less Work Than You Think

A common analytical stumbling block comes when an analyst tries to build a complicated general solution to a problem when only a limited number of options are present. To use a military example, you don't have to develop a general solution for identifying aircraft carriers because there are only 20 of them in active service. Instead of working on one big problem, you can solve 20 problems that are considerably smaller and mostly similar.

When dealing with hardware systems and applications, it often helps to stop, step back, and do some market research. The problem often becomes smaller when you find out, for example, that while there are a bunch of systems with embedded web servers, most of them are using Allegro RomPager.

MAC addresses operate entirely within the scope of the local network. To communicate beyond the borders of a router, the host must have an IP address. The relationship between a local MAC and an IP address is managed through the *address resolution protocol* (ARP). Individual hosts maintain *ARP tables* that contain mappings between IP addresses and MAC addresses on a network. For example, on my local host, I can query the ARP table using arp -a:

```
$ arp -a
wireless_broadband_router.home (192.168.1.1) at 0:1f:90:92:70:5a on en1 ifscope
/[ethernet]
new-host-2.home (192.168.1.3) at 0:1e:c2:a6:17:fb on en1 ifscope [ethernet]
new-host.home (192.168.1.4) at cc:8:e0:68:b8:a4 on en1 ifscope [ethernet]
apple-tv-3.home (192.168.1.9) at 7c:d1:c3:26:35:bf on en1 ifscope [ethernet]
? (192.168.1.255) at ff:ff:ff:ff:ff:ff on en1 ifscope [ethernet]
```

Do the lookups and you'll find that I *really* like Apple hardware. Or I prefer to keep my Windows and Linux boxes physically wired.

Analytically, MAC addresses (when you can get them, and you'll normally have them only for your local network, as already explained) are particularly useful for identifying and differentiating *hardware*, particularly networking hardware such as routers. IP addresses are considerably more fungible than MAC addresses, and if you need to track a mobile asset like a laptop or anything moderated through DHCP, the MAC address will be your best asset for doing so.

IP Addressing

IP addresses are the most commonly accessed piece of information about a host, and often the only piece of data you will have about a host.

IP is slowly transitioning from IPv4 to IPv6. IPv6 corrects a number of design errors in IPv4, the most notable being IP address exhaustion. An IPv4 address is a 32-bit value, conventionally written in "dotted quad" format: four bytes, written decimally, separated by periods (like 192.168.1.1). At the time of IPv4's original design, nobody seriously expected that the 4 billion addresses provided would be exhausted, and many of the early allocations of IPv4 addresses are comically generous, as you can see from the master list of /8 allocations (*http://bit.ly/8-allocations*). A /8 is a collection of 16 million + addresses (2^{24}) all of which have the same first octet, so 9.0.0.0 to 9.255.255.255 is all owned by IBM, for example. Looking at the list, you'll see that several of the blocks were assigned large and early to companies such as Xerox and Ford who don't really use the space they have. The situation has actually improved over the past few years, when several drug companies owned nearly empty /8s and have since returned them to IANA.

The majority of the English-speaking Internet still runs on IPv4, while in Asia and elsewhere, IPv6 is increasingly prevalent. The uneven allocation of IPv4 addresses forces countries who have come to the Internet historically later to build IPv6 infrastructure.

IPv4 Addresses, Their Structure, and Significant Addresses

IPv4 addresses can be expressed using a number of different notations. The most common is the dotted quad format discussed earlier: four integer values between 0 and 255, separated by periods. Addresses can also be referred to directly as a value, usually in hexadecimal. Consequently, the IP address 0xA1010203 is 161.1.2.3 as a dotted quad, and 2701197827 as a decimal integer.

Groups of IP addresses are usually described linearly (e.g., 128.2.11.3–128.2.3.14), or using a *Classless Internet Domain Routing (CIDR) block*. CIDR blocks, which are discussed in more depth later, are a mechanism for describing the addresses reachable by picking a particular route. Addresses in CIDR notation are represented by a *prefix*,[1] which is a dotted quad representation of the significant bits of an address, and then a *mask*, which indicates how many bits make up the prefix.

For example, the CIDR block 128.2.11.0/24 consists of all addresses whose first 24 bits are 128.2.11, so any address from 128.2.11.0 to 128.2.11.255 is in that block.

A number of IP addresses are either reserved or fixed by convention in network configuration. For an individual host on a network, the most important are the broadcast address, gateway, and netmask. IP networks are logically divided into subnets, a col-

---

1. Note that the prefix is the equivalent to a subnet's netmask.

lection of contiguous addresses that can all communicate with each other without the need for internal routing. When configuring an IP address, this range is specified using a *netmask*, which is an IP address with a certain number of its least significant bits zeroed out.

To communicate outside its subnet, a host will have to talk to a router, and does so using a preconfigured *gateway address*. The gateway address is simply the IP address of the router's interface to the subnet. Gateway addresses are customarily assigned the lowest value in the subnet, but this is not a requirement.

A network's *broadcast* address is set to the subnet mask, but with all the host bits high (e.g., for a network with subnet mask 192.168.1.0, the broadcast address is 192.168.1.255). Messages sent to the broadcast address are sent to every target within the network. The broadcast address is one of a number of addresses you should *never* see outside of local network traffic. Addresses ending in .255, for lack of a better term, smell funny.

A number of IPv4 addresses are reserved for specific networking functions. These addresses are specifically intended for local use and consequently should not be seen crossing networks. The most significant are:

Local identification addresses
These belong to the 0.0.0.0/8 CIDR block (0.0.0.0–0.255.255.255). Local identification addresses are used during the startup sequence for a host that doesn't have an IP address yet.

Loopback address
The loopback address of a host is 127.0.0.1. Traffic sent to the loopback address is sent back to the host without entering the network. IANA has reserved the entire 127.0.0.0/8 CIDR block (127.0.0.0–127.255.255.255) for loopback, so as with local identification, nothing from the 127.0.0.0/8 CIDR block should be seen crossing network boundaries.

RFC 1918 netblocks
This document defines a number of netblocks for private use. These addresses can be used within local networks with the intent that they never communicate directly with the global Internet. The RFC netblocks are 10.0.0.0/8, 192.168.0.0/16 and 172.16.0.0/12. Addresses within these blocks are often assigned automatically by local routing tools or DHCP.

Multicast addresses
Multicast addresses are used to classify specific groups of hosts within a subnet. For example, multicast address 224.0.0.2 is the "all routers" multicast address, and all routers within the subnet will receive traffic sent there. Multicast traffic is primarily the focus of routing and other Internet control protocols.

IPv6 Addresses, Their Structure and Significant Addresses

One of the most significant changes between IPv4 and IPv6 is the number of addresses they make available. IPv6 assigns 128 bits to each address; this ensures plenty of addresses, but introduces some problems in notation.

The default format for an address is eight 16-bit hexadecimal values separated by colons, such as 2001:0010:AF3A:FB31:09A8:08A1:1098:1101. Given that this is a long and clumsy representation, addresses are usually represented using a number of shorthand conventions. When writing IPv6 addresses, apply these rules:

- Leading zeroes in any group are omitted, so 01AA:0002 can be written as 1AA:2.

- Consecutive groups of zero may be replaced with a pair of colons, so 2001:0:0:0:0:0:0:1 is written as 2001::1. The double-colon reduction can be used only once, so 2001:0:0:0:11:0:0:1 is written as 2001::11:0:0:1.

The RIRs and IP Address Allocation

Researching an IP address often means tracing the chain of ownership from IANA to a specific organization. The process of reservation is hierarchical; at the top level, IP address allocation is controlled by the Internet Assigned Numbers Authority (IANA) (*http://www.iana.org*). IANA is a department of the Internet Corporation for Assigned Names and Numbers (ICANN), the US-based nonprofit in charge of managing IP address and DNS name assignment.

IANA delegates the control of blocks of numbers to the Regional Internet Registries (RIRs), continental organizations that manage the allocation of IP addresses and Autonomous System numbers within their continent. RIRs are the intermediary between IANA and the various national and TLD registrars that actually deal with the allocation of addresses (see Table 8-1).

Table 8-1. The RIRs

RIR	Domain	URL
ARIN	US and Canada	www.arin.net
LACNIC	Central and South America, the Caribbean	lacnic.net
RIPE	Europe, Russia, and the Middle East	www.ripe.net
APNIC	Asia and Oceana	www.apnic.net
AfriNIC	Africa	www.afrinic.net

IANA delegates address blocks to the RIRs, and the RIRs in turn allocate sections of those blocks to organizations within their domains. RIRs then allocate address blocks to their members, and those members can allocate subblocks or addresses as they see fit.

This allocation process means that every IP address has a chain of ownership. That ownership begins with IANA, is allocated to one of the RIRs, and then down through one or more ISPs until it reaches whatever party is currently using the address. Beyond the final ISP (generally, below a /24 or a /27), address ownership is more fungible—it's rare to be able to associate a specific address with a specific person unless that's a matter of public record via whois, or the ISP is willing to give up that information.

As with IPv4, multiple IPv6 blocks are reserved for specific functions. The most important reservation at this point is 2000::/3 (as with IPv4, CIDR block notation can be used with IPv6 addresses, and the mask can extend up to 128 bits). IPv6 space is *huge*, and to help keep routes reasonably close together, *all routable traffic in IPv6* should be in the 2000::/3 block. Further divisions within the 2000::/3 block are maintained by IANA as it does with the /8 registry for IPv4. The master reference is available on the IPv6 Global Unicast Address Assignments page (*http://bit.ly/ipv6-add*).

Additional address blocks of note include the ::/128 and ::1/128 blocks, which are the unspecified and loopback address (the equivalent of 0.0.0.0, and 127.0.0.0 for IPv4).

Of particular interest are the utility address blocks 2001:758::/29 and 2001:678::/29. 2001:758::/29 is specifically assigned to *Internet Exchange Points* (IXPs); an IXP is a physical location where multiple ISPs interconnect with each other. 2001:678::/29 represents a block of provider-independent addresses; users can contact their RIRs directly for these addresses.

For clarity, a summary of local and unroutable addresses is provided in Table 8-2.

Table 8-2. Notable addresses

IPv4 block	IPv6 block	Description
0.0.0.0/0	::/0	Default route; addresses from this block shouldn't be seen
0.0.0.0/32	::/128	Unspecified address
127.0.0.1/8	::1/128	Loopback
192.168.16.0/24	fc00::/7	Reserved for local traffic
10.0.0.0/8	fc00::/7	Reserved for local traffic
172.16.0.0/12	fc00::/7	Reserved for local traffic
224.0.0.0/4	ff00::/8	Multicast addresses

Checking Connectivity: Using ping to Connect to an Address

The most basic command-line tool for checking connectivity is *ping*. *ping* works by using ICMP (see "Packet and Frame Formats" on page 24) messages. *ping* sends an ICMP echo request (type 8, code 0) to the target. On receiving an echo request message, the target should respond with an echo reply (type 0, code 0). Example 8-1 shows the output of *ping* and a *pcap* of the contents.

Example 8-1. ping output

```
$ ping -c 1 nytimes.com
PING nytimes.com (170.149.168.130): 56 data bytes
64 bytes from 170.149.168.130: icmp_seq=0 ttl=252 time=29.388 ms

$ tcpdump -Xnr ping.pcap
reading from file ping.pcap, link-type EN10MB (Ethernet)
20:38:09.074960 IP 192.168.1.12 > 170.149.168.130:
                ICMP echo request, id 44854, seq 0, length 64
        0x0000:  4500 0054 0942 0000 4001 5c9b c0a8 010c  E..T.B..@.\.....
        0x0010:  aa95 a882 0800 0fb8 af36 0000 5175 d7f1  .........6..Qu..
        0x0020:  0001 24a6 0809 0a0b 0c0d 0e0f 1011 1213  ..$............
        0x0030:  1415 1617 1819 1a1b 1c1d 1e1f 2021 2223  .............!"#
        0x0040:  2425 2627 2829 2a2b 2c2d 2e2f 3031 3233  $%&'()*+,-./0123
        0x0050:  3435 3637                                4567
20:38:09.104250 IP 170.149.168.130 > 192.168.1.12:
                ICMP echo reply, id 44854, seq 0, length 64
        0x0000:  4500 0054 0942 0000 fc01 a09a aa95 a882  E..T.B.........
        0x0010:  c0a8 010c 0000 17b8 af36 0000 5175 d7f1  .........6..Qu..
        0x0020:  0001 24a6 0809 0a0b 0c0d 0e0f 1011 1213  ..$............
        0x0030:  1415 1617 1819 1a1b 1c1d 1e1f 2021 2223  .............!"#
        0x0040:  2425 2627 2829 2a2b 2c2d 2e2f 3031 3233  $%&'()*+,-./0123
        0x0050:  3435 3637                                4567
```

Note first the size of the packet and the `ttl` value. These values are usually set by default by the TCP stack. In the case of Mac OS X, the ICMP packet has a 56-byte payload, which results in an 84-byte packet (20 bytes of IP header, 8 bytes of ICMP header, and 56 bytes payload). The type and code are at 0x0014-0x0015 (08 for the request, 00 for the response). After the ICMP header, note that the contents of the packet are echoed. ICMP has a concept of a session, and in many cases, messages are sent in response to packets from entirely different protocols. Different ICMP messages use different techniques to indicate their point of origin; in the case of *ping*, this is done by echoing the packet's original contents.

ping is a simple application: it sends an echo request with an embedded sequence identifier. The application then waits until a specified timeout (usually on the order of 4,000 ms); if the response is received in that time, the response is printed and the next packet is sent. *ping* is a diagnostic tool, and any serious implementation will provide a number of command line switches for manipulating packet composition.

Sweeping Pings and Ping Sweeping

These are actually different terms, although Google gets confused when you enter a search for them. A *ping sweep* (or *ping sweeping*) is a scanning technique that systematically pings all the IP addresses assigned to a network to determine which ones are

---

present and which ones are not. Ping sweeping is supported by *nmap* and a number of other scanning tools, although you can write a script to do it in about 20 seconds.

A *sweeping ping*, in contrast, is a sequence of ping messages that undergo size increases with each packet. Sweeping pings are intended to diagnose channels by identifying traffic manipulation or MTU issues. Sweeping pings are enabled by a command-line option on most modern *ping* implementations.

It's not uncommon to find networks blocking ICMP messages. Ping sweeping is consequently a middling tool for finding hosts on a network; direct TCP or UDP scanning will generally be more effective.

Tracerouting

traceroute is a tool and technique to identify the routers that forward packets from point A to point B. *traceroute* produces a sequential list of routers by manipulating packet TTLs.

The TTL (time to live) field of an IP packet is a mechanism developed to prevent packets from bouncing through the Internet forever. Every time a packet is forwarded by a router, its TTL value decreases by one. When the TTL reaches zero, the forwarding router drops the packet and sends an ICMP time exceeded (type 11) message.

```
$traceroute www.nytimes.com
traceroute to www.nytimes.com (170.149.168.130), 64 hops max, 52 byte packets
 1  wireless_broadband_router (192.168.1.1)  1.189 ms  0.544 ms  0.802 ms
 2  l100.washdc-vfttp-47.verizon-gni.net (96.255.98.1)  2.157 ms  1.401 ms
    1.451 ms
 3  g0-13-2-7.washdc-lcr-22.verizon-gni.net (130.81.59.154)  3.768 ms  3.751 ms
    3.985 ms
 4  ae5-0.res-bb-rtr1.verizon-gni.net (130.81.209.222)  2.029 ms  2.314 ms
    2.314 ms
 5  0.xe-3-1-1.br1.iad8.alter.net (152.63.37.141)  2.731 ms  2.759 ms  2.781 ms
 6  xe-2-1-0.er2.iad10.us.above.net (64.125.13.173)  3.313 ms  3.706 ms  3.970 ms
 7  xe-4-1-0.cr2.dca2.us.above.net (64.125.29.214)  3.741 ms  3.668 ms
    xe-3-0-0.cr2.dca2.us.above.net (64.125.26.241)  4.638 ms
 8  xe-1-0-0.cr1.dca2.us.above.net (64.125.28.249)  3.677 ms
    xe-7-2-0.cr1.dca2.us.above.net (64.125.26.41)  3.744 ms
    xe-1-0-0.cr1.dca2.us.above.net (64.125.28.249)  4.496 ms
 9  xe-3-2-0.cr1.lga5.us.above.net (64.125.26.102)  24.637 ms
    xe-2-2-0.cr1.lga5.us.above.net (64.125.26.98)  10.293 ms  9.679 ms
10  xe-2-2-0.mpr1.ewr1.us.above.net (64.125.27.133)  20.660 ms  10.043 ms
    10.004 ms
11  xe-0-0-0.mpr1.ewr4.us.above.net (64.125.25.246)  15.881 ms  16.848 ms
    16.070 ms
12  64.125.173.70.t01646-03.above.net (64.125.173.70)  30.177 ms  29.339 ms
    31.793 ms
```

As the next code block shows, *traceroute* sends an initial 52-byte message, and then proceeds to receive sequential information about each address it contacts en route to 170.149.168.130. Let's look at the payload in more depth.

```
$ tcpdump -nXr traceroute.pcap  | more
21:06:51.202439 IP 192.168.1.12.46950 > 170.149.168.130.33435: UDP, length 24
        0x0000:  4500 0034 b767 0000 0111 ed85 c0a8 010c  E..4.g..........
        0x0010:  aa95 a882 b766 829b 0020 b0df 0000 0000  .....f..........
        0x0020:  0000 0000 0000 0000 0000 0000 0000 0000  ................
        0x0030:  0000 0000                                ....
21:06:51.203481 IP 192.168.1.1 > 192.168.1.12: ICMP time exceeded in-transit,
        length 60
        0x0000:  45c0 0050 a201 0000 4001 548e c0a8 0101  E..P....@.T.....
        0x0010:  c0a8 010c 0b00 09fe 0000 0000 4500 0034  ............E..4
        0x0020:  b767 0000 0111 ed85 c0a8 010c aa95 a882  .g..............
        0x0030:  b766 829b 0020 b0df 0000 0000 0000 0000  .f..............
        0x0040:  0000 0000 0000 0000 0000 0000 0000 0000  ................
21:06:51.203691 IP 192.168.1.12.46950 > 170.149.168.130.33436: UDP, length 24
        0x0000:  4500 0034 b768 0000 0111 ed84 c0a8 010c  E..4.h..........
        0x0010:  aa95 a882 b766 829c 0020 b0de 0000 0000  .....f..........
        0x0020:  0000 0000 0000 0000 0000 0000 0000 0000  ................
        0x0030:  0000 0000                                ....
21:06:51.204191 IP 192.168.1.1 > 192.168.1.12: ICMP time exceeded in-transit,
        length 60
        0x0000:  45c0 0050 a202 0000 4001 548d c0a8 0101  E..P....@.T.....
        0x0010:  c0a8 010c 0b00 09fe 0000 0000 4500 0034  ............E..4
        0x0020:  b768 0000 0111 ed84 c0a8 010c aa95 a882  .h..............
        0x0030:  b766 829c 0020 b0de 0000 0000 0000 0000  .f..............
        0x0040:  0000 0000 0000 0000 0000 0000 0000 0000  ................
```

Note that *traceroute* sends out UDP messages, starting at port 33435 and incrementing the port number by one with each additional message. The port number is incremented in order to reconstruct the order in which the packets are sent. Note that the ICMP packet from offset 0x001C onward contains the original UDP packet. As noted above, ICMP messages need to use a number of different techniques to provide context—error messages such as TTL exceeded include the IP header and the first 8 bytes of the original packet. This includes the UDP source port number. *traceroute* orders the ICMP messages in order of this port number in order to determine the order in which those messages were sent.

While *traceroute* uses UDP by default, the same technique can be used by TCP or any other protocol where there is a controllable value (such as ephemeral port number) in the first 8 bytes of the IP payload.

ping and *traceroute* are more useful if you can use them from different locations. To that end, a number of Internet service providers and other organizations provide *looking glass servers*. A looking glass server is a publicly accessible (generally via the Web) interface to any of a number of common Internet applications. Most looking glasses are managed by NOCs or ISPs, and provide access to multiple routers. There is no standard for implementation, and different looking glasses will provide different services. A comprehesive list is available at www.traceroute.org.

IP Intelligence: Geolocation and Demographics

A number of database and intelligence services provide further information about an IP address. This type of augmentation data includes ownership, geolocation, and demographic information.

It's important to distinguish this augmentation data from information such as autonomous system, domain name, and whois data. The latter is necessary for the upkeep of the network, and is maintained by Internet organizations related to ICANN. Geolocation, demographic data, and ownership are intelligence products. The companies that produce them use a variety of mechanisms including network scanning as well as shoe-leather investigation to produce it. This leads to several important qualities:

- The intelligence updates slowly, whereas DNS names can change very rapidly. It takes additional checking to find out that 128.2.11.214 is no longer involved in selling car parts and is now hosting malware.

- There is always some degree of approximation. As a rule of thumb, intelligence data gets less accurate as you delve down into finer detail. Country information is usually good, but I'm moderately skeptical about city information outside of the US and western Europe, and I never trust physical location.

- You get what you pay for. The companies that produce this data have customers who need it. Most of the companies started out providing demographic data for large websites, and it's still common to find limits on the number of queries you can conduct per license. You pay for accuracy and you pay for precision. There are free intelligence databases, but if you want to get finer detail than country codes, prepare to crack open your wallet.

The most commonly used open source reference is MaxMind's GeoIP (*http://bit.ly/geoip*), which provides a number of databases for city, country, region, organization, ISP, and network speed. They also provide free services in the form of "lite" databases for finding city and country. All of their products are downloadable databases and are updated regularly. MaxMind has been providing this service for years, along with a number of APIs in Python and other scripting languages that are available to access the database.

For more extensive information, options include Neustar (*http://www.neustar.biz*) and Digital Envoy's Digital Element (*http://www.digitalenvoy.com*). Both provide more precise measurement, as well as additional demographic data such as *Metropolitan Statistical Area* (MSA) (contiguous areas of high population density used by the government for statistical analysis) and *North American Industry Classification System* (NAICS) codes (a numerical identifier akin to a Dewey Decimal number for business type). These services are *not* cheap, however.

DNS

In a just world, each IP address would have a single DNS name, and finding the DNS name associated with an IP address would be a simple matter of consulting a database. This world is not just.

DNS is the glue that makes the Internet usable by human beings. As one of the older services making the Internet work, DNS overlaps a couple of other services (particularly mail). DNS is, at this point, a distributed database that provides lookup information for a number of different relationships, in particular DNS name to IP address, DNS name to DNS name, email address to mail server, and so on.

DNS Name Structure

A *domain name* consists of a hierarchical sequence of labels separated by periods, such as *www.oreilly.com*. Domain names become more general as you read from right to left, ending at the root domain (the root domain is ., but it's almost always implicit). Domain names do have limits. The total length of a name cannot exceed 253 characters, and individual labels are limited to 64.

Historically, labels were limited to a restricted subset of ASCII characters for the name. Since 2009, it has been possible to acquire *internationalized domain names*, which are encoded using character systems such as Chinese, Greek, and so on.[2] The mechanical limits of 253 characters per name still hold, though the encoding is more complex.

NICs and Domain Name Allocation

The authority to allocate domain names, as with IP addresses, begins with ICANN. ICANN controls the root zone and defines the *top-level domains* (TLDs) that lie just below the root of the tree. As with addresses, each TLD has a managing authority referred to as a *network information center* (NIC). Each NIC establishes different policies for name allocation—for example, anyone can get a *.com* address, but only accredited educational institutions qualify for a *.edu* address. Depending on NIC policy, registration authority may be further delegated to one or more *registrars*.

IANA defines four categories of TLD. The oldest category is the *generic TLDs* (gTLD); these are country-agnostic top-level domains such as *.com* or *.edu*. Following gTLDs is the one-domain *infrastructural TLD*, which contains the *.arpa* domain used for reverse

---

2. Internationalized domain names raise the risk of homographic attacks, such as creating a domain name that looks like *oreilly.com* but uses a Cyrillic O.

DNS lookups. A *country code TLD* (ccTLD) is a two-letter top-level domain for a countries (e.g., *.ie* for Ireland). A new set of *internationalized TLDs* (IDN ccTLD) allow non-Latin characters.

Each TLD has its own NIC. Table 8-3 below shows the NICs for a number of commonly consulted TLDs.

Table 8-3. Notable NICs

TLD	NIC	URL
.org	Public Interest Registry	www.pir.org
.biz	Neustar	www.neustar.biz/enterprise/domain-name-registry
.com	VeriSign	www.verisigninc.com/
.net	VeriSign	www.verisigninc.com/
.edu	Educause	www.educause.ed
.int	IANA	*www.iana.org/domains/int*
.fr	AFNIC	www.afnic.fr/
.uk	Nominet	www.nominet.org.uk
.ru	Coordination Center for TLD RU	www.cctld.ru/en/
.cn	CNNIC	www1.cnnic.cn/
.kr	KISA	www.kisa.or.kr/

This hierarchy of nameservers also serves to determine which servers are *authoritative*. Top-level registries assign authority to subregistries by granting them *zones*. Each zone has one master server that maintains its domain names and is authoritative when queried, but zones can be nested in order to give different servers authority.

Forward DNS Querying Using dig

The basic DNS query tool is *domain information groper* (*dig*), a command-line DNS client that enables you to query DNS for all of the major records. Begin by conducting a simple dig query:

```
$ dig oreilly.com
dig oreilly.com

; <<>> DiG 9.8.3-P1 <<>> oreilly.com
;; global options: +cmd
;; Got answer:
;; ->>HEADER<<- opcode: QUERY, status: NOERROR, id: 29081
;; flags: qr rd ra; QUERY: 1, ANSWER: 2, AUTHORITY: 0, ADDITIONAL: 0

;; QUESTION SECTION:
;oreilly.com.                    IN      A
```

```
;; ANSWER SECTION:
oreilly.com.            383     IN      A       208.201.239.101
oreilly.com.            383     IN      A       208.201.239.100

;; Query time: 10 msec
;; SERVER: 192.168.1.1#53(192.168.1.1)
;; WHEN: Sat Jul 20 19:11:17 2013
;; MSG SIZE  rcvd: 61
$ dig +short oreilly.com
208.201.239.101
208.201.239.100
```

We will consider dig's display options, and then the structure of the DNS response. As seen in the previous example, the basic dig command provides extensive information about the query, beginning with a list of options invoked, then a DNS header, and then several sections corresponding to the query. Note the QUERY, ANSWER, AUTHORITY, and ADDITIONAL fields in the header line, and how those correspond to the lines in the corresponding sections. Because this domain returned no AUTHORITY or ADDITIONAL records, none are shown in the output. The query is followed by a set of statistics about the query: the server, the time it took, and the size of the message.

dig provides an enormous number of output options; the previous example showed the default display. Individual sections of that display can be turned off using +nocomments (which kills all the comments beginning with a double semicolon), +nostats (killing the statistics at the end), and +noquestion and +noanswer (to eliminate the DNS responses). +short will simply remove all the cruft and show the responses.

dig is simply a DNS client, so the majority of information seen is from the DNS server itself. dig enables queries to different servers by using @ in the command line. For example:

```
$ # 8.8.8.8 is Google's public DNS server; let's query a CDN using it
$ dig @8.8.8.8 www.foxnews.com
; <<>> DiG 9.8.3-P1 <<>> @8.8.8.8 www.foxnews.com
; (1 server found)
;; global options: +cmd
;; Got answer:
;; ->>HEADER<<- opcode: QUERY, status: NOERROR, id: 18702
;; flags: qr rd ra; QUERY: 1, ANSWER: 4, AUTHORITY: 0, ADDITIONAL: 0

;; QUESTION SECTION:
;www.foxnews.com.                IN      A

;; ANSWER SECTION:
www.foxnews.com.            282     IN      CNAME   www.foxnews.com.edgesuite.net.
www.foxnews.com.edgesuite.net. 21582 IN CNAME   a20.g.akamai.net.
a20.g.akamai.net.           2       IN      A       204.245.190.42
a20.g.akamai.net.           2       IN      A       204.245.190.8
```

```
;; Query time: 141 msec
;; SERVER: 8.8.8.8#53(8.8.8.8)
;; WHEN: Sat Jul 20 19:48:01 2013
;; MSG SIZE  rcvd: 135

$ # Query using my default server
$ dig www.foxnews.com

; <<>> DiG 9.8.3-P1 <<>> www.foxnews.com
;; global options: +cmd
;; Got answer:
;; ->>HEADER<<- opcode: QUERY, status: NOERROR, id: 47098
;; flags: qr rd ra; QUERY: 1, ANSWER: 4, AUTHORITY: 0, ADDITIONAL: 0

;; QUESTION SECTION:
;www.foxnews.com.                IN      A

;; ANSWER SECTION:
www.foxnews.com.           189     IN      CNAME   www.foxnews.com.edgesuite.net.
www.foxnews.com.edgesuite.net. 9699 IN  CNAME   a20.g.akamai.net.
a20.g.akamai.net.          9       IN      A       23.66.230.160
a20.g.akamai.net.          9       IN      A       23.66.230.106

;; Query time: 97 msec
;; SERVER: 192.168.1.1#53(192.168.1.1)
;; WHEN: Sat Jul 20 19:48:09 2013
;; MSG SIZE  rcvd: 135
```

As you can see, querying a CDN-moderated site (Fox News uses Akamai) results in radically different IP addresses for the same name. CDNs manipulate the DNS to ensure that caches of published data are geographically close to their target. If you don't specify the server using @, dig will default to whatever server the system is configured to use (for example, in Unix systems this is maintained in */etc/resolv.conf*).

A CDN is a caching network that makes the Internet viable. Before the Web, a user might visit four to five hosts in an hour; after the Web, a request to a web page might launch a hundred different HTTP requests. The majority of these requests are redirected via DNS to caching servers that are located geographically nearby.

CDNs add an annoying wrinkle to web analysis, because a single CDN server may host multiple websites. Once an address is identified as a CDN, figuring out exactly what it is tends to be prohibitively difficult.

Now, let's look at the DNS data. DNS is a federated database system. So queries go first to a local DNS server, which sends a response if it possesses the answer to the query. If the server doesn't have the information, it uses the hierarchical structure of the name to figure out where to send the request, waits for a response, and sends the response back. DNS supports a number of different queries, termed *resource records* (RRs), and the options sent during the query specify the resource record requested as well as options for querying additional servers. The values with `As` or `CNAMES` in the lines above are resource records.

Note that the header lists eight fields:

opcode

> This field was intended to specify a number of different actions, such as queries, inverse queries, and server status. In practice, it should always be set to query. A number of other opcodes exist, but they are used to communicate information between servers.

status

> The status of the response. Three messages appear most often: NOERROR, NXDO MAIN, and SERVFAIL. NOERROR indicates that the query was successful, NXDOMAIN indicates that no domain was available, and SERVFAIL indicates that authoritative servers for the domain were unreachable.

id

> The message ID. DNS is a UDP-moderated protocol and uses message IDs to track queries and responses.

flags

> These provide information on the response, and include qr (set high for a response), aa (set high when the answer is from an authoritative server), ra (recursion desired), and rd (recursion available).

The remaining four fields refer to the categories of records sent in response. These four are:

QUERY

> This record is simply a copy of the original request; you can see in this case that the query is echoed in what dig refers to as the QUESTION section.

ANSWER

> Contains the response.

AUTHORITY

> Reserved for records that identify other servers.

ADDITIONAL

> Provides additional information, such as the expected responses to future queries.

Additional information is very much a function of the nameserver's administrators. A common example of its use follows, where the information provides a name lookup for the mail server identified by an MX query:

```
$ dig +nostats +nocmd mx cmu.edu
;; Got answer:
;; ->>HEADER<<- opcode: QUERY, status: NOERROR, id: 30852
```

```
;; flags: qr rd ra; QUERY: 1, ANSWER: 4, AUTHORITY: 0, ADDITIONAL: 3

;; QUESTION SECTION:
;cmu.edu.                        IN      MX

;; ANSWER SECTION:
cmu.edu.                 20051   IN      MX      10 CMU-MX-02.ANDREW.cmu.edu.
cmu.edu.                 20051   IN      MX      10 CMU-MX-03.ANDREW.cmu.edu.
cmu.edu.                 20051   IN      MX      10 CMU-MX-04.ANDREW.cmu.edu.
cmu.edu.                 20051   IN      MX      10 CMU-MX-01.ANDREW.cmu.edu.

;; ADDITIONAL SECTION:
CMU-MX-03.ANDREW.cmu.edu. 20412 IN      A       128.2.155.68
CMU-MX-01.ANDREW.cmu.edu. 20232 IN      A       128.2.11.59
CMU-MX-02.ANDREW.cmu.edu. 20051 IN      A       128.2.11.60
```

Now, let's discuss what those resource records actually mean. DNS has upward of 20 resource records for different functions. The major ones are:

A

An answer record, providing the IP address associated with a particular name.

AAAA

Like A, but provides an IPv6 address for a name.

CNAME

Relates two names, a canonical name and an alias.

MX

Returns the mailserver for a domain.

PTR

Points to a canonical name; mostly used for DNS reverse lookups.

TXT

Contains arbitrary text data.

NS

Describes the nameserver for an address.

SOA

Provides information about the authoritative nameserver for an address.

dig starts all resource records with the same four values: a name, a time to live (TTL), a class, and an identifier for the RR (for example: cmu.edu, 20051, IN, MX). The name is passed with the query. The TTL indicates for how long (in seconds) the value of the name can be trusted; DNS relies heavily on caching and the TTL provides instructions on when to refresh the cache. The class will almost invariably be IN (Internet); other class names are possible, but outside the scope of this book.

A and AAAA provide basic DNS functionality: they associate the queried name with an IP address. A records provide IPv4 addresses, and AAAA records provide IPv6 addresses. By default, dig queries for A records, while other record types are specified by adding them to the command line, seen here:

```
$ dig +nocomment +noquestion +nostats +nocmd www.google.com
www.google.com.          55      IN      A       74.125.228.81
www.google.com.          55      IN      A       74.125.228.83
www.google.com.          55      IN      A       74.125.228.84
www.google.com.          55      IN      A       74.125.228.80
www.google.com.          55      IN      A       74.125.228.82
$ dig +nocomment +noquestion +nostats +nocmd aaaa www.google.com
www.google.com.          18      IN      AAAA    2607:f8b0:4004:802::1014
```

Note that the query to Google responds with five A records. This is an example of *round robin DNS allocation*, a common load balancing technique. In round robin allocation, the same domain name is assigned to multiple IP addresses. Consequently, when a query chooses an IP address to contact for the name, it effectively picks the name randomly from the set of targets. Round robin DNS allocation is one of many DNS hacks that makes reverse lookups (IP addresses from names) incredibly annoying.

Note also the short TTL values. If a particular Google server goes down, the TTL guarantees that in 55 seconds, the user has good odds of contacting another server.

Canonical name (CNAME) records are used to associate an alias to a canonical name. For example, consider lookups for *www.oreilly.com*:

```
dig +nocomment +noquestion +nostats +nocmd www.oreilly.com
www.oreilly.com.         3563    IN      CNAME   oreilly.com.
oreilly.com.             506     IN      A       208.201.239.101
oreilly.com.             506     IN      A       208.201.239.100
```

As this shows, the name *www.oreilly.com* actually points to *oreilly.com*. *www.oreilly.com* does *not* have an IP address; it points to *oreilly.com*, and *that* name has an IP address. Canonical names are used for shortcuts (as in the previous example), and also to manage content distribution. The example using Fox News showed how Akamai first aliases all of Fox News' sites into its own network names using CNAME.

DNS provides the lookup functions for email, through the agency of the *mail exchange* (MX) record. MX records record the addresses of mail servers for a particular domain. For example, if I decide to mail *jbro@andrew.cmu.edu*, I can find the mail server for doing so by looking up the MX records for *cmu.edu*:

```
$dig  +noquestion +nostats +nocmd mx cmu.edu
;; Got answer:
;; ->>HEADER<<- opcode: QUERY, status: NOERROR, id: 49880
;; flags: qr rd ra; QUERY: 1, ANSWER: 4, AUTHORITY: 0, ADDITIONAL: 2

;; ANSWER SECTION:
cmu.edu.                 21560   IN      MX      10 CMU-MX-03.ANDREW.cmu.edu.
```

```
cmu.edu.                        21560   IN      MX      10 CMU-MX-04.ANDREW.cmu.edu.
cmu.edu.                        21560   IN      MX      10 CMU-MX-01.ANDREW.cmu.edu.
cmu.edu.                        21560   IN      MX      10 CMU-MX-02.ANDREW.cmu.edu.

;; ADDITIONAL SECTION:
CMU-MX-01.ANDREW.cmu.edu. 21519 IN      A       128.2.11.59
CMU-MX-02.ANDREW.cmu.edu. 21159 IN      A       128.2.11.60
```

MX records include a server name (such as CMU-MX-03.ANDREW.cmu.edu), as well as a priority value for the email server. The weighting value is used to choose a mail server: mail clients should pick mail servers in order of ascending priority (i.e., 1 should be chosen before 10).

Of note in this example are the A records shoved into the additional section. These records resolve the CMU-MX-01 and CMU-MX-02 addresses. This is a conscious decision by CMU's DNS administrators to include this information and reduce the number of lookups done.

NS records are used to find the authoritative nameserver for a zone. For example, for O'Reilly Media:

```
$ dig +nostat ns oreilly.com

; <<>> DiG 9.8.3-P1 <<>> +nostat ns oreilly.com
;; global options: +cmd
;; Got answer:
;; ->>HEADER<<- opcode: QUERY, status: NOERROR, id: 32310
;; flags: qr rd ra; QUERY: 1, ANSWER: 2, AUTHORITY: 0, ADDITIONAL: 0

;; QUESTION SECTION:
;oreilly.com.                   IN      NS

;; ANSWER SECTION:
oreilly.com.            3600    IN      NS      nsautha.oreilly.com.
oreilly.com.            3600    IN      NS      nsauthb.oreilly.com.
```

Now look at the NS record for a site managed by a CDN, such as Fox News again:

```
$ dig +nostat ns foxnews.com

; <<>> DiG 9.8.3-P1 <<>> +nostat ns foxnews.com
;; global options: +cmd
;; Got answer:
;; ->>HEADER<<- opcode: QUERY, status: NOERROR, id: 38538
;; flags: qr rd ra; QUERY: 1, ANSWER: 8, AUTHORITY: 0, ADDITIONAL: 5

;; QUESTION SECTION:
;foxnews.com.                   IN      NS

;; ANSWER SECTION:
foxnews.com.            300     IN      NS      usc2.akam.net.
foxnews.com.            300     IN      NS      ns1.chi.foxnews.com.
```

```
foxnews.com.              300     IN      NS      ns1-253.akam.net.
foxnews.com.              300     IN      NS      dns.tpa.foxnews.com.
foxnews.com.              300     IN      NS      usw1.akam.net.
foxnews.com.              300     IN      NS      usw3.akam.net.
foxnews.com.              300     IN      NS      asia3.akam.net.
foxnews.com.              300     IN      NS      usc4.akam.net.

;; ADDITIONAL SECTION:
usw1.akam.net.            28264   IN      A       96.17.144.195
usw3.akam.net.            50954   IN      A       69.31.59.199
asia3.akam.net.           28264   IN      A       222.122.64.134
usc4.akam.net.            28264   IN      A       96.6.112.196
usc2.akam.net.            88188   IN      A       69.31.59.199
```

Note that in this case, the authoritative nameservers are largely owned by *akam.net* (Akamai). Fox News is hosted by Akamai's CDN, and Akamai modifies the names of the hosts as necessary in order to boost performance.

SOA records contain summary information about the authoritative server for a domain. These records are most commonly encountered during failed lookups. When an address isn't found, the SOA information for that zone's server is returned instead.

```
dig @8.8.4.4 +multiline +nostat zlkoriongomk.com

; <<>> DiG 9.8.3-P1 <<>> @8.8.4.4 +multiline +nostat zlkoriongomk.com
; (1 server found)
;; global options: +cmd
;; Got answer:
;; ->>HEADER<<- opcode: QUERY, status: NXDOMAIN, id: 11857
;; flags: qr rd ra; QUERY: 1, ANSWER: 0, AUTHORITY: 1, ADDITIONAL: 0

;; QUESTION SECTION:
;zlkoriongomk.com.        IN A

;; AUTHORITY SECTION:
com.                      899 IN SOA a.gtld-servers.net. nstld.verisign-grs.com. (
                          1374373035 ; serial
                          1800       ; refresh (30 minutes)
                          900        ; retry (15 minutes)
                          604800     ; expire (1 week)
                          86400      ; minimum (1 day)
                          )
```

The SOA field begins with the source host, followed by a contact email address. After this address comes a serial number, which indicates how many times the source file has been modified, and then timeout statistics. Note the \+multiline option for dig; this will provide a multiple line, more human-readable output for the SOA record.

The TXT field is a wildcard field used for any text output that the server administrator feels like passing. For example, Google passes strings for managing Google Apps:

```
$ dig +short txt google.com
"v=spf1 include:_spf.google.com ip4:216.73.93.70/31 ip4:216.73.93.72/31 ~all"
```

The DNS Reverse Lookup

A *reverse lookup* is the process of reconstructing a DNS name from an IP address. For example, if I want to find out who owns 208.201.139.101, I do so using dig -x:

```
$ dig +nostat -x 208.201.139.101

; <<>> DiG 9.8.3-P1 <<>> +nostat -x 208.201.139.101
;; global options: +cmd
;; Got answer:
;; ->>HEADER<<- opcode: QUERY, status: NOERROR, id: 7519
;; flags: qr rd ra; QUERY: 1, ANSWER: 1, AUTHORITY: 0, ADDITIONAL: 0

;; QUESTION SECTION:
;101.139.201.208.in-addr.arpa.    IN       PTR

;; ANSWER SECTION:
101.139.201.208.in-addr.arpa. 21600 IN  PTR     host-d101.studley.com.
```

Reverse lookups are requests to get DNS names from IP addresses. Note that the question section does not request the IP address, 208.201.139.101, but 101.139.201.208.in-addr.arpa, which lists the fields of the IP address in reverse order. When DNS does a reverse lookup, it creates a special domain name to query in the *in-addr.arpa* TLD.[3] The string of digits and periods used for a reverse lookup is the original IP address reversed. The is because DNS names and IP addresses are defined in a contradictory fashion. A DNS name becomes more finely defined (from TLD to domain to individual host) by reading from right to left, while IP addresses are more finely defined reading from left to right.

Reverse lookups are a kludge. Note that the record returned in the answer is a Pointer (PTR) record. PTR records are not automatically created with the canonical A records, but are instead registered separately by the NIC. More important, there's no requirement that a PTR record be registered, and the relationship between names and IP addresses is tenuous at best.

For example, consider a CDN. If I look up one of Fox News' IP addresses, such as 23.66.230.66, I get this:

```
dig +nostat +nocmd -x 23.66.230.66
;; Got answer:
;; ->>HEADER<<- opcode: QUERY, status: NOERROR, id: 56379
;; flags: qr rd ra; QUERY: 1, ANSWER: 1, AUTHORITY: 0, ADDITIONAL: 0
```

3. *.arpa* officially stands for Address and Routing Parameter area. This name is a backronym, because the abbreviation originally meant Advanced Research Projects Agency, the DoD agency that originally funded Internet development

```
;; QUESTION SECTION:
;66.230.66.23.in-addr.arpa.        IN        PTR

;; ANSWER SECTION:
66.230.66.23.in-addr.arpa. 290  IN
PTR      a23-66-230-66.deploy.static.akamaitechnologies.com.
```

The CDN becomes an informational dead end; the answer from the reverse lookup has no meaningful relation to the names in the original query.

In general, DNS information is best collected at the time of the original query. The uncertainty of reverse lookups is part of the reason for this. However, even if reverse lookups worked perfectly, attackers often use very short-lived names. Where possible, record domain names as they're used (such as the URL in HTTP logs) rather than trying to reconstruct them after the fact.

Using whois to Find Ownership

While DNS can provide information on a domain's name, the meat of ownership information is provided by whois. This is a federated protocol (RFC 3921 (*http://bit.ly/rfc-3921*)) that lists the putative owners of DNS names. The standard whois query on a domain will return ownership and contact information for a domain, as seen in Example 8-2.

Example 8-2. A whois query for oreilly.com

```
$whois oreilly.com

<boilerplate>

   Domain Name: OREILLY.COM
   Registrar: GODADDY.COM, LLC
   Whois Server: whois.godaddy.com
   Referral URL: http://registrar.godaddy.com
   Name Server: NSAUTHA.OREILLY.COM
   Name Server: NSAUTHB.OREILLY.COM
   Status: clientDeleteProhibited
   Status: clientRenewProhibited
   Status: clientTransferProhibited
   Status: clientUpdateProhibited
   Updated Date: 26-may-2012
   Creation Date: 27-may-1997
   Expiration Date: 26-may-2013

<more boilerplate>

   Registered through: GoDaddy.com, LLC (http://www.godaddy.com)
   Domain Name: OREILLY.COM
      Created on: 26-May-97
      Expires on: 25-May-13
```

```
Last Updated on: 26-May-12

Registrant:
O'Reilly Media, Inc.
1005 Gravenstein Highway North
Sebastopol, California 95472
United States

Administrative Contact:
   Contact, Admin  nic-ac@oreilly.com
   O'Reilly Media, Inc.
   1005 Gravenstein Highway North
   Sebastopol, California 95472
   United States
   +1.7078277000      Fax -- +1.7078290104

Technical Contact:
   Contact, Tech  nic-tc@oreilly.com
   O'Reilly Media, Inc.
   1005 Gravenstein Highway North
   Sebastopol, California 95472
   United States
   +1.7078277000      Fax -- +1.7078290104

Domain servers in listed order:
   NSAUTHA.OREILLY.COM
   NSAUTHB.OREILLY.COM
```

You'll note that a whois entry for a domain returns an enormous amount of boilerplate information. You will also find that the information returned has no particular fixed format—whois information is the electronic equivalent of 3×5 index cards. Depending on who owns the card and how they decide to administer it, you may get phone numbers and biographies, or nothing at all.

A good way to get a feel for the differences in registration is to take a look at the registration files for different countries. There is no central whois database—instead, depending on the top-level domain, whois information may be maintained by any of a number of whois servers. For example, Russian whois data (the *.ru* domain) is maintained by *whois.ripn.net*, French by *lvs-vip.nic.fr*, and Brazilian by *registro.br*. Fortunately, the good folks at *whois-servers.net* provide aliases for every country and TLD, and depending on your whois implementation, the information may be baked into the executable for you already.

At the minimum, any whois implementation will provide the ability to specify a lookup server using the -h switch. So whois -h ru.tld-servers.net is identical to whois -h whois.ripn.net. Several whois implementations offer a country-specific -c option, making whois -c RU identical to both of the previous examples.

In addition to providing information on domain names, whois is also useful for providing information on address allocation and ownership. If whois is called with an IP address rather than a name, like in Example 8-3, it will provide information on the organization that owns that address, often in the form of a netblock. For example, if I look up the whois information for Voila, a French search engine, I get different information based on whether I look at RIPE (the European top-level registry) or the French NIC. RIPE is informative; the French NIC is considerably less so.

Example 8-3. Using whois with an IP address

```
$dig +short voila.fr
193.252.148.80

$ whois -h whois.ripe.net 193.252.148.80
% This is the RIPE Database query service.
% The objects are in RPSL format.
%
% The RIPE Database is subject to Terms and Conditions.
% See http://www.ripe.net/db/support/db-terms-conditions.pdf

% Note: this output has been filtered.
%       To receive output for a database update, use the "-B" flag.

% Information related to '193.252.148.0 - 193.252.148.255'

% Abuse contact for '193.252.148.0 - 193.252.148.255' is 'gestionip.ft@orange.com'

inetnum:        193.252.148.0 - 193.252.148.255
netname:        ORANGE-PORTAILS
descr:          France Telecom
descr:          internet portals for multiple services
country:        FR
admin-c:        WPTR1-RIPE
tech-c:         WPTR1-RIPE
status:         ASSIGNED PA
remarks:        for hacking, spamming or security problems send mail to
remarks:        abuse@orange.fr
mnt-by:         FT-BRX
source:         RIPE # Filtered

role:           Wanadoo Portails Technical Role
address:        France Telecom - OPF/Portail/DOP/Hebex
address:        48, rue Camille Desmoulins
address:        92791 Issy Les Moulineaux Cedex 9
address:        FR
phone:          +33 1 5888 6500
fax-no:         +33 1 5888 6680
admin-c:        WPTR1-RIPE
tech-c:         WPTR1-RIPE
nic-hdl:        WPTR1-RIPE
mnt-by:         FT-BRX
```

```
source:         RIPE # Filtered

% This query was served by the RIPE Database Query Service version 1.60.2 (WHOIS4)

$ whois -h fr.whois-servers.net 195.152.120.129
%%
%% This is the AFNIC Whois server.
%%
%% complete date format : DD/MM/YYYY
%% short date format     : DD/MM
%% version               : FRNIC-2.5
%%
%% Rights restricted by copyright.
%% See http://www.afnic.fr/afnic/web/mentions-legales-whois_en
%%
%% Use '-h' option to obtain more information about this service.
%%
%% [96.255.98.126 REQUEST] >> 195.152.120.129
%%
%% RL Net [##########] - RL IP [#########.]
```

You will find that the situation is reversed with Asian information. The APNIC whois is often fairly sparse, but the whois entries at the country level are usually informative.

Whois information is particularly useful when you can't get much useful data out of a DNS reverse lookup. If you can't find the specific domain name, you can use whois to at least find the block of addresses that host the domain.

Additional Reference Tools

In addition to network and routing information, there exist a number of commonly accessible sites containing information on exploits, attacks, and the reputation of particular IP addresses. These sites are usually small, volunteer-run and have a fair degree of turnover to them.

DNSBLs

A *DNS Blackhole List* (DNSBL) is a DNS-based IP address database used primarily as an antispam technique. The first DNSBLs were actually implemented using BGP, and were intended to actively drop routes associated with spammer IP addresses. DNSBLs are instead DNS-moderated, they serve as reputation databases for email software. For example, a mail transfer agent can consult a DNSBL to determine if the sending IP is a spammer and react accordingly.

DNSBLs work by providing a reverse-lookup style functionality on their DNS servers. For example, I can look up an echo address on a DNSBL using dig:

```
$ dig 2.0.0.127.sbl.spamhaus.org

; <<>> DiG 9.8.3-P1 <<>> 2.0.0.127.sbl.spamhaus.org
;; global options: +cmd
;; Got answer:
;; ->>HEADER<<- opcode: QUERY, status: NOERROR, id: 45434
;; flags: qr rd ra; QUERY: 1, ANSWER: 1, AUTHORITY: 0, ADDITIONAL: 0

;; QUESTION SECTION:
;2.0.0.127.sbl.spamhaus.org.     IN      A

;; ANSWER SECTION:
2.0.0.127.sbl.spamhaus.org. 300 IN      A       127.0.0.2

;; Query time: 39 msec
;; SERVER: 192.168.1.1#53(192.168.1.1)
;; WHEN: Sun Jul 28 15:10:23 2013
;; MSG SIZE  rcvd: 60
```

The address I intended to query was 127.0.0.2. Note that, as with a reverse lookup, I reverse the IP address. After reversing the address, I attach it to the name of the list and query. This process is effectively a reverse lookup without relying on the hard-coded *.arpa* TLD. Instead, the response is provided by an A record provided by Spamhaus's SBL server.

DNSBLs differ depending on the list and provider. Providers may provide several different forms of lists for different categories of traffic. Different providers will also provide different policies for adding or removing addresses from the DNSBL. How different organizations handle *delisting* (address removal) radically impacts the character of the list. Most automatically drop an address a fixed number of days after the last abuse; others require manual intervention.

Some notable DNSBLs include:

Spam and Open Relay Blocking System (SORBS) (http://www.sorbs.net)
Provides over 15 different DNSBLs that categorize hosts into a number of different behaviors. SORBS is particularly useful for categorizing dynamic addresses such as dialup and DSL addresses through a specialized list, the Dynamic User and Host List (DUHL).

Spamhaus (http://www.spamhaus.org)
A nonprofit private company that produces a number of distinct blacklists and whitelists. Spamhaus's most commonly used lists are the PBL (end-user addresses), SBL (spam addresses), and XBL (hijacked IP addresses and bots). These lists are accessible as a single combined service, ZEN.

SpamCop
> Currently owned by Cisco Systems, SpamCop began as a private effort and eventually became part of IronPort's email reputation system. Currently, SpamCop provides one public list, the SpamCop Block List (*SCBL*).

DNSBLs are useful as a categorized source of hostile activity. Using a DNSBL, an analyst can determine whether a particular address has been doing something hostile elsewhere on the Internet and possibly what kind of activity it was. They supplement the more basic lookup information discussed earlier by providing some idea of a site's past history.

DNSBLs are designed to be real-time tools that work primarily with mail agents, not to support forensic analysis. Records will change quickly and unpredictably, so an address may be recognized by the DNSBL as hostile at the time of an event, but be delisted when an analyst examines it later. Most of the blacklists sell some kind of feed or data dump that, for forensic purposes, is preferable.

## CHAPTER 9

More Tools

As discussed at the beginning of the book, there are a lot of tools that you will end up using for one or two specific purposes. In this section, I discuss other tools that I find handy for analysis and include a brief explanation about how to use them.

Many of these tools are pretty powerful—far more than in a three-page summary can describe. I will touch on each of these tools very briefly and try to provide an example for each. However, be prepared to look for additional material and supplemental documentation.

Visualization

While R is my primary tool for graph visualization, there are several additional tools that are handy under specific circumstances. Graphviz is toolkit for visualizing graphs. Gnuplot is the utility knife of plotting tools: powerful, scriptable, and profoundly unfriendly.

Graphviz

Graphviz (*http://www.graphviz.org*) is a graph layout and visualization package. Originally developed by AT&T Labs, the package is now released under the Eclipse license and is actively maintained.

Graphviz is actually a suite of tools, each of which provides a different mechanism for automatically laying out graphs. With each tool, you provide a graph specification, and the tool automatically lays out the graph based on the specification. Graphs are specified via a language called *dot*, which specifies nodes of various attributes and then links connecting them. An example dot command and output are shown in Example 9-1, with the results illustrated in Figure 9-1.

Example 9-1. A sample graph in dot

```
# This is a simple dotfile showing the basic features of a graph
digraph sample_graph {
        # Nodes are specified with the node command, if note labeled seperately
        # Their labels are their names
        node [shape=circle] node_a, node_b;
        # The shape will automatically be a circle
        node [label="Node Gamma"] node_c;
        # Node attributes are passed down the line, so if I want to
        # avoid everything being called 'Node gamma', I have to reset
        # the label to the node name
        node [shape=square, label="\N"] node_1, node_2;
        node [shape=doublecircle] node_3;
        # Edge attributes are put in square brackets; label is the text label
        # for the graph
        node_1 -> node_a [ label="Transition 1,A" ];
        node_a -> node_1;
        node_b -> node_b [ label="Transition B,B" ];
        node_c -> node_2;
        node_2 -> node_1;
        # Color is controlled with the color attribte
        node_2 -> node_3 [color = "blue"];
        node_2 -> node_a;
        # Style lets you specify dotted, bold, &c.
        node_2 -> node_b [style = "dotted"];
        node_2 -> node_c;
        label="Sample Graph";
        fontsize=14;
}
```

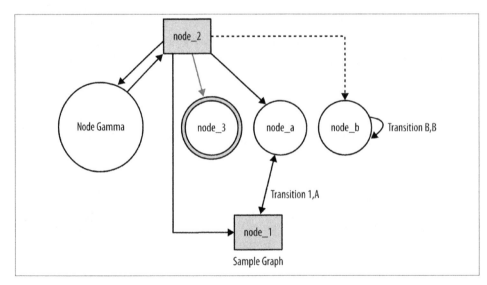

Figure 9-1. Resulting layout in dot

It's very easy to convert log records from their own formats to dot, and the resulting graphs can often be used to visually signify features such as central nodes. Example 9-2 shows the code that converts HTTP page and referrer sites into links and then plots the progression of surfing using dot. An example graph is shown in Figure 9-2.

Example 9-2. Convert Web Log Records into Dot Graphs

```python
#!/usr/bin/env python
#
# log2dot.py
#
# Input:
# Log files from stdin.  We assume these files have been processed to
# provide the URL and Referer URL
#
# Output
# Stdout produces a dot file which can be run through graphviz
import sys, re
host_id = re.compile('^http://([^/]+)/.*$')
pairs = {}
nodes = {}
def graph_output(nodes, pairs):
    graph_header = """
    digraph graph_output {
        rotate = 90;
        size="7.5,10";
        """
    print graph_header
    a = nodes.keys()
    a.sort()
    for i in a:
        print "node [shape = circle] i;"
    a = pairs.keys()
    a.sort()
    for i in a:
        for j in pairs[i].keys():
            # Prints each link then labels it with the number of occurrences
            print '%s -> %s [label="%d"] ;' % (i,j,pairs[i][j])
    print "}"

if __name__ == '__main__':
    for i in sys.stdin.readlines():
        values = i[:-1].split()
        host = values[-2][:-1]
        referrer = values[-1]
        if host_id.match(referrer):
            refname = host_id.match(referrer).groups()[0]
        else:
            refname = referrer
        a = host.split('.')
        if a[0] == 'www':
            host = '.'.join(a[1:])
```

```
    a = refname.split('.')
    if a[0] == 'www':
        refname = '.'.join(a[1:])

    host = host.replace('-','_')
    host = host.replace('.','_')
    refname = refname.replace('-','_')
    refname = refname.replace('.','_')
    nodes[host] = 1
    nodes[refname] = 1
    if pairs.has_key(refname):
        if pairs[refname].has_key(host):
            pairs[refname][host] += 1
        else:
            pairs[refname][host] = 1
    else:
        pairs[refname] = {host:1}
graph_output(nodes, pairs)
```

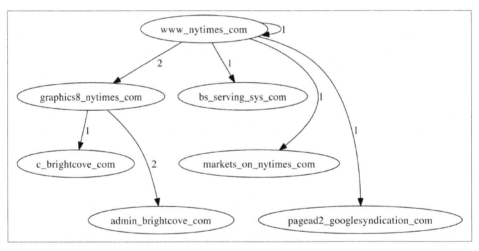

Figure 9-2. Sample output of the log2dot script

Communications and Probing

Network monitoring, as I've discussed it in this book, is largely passive. There are a number of situations where more active monitoring and testing is warranted, however. The tools in this section are used for actively poking and probing at a network.

In the context of this book, I've focused on tools that are used to actively supplement monitoring infrastructure. They're used to provide example sessions (*netcat*), supplement passive monitoring with active probing (*nmap*), or to provide crafted sessions to test specific monitoring configurations (Scapy).

netcat

netcat (http://nc110.sourceforge.net) is a Unix command-line tool that redirects output to TCP and UDP sockets. The power of *netcat* is that it turns sockets into just another pipe-accessible Unix FIFO. Using *netcat*, it is possible to quickly implement clients, servers, proxies, and portscanners.

netcat's simplest invocation is `netcat host port`, which creates a TCP socket to the specified host and port number. Input can be passed to *netcat* and output read using standard Unix redirects, like this:

```
$echo "GET /" | netcat www.oreilly.com 80
<!DOCTYPE HTML PUBLIC "-//IETF//DTD HTML 2.0//EN">
<html><head>
...
```

In this example, we use *netcat* to fetch the index page of a website. The `GET /` is standard HTTP syntax.[1] If you know how to create a session using a particular protocol such as HTTP, SMTP, or the like, you can send it through *netcat* to create a client.

On the same principle, you can use *netcat* for banner grabbing (see Chapter 15). For example, I can grab an *ssh* banner by sending a bogus session through *netcat* to an SSH server:

```
$ echo "WAFFLES" | nc fakesite.com 22
SSH-2.0-OpenSSH_6.2
Protocol mismatch.
```

Note the use of nc in the example; on most *netcat* packages, the two applications will be aliases to each other. By default, *netcat* opens a TCP connection, this can be modified using the -u option.

netcat provides a number of command-line options for finer control of the tool. For example, to improve banner grabbing, we can use a range of ports:

```
echo "WAFFLES" | nc -w1 -v fakesite.com 20-30
fakesite.com [127.0.0.1] 21 (ftp) open
220 fakesite.com NcFTPd Server (licensed copy) ready.
500 Syntax error, command unrecognized.
fakesite.com [127.0.0.1] 22 (ssh) open
SSH-2.0-OpenSSH_6.2
```

The -v option specifies verbosity, adding the lines about which ports are opened. The -w1 command specifies a 1-second wait, and the 20-30 specifies to check the ports 20 through 30.

---

1. HTTP is an extremely robust protocol and tolerates any combination of session attempts, so this is a bit of a straw man for the sake of example.

Simple portscanning can be done using the -z option, which simply checks to see if a connection is open. For example:

```
$ nc -n -w1 -z -vv 192.168.1.9 3689-3691
192.168.1.9 3689 (daap) open
192.168.1.9 3690 (svn): Connection refused
192.168.1.9 3691 (magaya-network): Connection refused
Total received bytes: 0
Total sent bytes: 0
```

Which, in this case, scans an Apple TV.

netcat is a very handy tool for banner grabbing and internal analytics because it enables you to build an ad hoc client for any application very quickly. When new internal sites are identified, *netcat* can be used to scan and probe them for more information if a better tool isn't available.

nmap

Passive security analysis will only go so far, and every effective internal security program should have at least one scanning tool available to them. Network Mapper (*nmap*) (*http://www.nmap.org*) is the best open source scanning tool available.

The reason to use *nmap*, or any other scanning tool, is because these tools contain a huge amount of information about vulnerabilities and operating systems. The goal of any scanning effort is to gain intelligence about a targeted host or network. While a simple half-open scan can be easily implemented using just about anything with a command line, professional scanning tools benefit from expert systems that can combine banner grabbing, packet analysis, and other techniques to identify host information. For example, consider a simple *nmap* scan on the Apple TV used in the previous example (address 192.168.1.9):

```
$ nmap -A 192.168.1.9

Starting Nmap 6.25 ( http://nmap.org ) at 2013-07-28 19:44 EDT
Nmap scan report for Apple-TV-3.home (192.168.1.9)
Host is up (0.0058s latency).
Not shown: 995 closed ports
PORT     STATE SERVICE    VERSION
3689/tcp open  daap       Apple iTunes DAAP 11.0.1d1
5000/tcp open  rtsp       Apple AirTunes rtspd 160.10 (Apple TV)
| rtsp-methods:
|_  ANNOUNCE, SETUP, RECORD, PAUSE, FLUSH, TEARDOWN, OPTIONS, \
    GET_PARAMETER, SET_PARAMETER, POST, GET
7000/tcp open  http       Apple AirPlay httpd
| http-methods: Potentially risky methods: PUT
|_See http://nmap.org/nsedoc/scripts/http-methods.html
|_http-title: Site doesn't have a title.
7100/tcp open  http       Apple AirPlay httpd
|_http-methods: No Allow or Public header in OPTIONS response (status code 400)
```

```
|_http-title: Site doesn't have a title.
62078/tcp open  tcpwrapped
Service Info: OSs: OS X, Mac OS X; Device: media device;
CPE: cpe:/o:apple:mac_os_x

Service detection performed. Please report any incorrect results at
http://nmap.org/submit/ .
Nmap done: 1 IP address (1 host up) scanned in 69.63 seconds
```

The *nmap* scan contains information about open ports, the version of the server software on those ports, potential risks, and additional data such as the CPE string.[2]

Analytically, scan tools are used immediately after a new host is discovered on a network in order to figure out exactly what the host is. In particular, this is done by using the following process:

1. Audit flow data to see if any new host/port combinations are appearing on the network.

2. If new hosts are found, run *nmap* on the hosts to determine what they're running.

3. If *nmap* can't identify the service on the port, run nc to do some basic banner grabbing and find out what the new port is.

Scapy

Scapy (*http://bit.ly/scapy*) is a Python-based packet manipulation and analysis library. Using Scapy, you can rip apart packets in a Python-friendly structure, visualize their contents and create new correct IP packets that can be appended or injected into a collection of packets. Scapy is my go-to tool for converting and manipulating *tcpdump* records.

Scapy provides a Python-friendly representation of *tcpdump* data. Once you've loaded the data, you can view it using a number of display functions or examine the various layers of each packet, which are represented as their own elements in a dictionary. In Example 9-3, we read in and examine some packet contents using Scapy's provided text features and produce the image accompanying it. Figure 9-3 shows the output.

Example 9-3. Reading and examining packet contents

```
>>> # we start by loading up a dump file using rdpcap
>>> >> s=rdpcap('web.pcap')
>>> # We look for the first packet with TCP payload
>>> for i in range(0,100):
...     if len(s[i][TCP].payload) > 0:
...         print i
```

---

2. CPE (*http://1.usa.gov/cpe-nist*) is a NIST project to provide a common framework for describing platforms.

```
...          break
...
63
>>> # We look at its contents using show()
>>> >>> s[63].show()
###[ Ethernet ]###
  dst= 00:1f:90:92:70:5a
  src= 8c:2d:aa:46:f9:71
  type= 0x800
###[ IP ]###
     version= 4L
     ihl= 5L
     tos= 0x0
     len= 1110
     id= 10233
     flags= DF
     frag= 0L
     ttl= 64
     proto= tcp
     chksum= 0xbe42
     src= 192.168.1.12
     dst= 157.166.241.11
     \options\
###[ TCP ]###
        sport= 50300
        dport= http
        seq= 4157917086
        ack= 3403794807
        dataofs= 8L
        reserved= 0L
        flags= PA
        window= 8235
        chksum= 0x5dd5
        urgptr= 0
        options= [('NOP', None), ('NOP', None), ('Timestamp',
               (560054364, 662137900))]
###[ Raw ]###
           load= 'GET / HTTP/1.1\r\nHost: www.cnn.com\r\nConnection:...'
>>> # Dump the contents using PDFdump
>>> s[63].pdfdump('http.pdf')
```

Ethernet		
dst	00:1f:90:92:70:5a	
src	8c:2d:aa:46:f9:71	
type	0x800	
IP		
version	4L	
ihl	5L	
tos	0x0	
len	1110	
id	10233	
flags	DF	
frag	0L	
ttl	64	
proto	tcp	
chksum	0xbe42	
src	192.168.1.12	
dst	157.166.241.11	
options	[]	
TCP		
sport	50300	
dport	http	
seq	4157917086	
ack	3403794807	
dataofs	8L	
reserved	0L	
flags	PA	
window	8235	
chksum	0x5dd5	
urgptr	0	
options	[('NOP', None), ('[...]	
Raw		
load	'GET / HTTP/1.1\r\[...]	

```
00 1f 90 92 70 5a 8c 2d aa 46 f9 71 08 00 45 00
04 56 27 f9 40 00 40 06 be 42 c0 a8 01 0c 9d a6
f1 0b c4 7c 00 50 f7 d4 c7 9e ca e1 c9 77 80 18
20 2b 5d d5 00 00 01 01 08 0a 21 61 c0 5c 27 77
6c 2c 47 45 54 20 2f 20 48 54 54 50 2f 31 2e 31
0d 0a 48 6f 73 74 3a 20 77 77 77 2e 63 6e 6e 2e
63 6f 6d 0d 0a 43 6f 6e 6e 65 63 74 69 6f 6e 3a
20 6b 65 65 70 2d 61 6c 69 76 65 0d 0a 41 63 63
65 70 74 3a 20 74 65 78 74 2f 68 74 6d 6c 2c 61
70 70 6c 69 63 61 74 69 6f 6e 2f 78 68 74 6d 6c
2b 78 6d 6c 2c 61 70 70 6c 69 63 61 74 69 6f 6e
2f 78 6d 6c 3b 71 3d 30 2e 39 2c 2a 2f 2a 3b 71
3d 30 2e 38 0d 0a 55 73 73 65 72 2d 41 67 65 6e 74
3a 20 4d 6f 7a 69 6c 6c 61 2f 35 2e 30 20 28 4d
61 63 69 6e 74 6f 73 68 3b 20 49 6e 74 65 6c 20
4d 61 63 20 4f 53 20 58 20 31 30 5f 38 5f 33 29
20 41 70 70 6c 65 57 65 62 4b 69 74 2f 35 33 37
2e 33 31 20 28 4b 48 54 4d 4c 2c 20 6c 69 6b 65
20 47 65 63 6b 6f 29 20 43 68 72 6f 6d 65 2f 32
36 2e 30 2e 31 34 31 30 2e 34 33 20 53 61 66 61
72 69 2f 35 33 37 2e 33 31 0d 0a 41 63 63 65 70
74 2d 45 6e 63 6f 64 69 6e 67 3a 20 67 7a 69 70
2c 64 65 66 6c 61 74 65 2c 73 64 63 68 0d 0a 41
63 63 65 70 74 2d 4c 61 6e 67 75 61 67 65 3a 20
65 6e 2d 55 53 2c 65 6e 3b 71 3d 30 2e 38 0d 0a
41 63 63 65 70 74 2d 43 68 61 72 73 65 74 3a 20
49 53 4f 2d 38 38 35 39 2d 31 2c 75 74 66 2d 38
3b 71 3d 30 2e 37 2c 2a 3b 71 3d 30 2e 33 0d 0a
43 6f 6f 6b 69 65 3a 20 75 67 3d 35 31 36 36 33
36 34 36 30 62 38 65 63 63 30 61 33 64 31 34 36
63 31 36 65 34 30 30 32 32 33 36 3b 20 6f 70 74
69 6d 69 69 7a 65 6c 79 53 65 67 6d 65 6e 74 73 3d
25 37 42 25 32 32 31 37 30 39 36 32 33 34 30 25
32 32 25 33 41 25 32 32 66 61 6c 73 65 25 32 32
25 32 43 25 32 32 31 37 31 36 35 37 39 36 31 25
32 32 25 33 41 25 32 32 67 63 25 32 32 25 32 43
25 32 32 31 37 32 31 34 38 36 37 39 25 32 32 25
```

Figure 9-3. When fully installed, Scapy can produce graphical disassemblies of a packet

I use Scapy primarily to convert and reformat *tcpdump* records. The following example is a very simple application of this. The supplied script, shown in Example 9-4, provides a columnar output for *pcap* files similar to *rwcut*'s output.

Example 9-4. tcpcut.py script

```python
#!/usr/bin/env python
#
#
# tcpcut.py
#
# This is a script that takes a tcpdump file as input and dumps
# the contents to screen in a format similar to rwcut.
# It supports only nine fields and no prompts for the standard
# pedagogical reason.
#
# Input
# tcpcut.py data_file
#
# Output
```

```
# Columnar output to stdout

from scapy.all import *

import sys, time

header = '%15s|%15s|%5s|%5s|%5s|%15s|' % ('sip','dip','sport','dport',
        'proto','bytes')
tfn = sys.argv[1]

pcap_data = rdpcap(tfn)

for i in pcap_data:
    sip = i[IP].src
    dip = i[IP].src
    if i[IP].proto == 6:
        sport = i[TCP].sport
        dport = i[TCP].dport
    elif i[IP].proto == 17:
        sport = i[UDP].sport
        dport = i[UDP].dport
    else:
        sport = 0
        dport = 0
    bytes = i[IP].len
    print "%15s|%15s|%5d|%5d|%5d|%15d" % (sip, dip, sport, dport,
      i[IP].proto, bytes)
```

I also use Scapy to generate data for session testing. For example, if presented with a new logging system, I'll generate a session using *pcap* and run that against the logging system, then tweak the session using Scapy to see how my changes affect the logged records.

Packet Inspection and Reference

The tools discussed in this section are all focused on enhancing packet inspection and analysis. Wireshark is arguably the most useful packet inspection tool available, and *geoip* is a handy reference tool for figuring out where traffic data came from.

Wireshark

I'm not going to burn a lot of space on Wireshark because, like Snort and *nmap*, it's one of the most common and well-documented tools available for traffic analysis. Wireshark is a graphical protocol analyzer that provides facilities for examining packets and collecting statistics on them, as well as a number of tools for meaningfully exploring the data.

Wireshark's real strength is in its extensive library of *dissectors* for analyzing packet data. A dissector is a set of rules and procedures for ripping apart packet data and reconstructing the session underneath. An example of this is shown in Figure 9-4, which shows how Wireshark can extract and display the contents of an HTTP session.

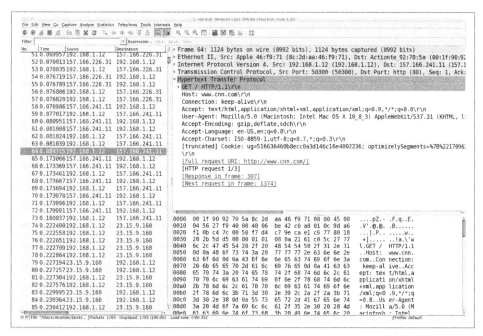

Figure 9-4. An example Wireshark screen showing session reconstruction

GeoIP

Geolocation services take IP addresses and return information on the physical location of the address. Geolocation is an intelligence process: researchers start with the allocation from NICs and then combine a number of different approaches ranging from mapping transmission delays to calling up companies and finding their mailing addresses.

MaxMind's GeoIP (*http://www.maxmind.com*) is the default free geolocation database. The free version (GeoLite) will provide you with city, country, and ASN information.

Applied Security (*http://www.appliedsec.com*) has produced a good GeoIP library in Python (*pygeoip* (*http://bit.ly/pygeoip*), also available in *pip*). *pygeoip* works with both the commercial and free database instances. The following sample script, *pygeoip_lookup.py*, shows how the API works:

```
#!/usr/bin/env python
#
```

```
# pygeoip_lookup.py
#
# Takes any IP addresses passed to it as input,
# runs them through the maxminds geoip database and
# returns the country code.
#

include sys,string,pygeoip

gi_handle = None
try:
    geoip_dbfn = sys.argv[1]
    gi_handle = pygeoip.GeoIP(geoip_dbfn,pygeoip.MEMORY_CACHE)
except:
    sys.stderr.write("Specify a database\n")
    sys.exit(-1)

for i in sys.stdin.readlines():
    ip = i[:-1]
    cc = gi_handle.country_code_by_addr(ip)
    print "%s %s" % (ip, cc)
```

Geolocation is big business, and there are a number of commercial geolocation databases available. MaxMind offers their own, and other options include Neustar's IP Intelligence (*http://bit.ly/ip-intel*), Akamai (*http://www.akamai.com*), and Digital Envoy (*http://www.digitalenvoy.com*).

The NVD, Malware Sites, and the C*Es

The *National Vulnerability Database* (NVD) is a public service maintained by NIST to enumerate and classify vulnerabilities in software and hardware systems. The NVD project has been operating under several different names for years, and there are several distinct components to the database. The most important started at MITRE under a variety of names beginning with C and ending with E:

CVE

The Common Vulnerabilities and Exposures database is a mechanism for enumerating software vulnerabilites and exploits.

CPE

The Common Platform Enumeration database provides a mechanism for describing software platforms using a hierarchical string. CVE entries use the CPE to refer to the specific vulnerable software releases covered by the CVE.

CCE

The Common Configuration Enumeration describes and enumerates software configurations, such as an Apache Install. CCE is still under construction.

NVD manages all of these enumerations under the *Security Content Automation Protocol* (SCAP), an ongoing effort to automate security configuration. For analysis purposes, the CVE is the most critical part of this entire mishegas. A single vulnerability may have dozens or hundreds of different exploits written for it, but the CVE number for that vulnerability ties them all together.

In addition to the government funded efforts, there are a number of other common exploit listings. These include:

BugTraq IDs
> BugTraq is a vulnerability mailing list that covers new exploits and vulnerabilities sent in by a large number of independent researchers. BugTraq uses a simple numerical ID and maintains a list (*http://bit.ly/vuln-list*) for each new vulnerability identified. BugTraq's bug reports tend to heavily overlap the NVD.

OSVDB (http://www.osvdb.org/)
> A vulnerability database maintained by the *Open Security Foundation* (OSF), a nonprofit organization for managing vulnerability data.

Symantec's Security Response (http://bit.ly/sec-resp)
> This site contains a database and summary for every malware signature produced by Symantec's AV software.

McAfee's Threat Center (http://bit.ly/mcafee-threat)
> The Threat Center serves the same purpose as Symantec's site; it's a frontend to the currently identified threats and malware that McAfee's AV software tracks.

Kaspersky's Securelist Threat Descriptions (http://bit.ly/securelist)
> Kaspersky's list of signatures.

These databases are more directly useful to malware researchers, who are obviously more focused on exploits and takeover. For network security analysis, these sites are primarily useful for identifying the vectors by which a worm or other malware propagates through a network, and consequently getting a good first approximation of what the traffic feed for malware will look like. For example, if a piece of malware propagates over HTTP and NetBIOS,[3] then you have some network services and port numbers to start poking at.

Search Engines, Mailing Lists, and People

Here's the difference between an average analyst and a good one. The average analyst will receive data from *pcap* or weblogs and come to a conclusion with the data provided.

---

3. Which, admittedly, describes a lot of malware.

The good analyst will seek out other information, whether from weblogs, mailing lists, or by communicating with analysts in other forums.

Computer security is a constantly changing field, and attacks are a constant moving target. It is very easy to grow complacent as an analyst because there are so many simple attacks to track and monitor, while attackers evolve to use new tools and approaches. Internet traffic changes for many reasons, many of them nontechnical—I've found the explanations for traffic jumps on mailing lists such as NANOG as well as the *New York Times* front page.

Further Reading

1. Laura Chappell and Gerald Combs, "Wireshark 101: Essential Skills for Network Analysis."

2. Graphviz (*http://www.graphviz.org*)

3. Gordon "Fyodor" Lyon, "Nmap Network Scanning," Nmap Project, 2009.

4. The Nmap project (*http://www.insecure.org*)

5. Scapy (*http://bit.ly/scapy*)

6. Wireshark (*http://www.wireshark.org*)

## PART III

Analytics

In the previous two sections of the book, we've discussed the types of data you can collect, and tools for manipulating that data. In this section, we focus on taking that data and conducting analyses on that.

Each chapter in the following section focuses on a different family of mathematical and analytical techniques that can be used on data. The focus of each chapter is on providing information that is more security-relevant or floor-relevant. Chapter 10 focuses on the process of *Exploratory Data Analysis* (EDA), and should be read before anything else. Chapter 11, Chapter 12, Chapter 13, and Chapter 14 provide examples of behaviors, relate them to attacks, and discuss ways that these behaviors can be used to construct alarms or be used for forensics and investigation. Chapter 15 looks at the problem of mapping a network, applying the techniques in the previous chapters to provide situational awareness.

## CHAPTER 10

Exploratory Data Analysis and Visualization

Exploratory Data Analysis (EDA) is the process of examining a dataset without pre-conceived assumptions about the data and its behavior. Real-world datasets are messy and complex, and require progressive filtering and stratification in order to identify phenomena that are worth using for alarms, anomaly detection, and forensics. Attackers and the Internet itself are a moving target, and analysts face a constant influx of weirdness. For this reason, EDA is a constant process.

The point of EDA is to get a better grip on a dataset before pulling out the math. To understand why this is necessary, I want to walk through a simple statistical exercise. In Table 10-1, there are four datasets, each consisting of a vector X and a vector Y. For each dataset, calculate these values:

- The mean of X and Y
- The variance of X and Y
- The correlation between X and Y

Table 10-1. Four datasets

I		II		III		IV	
X	Y	X	Y	X	Y	X	Y
10.0	8.04	10.0	9.14	10.0	7.46	8.0	6.58
8.0	6.95	8.0	8.14	8.0	6.77	8.0	5.76
13.0	7.58	13.0	8.74	13.0	12.74	8.0	7.71
9.0	8.81	9.0	8.77	9.0	7.11	8.0	8.84
11.0	8.33	11.0	9.26	11.0	7.81	8.0	8.47
14.0	9.96	14.0	8.10	14.0	8.84	8.0	7.04
6.0	7.24	6.0	6.13	6.0	6.08	8.0	5.25
4.0	4.26	4.0	3.10	4.0	5.39	19.0	12.50

I		II		III		IV	
12.0	10.84	12.0	9.13	12.0	8.15	8.0	5.56
7.0	4.82	7.0	7.26	7.0	6.42	8.0	7.91
5.0	5.68	5.0	4.74	5.0	5.73	8.0	6.89

You will find that the mean, variance, and correlation are identical for each dataset, but simply by looking at the numbers, you should suspect something fishy. A visualization will show just how diverse they are. Figure 10-1 plots these sets and shows how each dataset results in a radically different distribution. The *Anscombe Quartet* was designed to show the impact of outliers (such as in dataset IV) and visualization on data analysis.

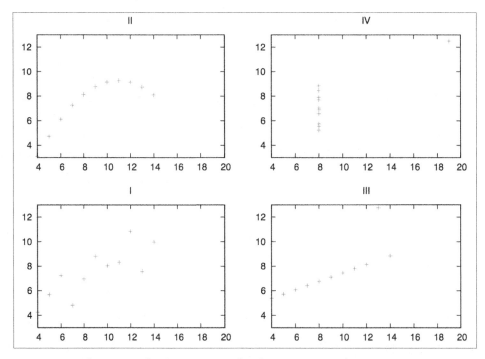

Figure 10-1. The Anscombe Quartet, visualized

As this example shows, simple visualization will identify significant features of the dataset that aren't identified by reaching for the stats. The classic mistake in statistical analysis involves pulling out the math before looking at the data. For example, analysts will often calculate the mean and standard deviation of a dataset in order to produce a threshold value (normally around 3.5 standard deviations from the mean). This threshold is based on the assumption that the dataset is normally distributed; if it isn't (and it rarely is), then simple counting will produce more effective results.

The Goal of EDA: Applying Analysis

The point of any EDA process is to move toward a model; that model might be a formal representation of the data, or it might be as simple as "raise an alarm when we see too much stuff" (where "too much" and "stuff" are, of course, exquisitely quantified). For information security, we will discuss four basic goals for data analysis: alarm construction, forensics, defense construction, and situational awareness.

When used as an alarm, an analytic process involves generating some kind of number, comparing it against a model of normal activity, and determining if the observed activity *requires an analyst's attention*. An anomaly isn't necessarily an attack, and an attack doesn't necessarily merit a response. A good alarm will be based on phenomena that are predictable under normal circumstances, which the defender can do something about, and which the attacker must disrupt to reach his goals.

The problem in operational informational security isn't *creating* alarms—it's making them manageable. The first thing an analyst has to do when she receives an alarm is provide context—validating that the threat is real, ensuring that it's relevant, determining the extent of the damage, and recommending actions to take place. False positives are a signficant problem, but they do not represent the whole scope of failure modes for alarms. Good analysis can increase the efficacy of alarms. See Chapter 7 for a more extensive discussion of this.

The majority of security analysis is forensic analysis, taking place after an event has occurred. Forensic analysis may begin in response to information from anywhere: alarms, IDS signals, user reports, or newspaper articles.[1]

A forensic analysis begins with some datum, such as an infected IP address or a hostile website. From there, the investigator has to find out as much as possible about the attack —the extent of the damage, other activities by the attacker, a timeline of the attack's major events. Forensic analysis is often the most data-intensive work an analyst can do, as it involves correlating data from multiple sources ranging from traffic logs to personnel interviews and looking through archives for data stored years ago.

Alarms and forensic analysis are both reactive measures, but an analyst can also use data proactively and construct defenses. As analysts, we have a set of tools, such as policy recommendations, firewall rules, and authentication, that can be used to implement defenses. The challenge when doing so is that these measures are fundamentally restrictive; from a user's perspective, security is a set of rules that limit their behavior now in order to prevent some abstract bad thing from happening later.

---

1. There's nothing quite like the day you start an investigation based on the attacker being written up in the *New York Times*.

People are always the last line of defense in information security. If security is implemented poorly or arbitarily, it encourages an adversarial relationship between system administrators and users, and before long, everything is moving on port 80. Analysis can be used to determine reasonable constraints that will limit attackers without imposing an undue burden on users.

Alarms, forensics, and redesign are all focused on the attack cycle—detecting attacks, understanding attacks, and recovering from attacks. Throughout this cycle, however, there is a constant dependence on knowledge management. Knowledge management in the form of inventories, past history, lookup data, and even phone books changes processes from rolling disasters into manageable disasters.

Knowledge management affects everything. For example, almost all intrusion detection systems (especially signature management systems) focus on packet contents without knowing, for example, that the IIS exploit they've helpfully identified was aimed at an Amiga 3000 running Apache.[2] In IDSes, a false positive is usually a sign that the IDS copped out early. Maintaining inventory and mapping information is a necessary first step toward developing effective alarms; many attacks are failures, and that failure can be identified through context and the alert trashed before it annoys analysts.

Good inventory and past history data can also be used to speed a forensic investigation. Many forensic analyses are cross-referencing different data sources in order to provide context, and this information is predictable. For example, if I have an internal IP address, I'll want to know who owns it and what software it's running.

Knowledge management requires pulling data from a number of discrete sources and putting it in one place. Information like ASNs, whois data, and even simple phone numbers are often stored in dozens if not hundreds of variably maintained databases and subject to local restrictions and politics. Internal network status is often just as chaotic, if not more so because almost invariably people are running services on the network that nobody knows about. Often, the very process of identifying assets for an ops floor will help network management and IT concerns in general.

As you look at data, keep in mind the goals of the data analysis. In the end, you have to figure out what the process is for—whether it's an alarm, timeline reconstruction, or figuring out whether you can introduce a firewall rule without dealing with pitchforks and torches.

EDA Workflow

Figure 10-2 is a workflow diagram for EDA in infosec. As this workflow shows, the core EDA process is a loop involving EDA techniques, extracting phenomena and analyzing

---

2. It exists.

them in more depth. EDA begins with a question, which can be as open-ended as "What does typical activity look like?" The question drives the process of data selection. For example, addressing a question such as "Can BitTorrent traffic be identified by packet size?" could involve selecting traffic communicated with known BitTorrent trackers or traffic that communicated on ports 6881–6889 (the common BitTorrent ports).

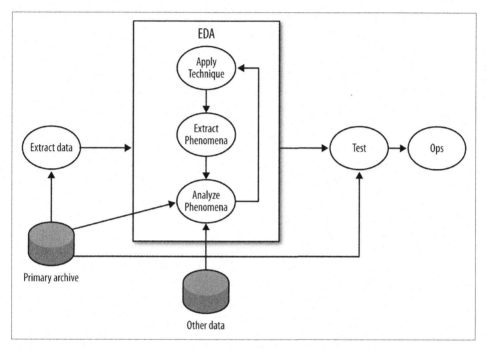

Figure 10-2. A workflow for exploratory data analysis

In the EDA loop, an analyst repeats three steps: summarizing and examining the data using a technique, identifying phenomena in the data, and then examining those phenomena in more depth. An *EDA technique* is a process for taking a dataset and summarizing it in some way that allows a *person* to identify phenomena worth investigating. Many EDA techniques are visualizations, and the majority of this chapter is focused on visual tools. Other EDA techniques include data-mining approaches such as clustering, and classic statistical techniques such as regression analysis.

EDA techniques provide behavioral cues that can then be used to go back to the original data, extract particular phenomena from that dataset and examine them in more depth. For example, looking at port 6881–6889 traffic, an analyst finds that hosts often have flows containing between 50 and 200 bytes of payload. Using that information, he goes back to the original data and uses Wireshark to find out that those packets are BitTorrent control packets.

This technique-extract-analyze process can be repeated indefinitely; finding phenomena and knowing when to stop are arts learned through experience. Analysis involves an enormous number of false positives because the most effective initial formulations are broad and prone to false positives. The EDA process will often require looking at multiple data sources. For example, an analyst looking at BitTorrent data could consult the protocol definition or run a BitTorrent client himself to determine whether the properties observed in the data hold true.

At some point, the EDA process has to stop. On the completion of EDA, an analyst will usually have multiple potential mechanisms for answering the initial question. For example, when looking for periodic phenomena such as dial-homes to botnet C&Cs, it's possible to use autocorrelation, Fourier analysis, or simply count time in bins. Once an analyst has options, the real question is which one to use, which is determined by a process usually driven by testing and operational demand.

The testing process should take the techniques developed during EDA and determine which ones are most suitable for operational use. This phase of the process involves constructing alarms and reports. See Chapter 7 on anomaly detection for more information about the criteria that make a good alarm.

Variables and Visualization

The most accessible and commonly approached EDA techniques are visualizations. Visualizations are tools, and based on the type of data examined and the goal of the analysis, there are a number of specific visualizations that can be applied to the task. In order to understand data, we have to start by understanding *variables*.

A variable is a characteristic of an entity that can be measured or counted, such as weight or temperature. Variables can change between entities or over time; the height of a person changes as she ages, and different people have different heights.

There are four categories of variables, which readers who have had an elementary statistics course will be familiar with. I'll review them briefly here, in descending order of rigor:

Interval
  An interval variable is one where the difference between two values is meaningful, but the ratio between two values has no meaning. In network traffic data, the start time of an event is the most common form of interval data. For example, an event may be recorded at 100 seconds after midnight, and another one at 200 seconds after midnight. The second event takes place after the first one, but it isn't meaningful to talk about it taking place "twice as long" after the first one since there's no real concept of "zero start time."

Ratio

A ratio variable is like an interval variable, but also has a meaningful form of "zero," which enables us to discuss ratio variables in terms of multiplication and division. One form of a ratio variable is the number of bytes in a packet. For example, we can have a packet with 200 bytes, and another one with 400 bytes. As with interval variables, we can describe one as larger than the other, and we can also describe the second packet as "twice as large" as the second one.

Ordinal

Data is in numerical order, but does not have fixed intervals. Customer ratings fall in this category. A rating of 5 is higher than 4, and 4 is higher than 3, so you can be assured that 5 is also higher than 3. But you can't say that the degree of customer satisfaction goes up the same from 3 to 4 and from 4 to 5. (A common error is to base calculations on this, treating ratings as interval or ratio data.)

Nominal

This data is just named rather than numeric, as the term "nominal" indicates. There is no order to it. Data of this type that you commonly track include your hosts and your services (web, email, etc.).

Data isn't necessarily ordinal just because it's designated by numbers. Your ports are nominal data. Port 80 is not "higher" in some way than port 25; it's best just to think of the numbers as alternative names for your HTTP port, your SMTP port, etc.

Interval, ratio, and ordinal variables are also referred to as *quantitative*, while nominal variables are also called *qualitative*. Interval and ratio variables can be further divided into *discrete* and *continuous* variables. A discrete variable has an indivisible difference between every value, while continuous variables have infinitely divisible differences. In network traffic data, almost all data collected is discrete. For example, a packet can contain 9 or 10 bytes of payload, but nothing in between. Even values such as start time are discrete, even if the subdivisions are extremely fine. Continuous variables are generally derived in some way, such as the average number of bytes per packet.

Univariate Visualization: Histograms, QQ Plots, Boxplots, and Rank Plots

Based on the type of variable measured, we can choose different visualizations. The most basic visualizations are applied to *univariate* data, which consists of one observed variable per unit measured. Examples of univariate measurements include the number of bytes per packet or the number of IP addresses observed over a period.

Histograms

A *histogram* is the fundamental plot for ratio and interval data; it is a count of how often a variable takes each possible value. A histogram consists of a set of *bins*, which are discrete ranges of values, and *frequencies*. Thus, if you can receive packets at any rate from 0 to 10,000 a second, you can create 10 bins for the ranges 0 to 999, 1,000 to 1,999, and so on. A frequency is the number of times that the observed value occurred within the range of the bin.

Generating a Histogram

The base material for a histogram is a set of quantitative observations. At the R prompt, for example, a quick and dirty histogram can be generated from raw data.

```
> sample <- rnorm(10,25,5)
> sample
 [1] 30.79303 25.52480 22.29529 29.20203 21.88355 19.73429 24.99312
 [8] 20.79997 22.24344 24.29335
> hist(sample)
```

The `rnorm` function in R takes the sample size, the mean of the values, and their standard deviation as parameters and generates a set of random observations. As is normal with R, the `hist` function holds your hand a lot, automatically assigning bin widths, for example.

Handy arguments to remember with the `hist` function include:

`prob` *(takes a Boolean)*
> When set to `True`, the histogram will be plotted to have an area of 1. When set to `False`, the histogram will plot the frequencies.

`breaks` *(takes multiple options)*
> `breaks` defines how the histogram bins up data. If set to a numeric value, it specifies the number of bins. If set to a vector, it uses the values of the vector as the breakpoints. It can also be set to a string to specify a predefined algorithm, or to a function pointer.

A histogram is valuable for data analysis because it helps you find structure in a variable's distribution, and structure provides material for further investigation. In the case of the histogram, that structure is generally a *mode*, the most commonly occuring value in a distribution. In a histogram, modes appear as peaks. Histogram analysis almost invariably consists of two questions:

1. Is the distribution normal or another one I know how to use?

2. What are the modes?

As an example of this type of analysis, take a look at the histogram in Figure 10-3. This is a histogram of flow size distributions for BitTorrent sessions, showing a distinctive peak between about 78–82 bytes. This peak is defined by the BitTorrent protocol: it's the result of a BitTorrent peer asking another peer if it has a particular piece of a file, and getting back "no" as an answer.

Modes enable you to ask new questions. Once you've identified modes in a distribution, you can go back to the source data and examine the records that produced the mode. In the example in Figure 10-3, you could go back to the times in the second mode (the 250–255 peak) and see whether the traffic showed any distinctive characteristics—short flows, long flows, communications with empty addresses, and so on. Modes direct your questions.

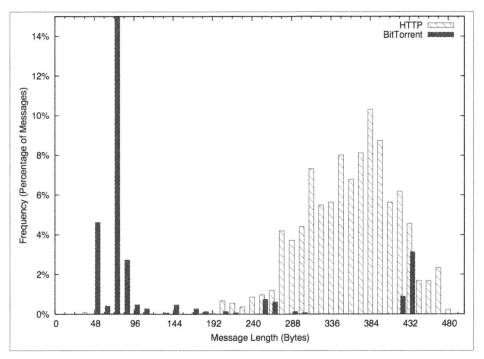

Figure 10-3. A distribution of BitTorrent flow sizes

This process of visualizing, then returning to the repository and pulling more detailed data is a good example of the iterative analysis shown in Figure 10-2. EDA is a cyclic process where analysts will return to the source (or multiple sources) repeatedly to understand why something is distinctive.

Bar Plots (Not Pie Charts)

A *bar plot* is the analog to a histogram when working with univariate qualitative data. Like a histogram, it plots the frequency of values observed in the dataset by using the height of various bars. Figure 10-4 is an example of such a plot, in this case showing the count of various services from network traffic data.

The difference between bar plots and histograms lies in the binning. Qualitative data can be grouped into ranges, and in histograms, the bins represent those ranges. These bins are approximations, and the range of values they contain can be changed in order to provide a more descriptive image. In the case of bar plots, the different potential values of the data are discrete, enumerable, and often have no ordering. This lack of ordering is a particular issue when working with multiple bar plots—when doing so, make sure to keep the same order in each plot and to include zero values.

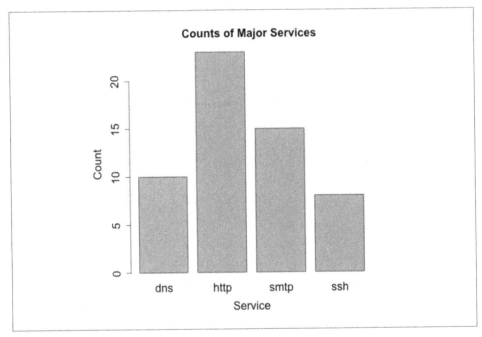

Figure 10-4. A bar plot showing the distribution of major services

In scientific visualization, bar plots are preferred over pie charts. Viewers have a hard time differentiating fine variations in pie slice sizes, variations that are much more apparent in bar plots.

The Quantile-Quantile (QQ) Plot

A *Quantile-Quantile* (QQ) plot compares the distributions of two variables against each other. A QQ plot is a two-dimensional plot, with the x-axis being the values of one distribution normalized as quantiles, and the y-axis being values of the second distribution again normalized as quantiles. For example, if I break each distribution into 100 centiles, the first point is the first percentile for each, the 50th point is the 50th percentile for each, and so on.

Figure 10-5 and Figure 10-6 show two QQ plots with the companion code following. These plots, generated using R's qqnorm function, plot each distribution against a normal distribution. The first plot, a normal distribution, shows the expected behavior when two similar distributions are plotted on a QQ plot—the values track the diagonal. There is some deviation but it isn't very severe. Compare the results with the uniform distribution in the second figure; in this one, significant deviations happen on the ends of the plot.

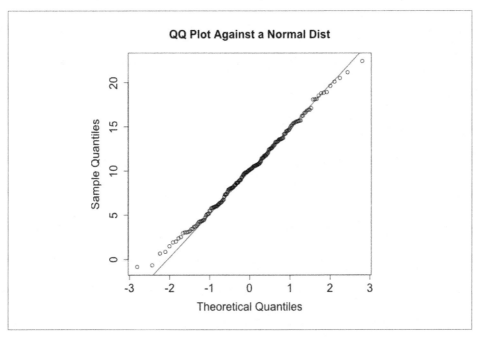

Figure 10-5. Example QQ plot against a normal distribution

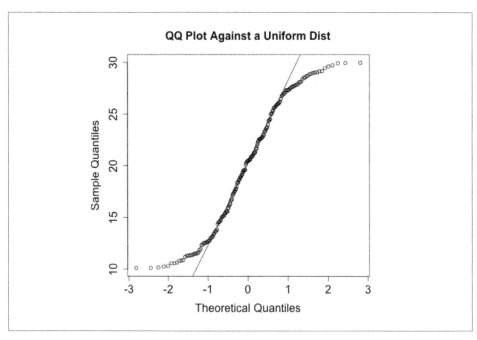

Figure 10-6. Example QQ plot against a uniform distribution

```
> # Generate a uniform and a normal distribution
> set.normal <- rnorm(n = 200, mean=10, sd = 5)
> set.unif <- runif(n = 200, min = 10, max = 30)
> # Plot against the norm for the normal set
> qqnorm(set.normal,main='QQ Plot Against a Normal Dist')
> qqline(set.normal)
> # Same drill for the uniform distribution
> qqnorm(set.unif, main='QQ Plot Against a Uniform Dist')
> qqline(set.unif)
```

R has a number of QQ plotting routines. The most important are qqnorm, which plots a dataset against the normal distribution; qqplot, which generates a qq plot comparing any two datasets; and qqline, which draws the reference line.

Is It Normal?

In Chapter 6 and this chapter, we've discussed a number of techniques for determining whether or not a dataset is normally distributed, or to be more precise, can be satisfactorily modeled using a normal distribution. Parametric distributions, if applicable, open up a number of tools to us. The problem is that in raw network data they're rarer than Yeti. Among the techniques listed are:

- The Shapiro-Wilk Test (Example 6-4), a statistical normality test.

- The Kolmogorov-Smirnov Test (Example 6-5), a general goodness-of-fit test.
- Histograms ("Histograms" on page 198), visualizing the distribution.
- QQ plots ("Bar Plots (Not Pie Charts)" on page 200), comparing the data against a normal.

Of all the tools available, I view visualization approaches (histograms and QQ plots) as the preferable option. My interest in acquiring a distribution is utilitarian. I'm looking for reasonable thresholds and something that matches the math well enough that I can use other tools because we don't have the control to make very sensitive measurements. Attackers will usually be fairly easy to identify once you've picked the right metric. The classic mistake with using means and standard distributions without looking at the data is that most network security datasets have a number of outliers. These outliers end up producing ridiculously large standard deviations, and the resulting threshold is triggered only for egregious events.

The Five-Number Summary and the Boxplot

The five-number summary is a standard statistical shorthand for describing a dataset. It consists of the following five values:

- The *minimum* value in a dataset
- The *first quartile* of the dataset
- The *second quartile* or *median* of the dataset
- The *third quartile* of the dataset
- The *maximum* value in the dataset

Quartiles are points that split the dataset into quarters, so the five numbers translate into the smallest value, the 25% threshold, the median, the 75% threshold, and the maximum. The five-number summary is a shorthand, and if you're looking at a lot of datasets very quickly, it can provide you with a quick feel for what the set looks like.

The five-number summary can be visualized using a *boxplot* (Figure 10-7), which is also called a *box-and-whiskers plot*. A boxplot consists of five lines, one for each value in the five-number summary. The center three lines are then connected as a box (the *box* of the plot) and the outer two lines are connected by perpendicular lines (the *whiskers*) of the plot.

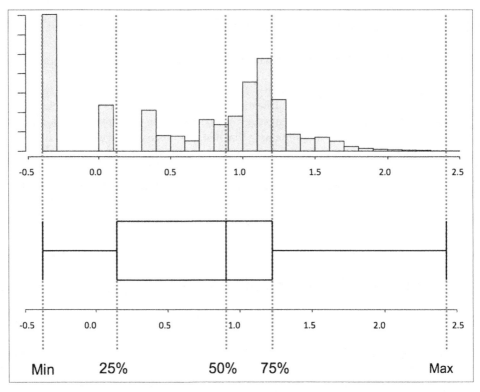

Figure 10-7. A boxplot and the corresponding histogram

Generating a Boxplot

In R, five-number summaries are generated using the fivenum command, as shown in the following example.

```
> s<-rnorm(100,mean=25,sd=5)
> fivenum(s)
[1] 14.61463 22.26498 24.50200 27.43826 37.99568
```

A basic boxplot is generated with the boxplot command, as follows, resulting in the image in Figure 10-8.

```
>boxplot(s)
```

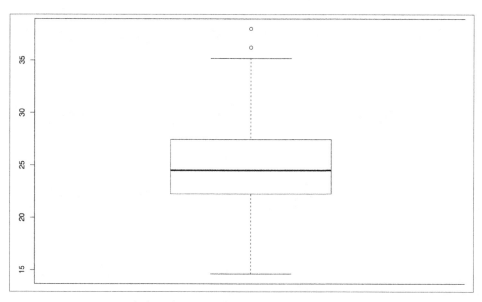

Figure 10-8. An example boxplot

Note that this plot produced a series of dots outside the whiskers. These are *outliers*, meaning they are far outside the first and third quartiles. By default, a low value is considered an outlier if its distance to the first quartile is more than 1.5 times the interquartile range (the difference between the first and third quartiles). Similarly, a high value is considered an outlier if its distance to the third quartile is more than 1.5 times the interquartile range.

Handy parameters to remember with `boxplot` include:

`notch` *(Boolean)*
> Set to `True`, it places a notch at the median value of the boxplot. If two plots notches don't overlap, it's a strong indicator that their medians differ.

`range` *(numeric)*
> Describes how far the whiskers will extend. The default value is 1.5, as described earlier in the sidebar. If you set `range` to zero, whiskers will extend as far as they need to and no values will be outliers.

When dealing with five-number summaries, it's not unusual to toss in the mean (Figure 10-9). Consequently, you will often see boxplots that include the mean with an extra character, usually an x. In R, you have to do multiple plots on the same canvas to produce this, as follows:

```
>boxplot(s)
>points(mean(s), pch='x')
```

In this example, the pch parameter sets the character of the point; in this case, an x.

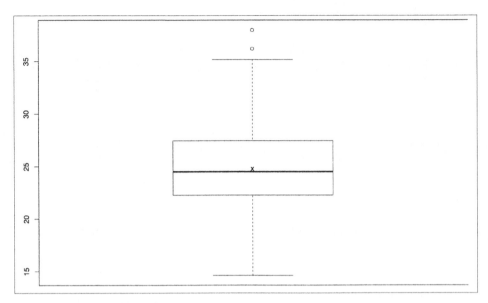

Figure 10-9. A boxplot with a mean

`boxplot` can take multiple vectors, making it a quick tool for comparing multiple discrete datasets. If, for example, you've identified several different phenomena in a dataset, you could split each one into a separate column for comparison. The following example shows this with some cooked scan data, producing the side-by-side boxplot in Figure 10-10.

```
> nonscan<-rnorm(100,mean=150,sd=30)
> scan<-runif(50,min=254,max=255)
> boxplot(nonscan,scan,names=c('nonscan','scan'))
```

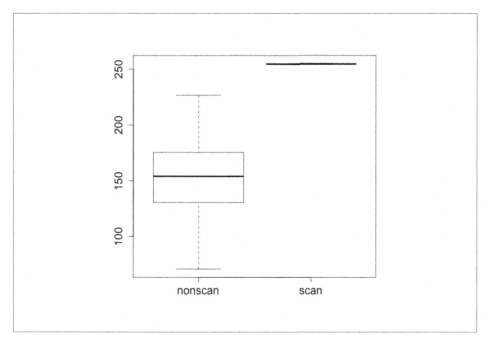

Figure 10-10. Side-by-side boxplots

I rarely find boxplots to be useful on their own. If I'm dealing with a single value, I'm going to get more information out of a histogram. Boxplots become more valuable when you start stacking bunches of them together, a situation where histograms are going to be just too busy to be meaningfully examined.

Bivariate Description

Bivariate data consists of two observed variables per unit measured. Examples of bivariate data include the number of bytes and packets observed in a traffic flow (which is an example of two quantitative variables), and the number of packets per protocol (an example of a quantitative and qualitative variable). The most common plots used for bivariate data are scatterplots (for comparing two quantitative variables), multiple boxplots (for comparing quantitative and qualitative variables), and contingency tables (for comparing two qualitative variables).

Scatterplots

Scatterplots are the workhorse of quantitative plots, and show the relationship between two ordinal, interval, or ratio variables. The primary challenge when analyzing scatterplots is to identify structure among the noise. Common features in a scatterplot are clusters, gaps, linear relationships, and outliers.

Let's start exploring scatterplots by looking at completely unrelated data. Figure 10-11 is an example of a noisy scatterplot, generated in this case by plotting two uniform distributions against each other. This is a boring plot.

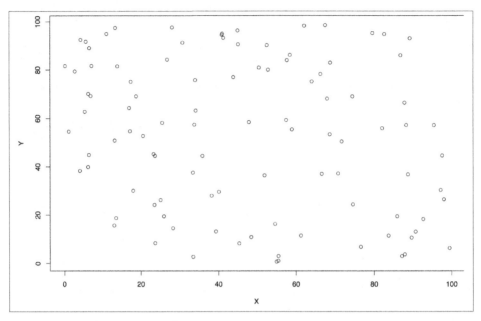

Figure 10-11. A boring scatterplot

Clusters and gaps are changes in the density of a scatterplot. The boring scatterplot in Figure 10-11 is a plot of uniform variables of unrelated density. If the two variables are related, then there should be a change in the density of the data somewhere on the plot. Figure 10-12 shows an example of clusters and gaps. In this example, there is a marked increase in activity in the lower-left quadrant, and a marked decrease in the upper-right quadrant.

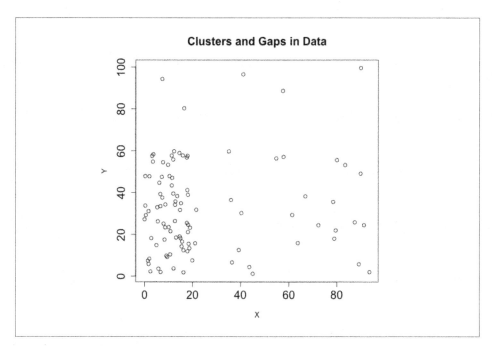

Figure 10-12. Clusters and gaps in data

Linear relationships, as the name indicates, appear in scatterplots as a line. The strength of the relationship can be estimated from the density of the points around the line. Figure 10-13 shows an example of three simple linear relationships of the form $y=kx$, but each relationship is progressively weaker and noisier.

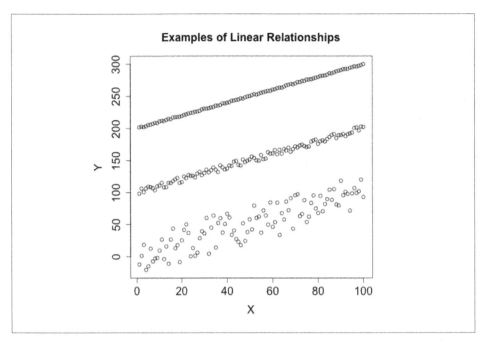

Figure 10-13. Linear relationships in data

Contingency Tables

Contingency tables are the preferred visualization when comparing categorical data against categorical data. A contingency table is simply a matrix: the rows list all the values one variable can have, the columns list all the values the other variable can have, and the entry in each cell is the number of observations that had both categories in common. Depending on the implementation, contingency tables also include a row and column containing the *marginals* for that row, a sum of all the values occurring in the row.

In R, contingency tables are constructed using the `table` command, which returns a table that can then be queried for marginals, as shown here:

```
# An example R table, created from two vectors of hosts and services
> hosts[0:3]
[1] "A" "B" "A"
> services[0:3]
[1] "http" "dns"  "smtp"
> # Table creation, hosts, and services have to be the same length
> info.table<-table(hosts,services)
> info.table
     services
hosts dns http smtp ssh
    A   2   15   10   0
```

```
    B   6   5   3   4
    C   3   3   1   2
> # You can access the marginals by calling margin.table
> margin.table(info.table)
[1] 54
> margin.table(info.table, 1)
hosts
 A  B  C
27 18  9
> margin.table(info.table, 2)
services
 dns http smtp  ssh
  11   23   14    6
```

Multivariate Visualization

A multivariate dataset is one that contains at least three variables per unit measured. Multivariate visualization is more of a technique rather than a specific set of plots. Most multivariate visualizations are built by taking a bivariate visualization and finding a way to add additional information. The most common approaches include colors or changing icons, plotting multiple images, and using animation.

Building good multivariate visualizations requires providing information from each of the datsets without drowning the reader in details. It's easy to plot a dozen different datasets on the same chart, but the results are often confusing.

The most basic approach for multivariate visualization is to overlay multiple datasets on the same chart, using different tickmarks or colors to indicate the originating dataset. As a rule of thumb, you can plot about four series on a chart without confusing a reader. When picking the colors or symbols to use, keep the following in mind:

- Don't use yellow; it looks too much like white and is often invisible on printouts and monitors.

- Choose symbols that are very different from each other. I personally like the open circle, closed circle, triangle, and cross.

- Choose colors that are far away from each other on the color wheel: red, green, blue, and black are my preferred choices.

- Avoid complex symbols. Many plotting packages offer a variety of asterisk-like figures that are hard to differentiate.

- Be consistent with your color and symbol choices, and don't overlap their domains. In other words, don't decide that red is HTTP and triangles are FTP.

For more information on plotting multiple series in R, consult "Annotating a Visualization" on page 120.

An alternative to plotting multiple sets on the same chart is to use multiple small plots next to each other. Commonly called *trellis plots*, Figure 10-14 is a good example generated by R's `pairs` command. When run on a data frame, `pairs` generates a matrix like the one shown in Figure 10-14—each pair of variables is a distinct scatterplot. Each scatterplot shows the relationship between the pair, and as this example shows it's very easy to quickly identify that volume and articles seem to have some relationship while everything else looks unrelated.

R's pairs plot is a powerful data exploration tool and is a good example of the expressive power of multiple visualizations. By relating multiple simple visualizations together in a well-defined and clear structure, you can process an enormous amount of data quickly. The key to building visualizations like this one is simplicity—small plots need to be careful with how they use real estate.

I find that trellis plots are usually the best option for plotting multivariate data because they provide a clean and user-controlled mechanism for showing the relationship between different variables. The minimal layout of Figure 10-14 is an important design feature to pay attention to in multivariate visualization. Trellis plots usually have an enormous amount of redundant metadata (e.g., axes, ticks, and labels) relative to the number of plots. To address this problem, use extremely minimal data representations in the plots: drop redundant axes, and remove internal labels and ticks.

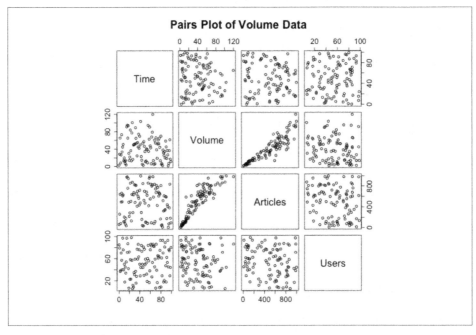

Figure 10-14. Trellis plot of volume data

Animation is pretty much what it says on the tin: you create multiple images and then step through them. In my experience, animation doesn't work very well. It reduces the amount of information directly observable by an analyst, who has to correlate what's going on in her memory as opposed to visually.

Operationalizing Security Visualization

EDA and visualization are part of the exploratory process and, as such, are somewhat rough around the edges. The EDA process involves a large number of dead ends and false starts. During the operationalization phase of an analytic process, the visualizations will need to be modified in order to supplement action and response. Additional processing and modification is needed to polish a visualization sufficiently for it to work on the floor. The following rules provide examples of good and bad visualizations and how to address the problems of visualizing data for information security.

Rule one: bound and partition your visualization to manage disruptions

When plotting security information, you need to expect and manage disruptions—after all, the whole point of looking for security events is to find disruptive activity. Plotting features like autoscaling can work against you by hiding data when something weird happens. For example, consider a count of anomalous events such as in Figure 10-15. This plot has two anomalies, but one is obscured by the need to plot the second.

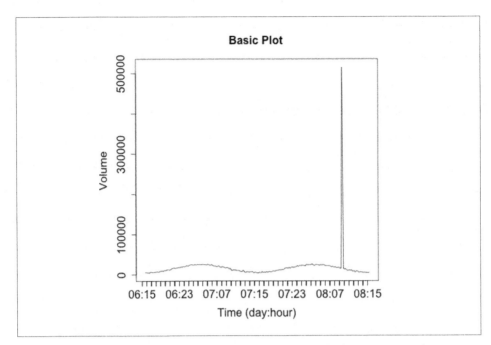

Figure 10-15. Autoscale's impact on disruptive event visualization

There are two strategies for dealing with these spikes. The first is to use *logarithmic scaling* on the dependent (y) axis. Log scaling replaces the linear scale with a logarithmic scale. For example, the ticks on the axis go from being 10, 20, 30, 40 to 10, 100, 1000, 10000. Figure 10-16 shows a logarithmic plot of the same phenomenon. Using a logarithmic scale will reduce the difference between the major anomaly and the rest of the data.

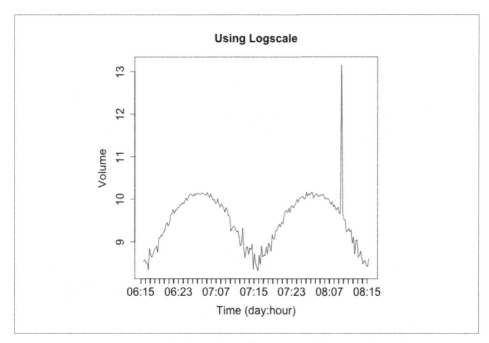

Figure 10-16. Using a log scale plot to limit the impact of large outliers

A logarithmic scale is suitable for EDA, and most tools provide an option to automatically plot data this way. With R, you pass in a log parameter to the plotting command to indicate which axis should be logarithmic (e.g., log="y").

I don't like using logarithmic scales when developing an operational visualization, however. With logarithmic scales you tend to lose information about typical phenomena—the curve for typical traffic in Figure 10-16 is deformed by the logarithmic scale. Also, the explanation of what a logarithmic scale is a bit recondite; I don't want to have to explain logarithmic scaling over and over again. When somebody is looking at the same data repeatedly, I'd prefer to keep it linear.

For these reasons, I prefer to keep the scaling on a plot consistent and identify and remove outliers. We've seen an example of this in Figure 10-8, where R automatically splits outliers from the boxplot. When developing an operational plot, I estimate the range of the plot, and usually set the upper limit displayed to the 98th percentile of the observed data. Then, when an anomaly occurs, I plot it separately and differently from the other data to indicate that it is an anomaly. Figure 10-17 shows a simple example of this.

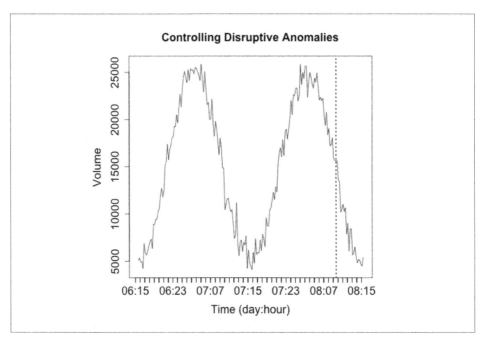

Figure 10-17. Partitioning anomalies out from normal data

The anomaly in Figure 10-17 is identified by the single line indicating that it's off the scale. The second anomaly (at 07:11) is not detected by that process, but the event is now obvious through visualization. That said, the anomaly marker is completely meaningless without further information and training, which leads into rule two.

Rule two: label anomalies

If rule one is in place, then you've already established some basic rules for discerning anomalies from normal traffic. Operational visualization is an aid to anomaly detection, so the same rules as constructing IDS (see Chapter 7) apply—prefetch data to reduce the operator's response time. As an example, the anomaly in Figure 10-18 is annotated with the information about what caused the anomaly as well as some statistics.

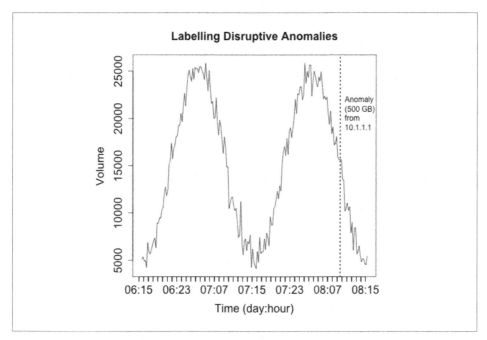

Figure 10-18. Labeling anomalies to aid investigation

Labeling anomalies on the plot can be useful for rapid reference, but if there are too many anomalies (and working off of rule one, you should expect that there will be too many anomalies). You can see this happening in Figure 10-18 where the label, while informative, is already consuming about a fifth of the horizontal space available. A better approach is to explain the anomalies in a separate table next to the visualization, which allows you to include as much data as necessary.

Rule three: use trendlines, distinguish artifacts from observations

Operational visualizations need to balance summarization and smoothing techniques that can help the analyst process data without getting mired in details, while at the same time providing the analyst with the actual data that happened and not thinking for him. As a result, when I operationally visualize data I prefer to include the raw data and then some kind of smoothing trendline at the same time. Figure 10-19 is a simple example of this kind of visualization, where a moving average is used to smooth out the observed disruptions.

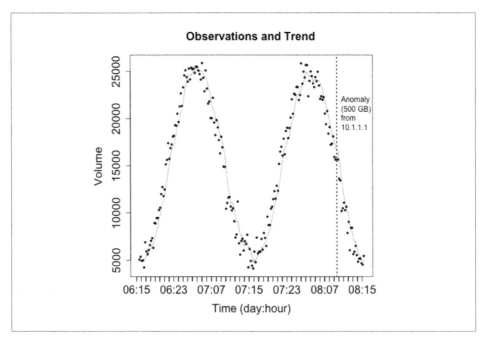

Figure 10-19. Moving average over direct observations

When creating visualizations like this, you need to ensure that the analyst can clearly differentiate between the data (the original) information and the artifacts you've created to aid analysis. You also need, as per rule one, to keep track of the impact of disruptive events—you don't want them interfering with your smoothing.

Rule four: be consistent across plots

Visualization exploits our pattern matching capabilities. However, those capabilities just *love* to run rampant on the vaguest hint. For example, you decide to pick a red line to represent HTTP traffic in a per-host activity. If you then decide to use a red line to represent incoming traffic in the same suite of visualizations, *somebody* is going to assume it's HTTP traffic again.

Rule five: annotate with contextual information

In addition to labeling anomalies, it's good to include unobtrusive contextual data that can help facilitate analysis. The example shown in Figure 10-20 adds some gray bars to indicate whether or not activity is taking place during or outside business hours.

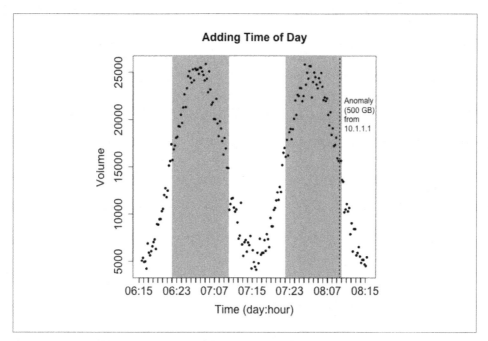

Figure 10-20. Adding some color to identify time of day

Rule six: avoid flash in favor of expressiveness

Finally, recognize that operational visualization is intended to be processed quickly and repeatedly. It's not a showcase for innovative graphic representation. The goal of operational visualization should be to express information quickly and clearly. Graphically excessive features like animation, unusual color choices, and the like will increase the time it takes to process the image without contributing information.

Be particularly careful about visualizations based on real-world or cyberspace metaphors. Whimsy wears thin *very* quickly, and we're not dealing with the physical world here. Metaphors such as "opening a desk" or "rattling all the doors in a building" (visualizations I've seen tried and the less said about them the better) often look neat in concept, but they usually require complex interstitial animations (which take up time) and lose information because of the metaphor. Focus on simple, expressive, serious displays.

Rule seven: when performing long jobs, give the user some status feedback

When I run SiLK queries, I have a habit of running them with the `--print-file` switch active, not because I care about which files are being accessed, but in order to have an indicator of whether the process is running or if the system is hung. When building visualizations, it's important to know how long it will take to complete one and to provide the user with some feedback that the visualization is actually being generated.

Further Reading

1. Greg Conti, *Security Data Visualization: Graphical Techniques for Network Analysis* (No Starch Press, 2001).

2. NIST Handbook of Explorator Data Analysis (*http://1.usa.gov/ex-data-an*)

3. Cathy O'Neil and Rachel Schutt, *Doing Data Science* (O'Reilly, 2013).

4. Edward Tufte, *The Visual Display of Quantitative Information* (Graphics Press, 2001).

5. John Tukey, *Exploratory Data Analysis* (Pearson, 1997).

## CHAPTER 11

On Fumbling

Up to this point, we have discussed a number of techniques for collecting and analyzing data. We must now marry this with attacker behavior.

Recall from the introduction the distinction between anomaly and signature detection. A focus of this book is on identifying viable mechanisms for detecting and dealing with anomalies, and to find these mechanisms, we must identify general attacker behaviors. *Fumbling*, which is the topic of this chapter, is the first of several such behaviors.

Fumbling refers to the process of systematically failing to connect to a target using a reference. That reference might be an IP address, a URL, or an email address. What makes fumbling *suspicious* is that a legitimate user should be given the reference he needs. When you start at a new company, they *tell* you the name of the email server; you don't have to guess it.

Attackers don't have access to that information. They must guess, steal, or scout that data from the system, and they will make mistakes. Often, those mistakes are huge and systematic. Identifying their mistakes and differentiating them from innocent errors is a valuable first step for analysis.

In this chapter, we will look at models of normal user behavior that are violated by attackers. This chapter integrates a variety of results from previous chapters, including material on email, network traffic, and social network analysis.

Attack Models

We need some vocabulary for talking about how attackers behave. There are a number of papers and studies on *attack models* that try to break the hacking process into a number of discrete steps. These models range from relatively simple linear affairs to extremely detailed *attack trees* that attempt to catalog each vulnerability and exploit. I'll start by laying out a simple but flexible model that contains steps common to a majority of attacks.

Reconnaissance

The attacker scouts out the target. Depending on the type of attack, reconnaissance may consist of googling, social engineering (posting on message boards to find and befriend users of a network), or active scanning using *nmap* or related tools.

Subversion

The attacker launches an exploit against a target and takes control. This may be done via a remote exploit, sending a Trojan file, or even password cracking.

Configuration

The attacker converts the target into a system more suitable for his own use. This may involve disabling antivirus packages, installing additional malware, taking inventory of the system and its capabilities, and/or installing additional defenses to prevent other attackers from taking over the target.

Exploitation

The attacker now uses the host for his own purposes. The nature of exploitation varies based on the attacker's original reason for being interested in the target (discussed shortly).

Propagation

The attacker will, if possible, use the host to attack other hosts. The host may serve as an expendable proxy, attacking neighbors (for example, other hosts behind a firewall on a 192.168.0.0/16 network).

This model isn't perfect, but it's a good general description of how attackers behave without getting bogged down in technical minutiae. There are always common tweaks, for example:

- Peer-to-peer worm propagation and phishing attacks rely on passive exploits and a bit of social engineering. These attacks rely on a target clicking a link or accessing a file, which requires that the bait (the filename or story surrounding it) be attractive enough to merit a click. At the time of this writing, for example, there's a spate of phishing attacks using credit ratings as the bait—the earliest informed me that my credit rating had risen and the latest batch is more ominously warning me of the consequences of a recently dropped credit rating. On peer-to-peer networks, attackers will drop Trojans with the names of current games or albums in order to attract victims. Even in this case, "surveillance" is still possible. The phishing attacks done in many APT attacks often depend on scouting out the population and posting habits of a site before identifying victims likely to respond to a crafted mail.

- Worms often merge the reconnaissance and subversion stages into one step. Some examples of this are shown later in the chapter (notably, in Example 11-1), where an attacker just launches exploits against well-known PHP URLs without checking to see if they actually exist.

Your Attacker Just Isn't That Into You: Interested and Uninterested Attackers

When we think about attackers, we tend to think of technically literate individuals figuring out specific weaknesses on a site in order to grab files or information off of it. This is the classic example of an *interested* attacker who wants to subvert and control a particular site in order to acquire cash, data, street cred, or who knows what. They make for great stories, but have been, if not a disappearing breed, a progressively minuscule portion of attacks for 10 years or more.

The vast majority of attacks today are conducted by *uninterested* attackers who want to take over as many hosts as possible and don't care about the fine details of any particular one. Uninterested attacks are largely automated; they have to be in order to tolerate their inordinately high failure rate. Because of this, the reconnaissance and subversion steps are often merged together. An automated worm may simply launch its attack against every host it encounters, regardless of whether the host is vulnerable.

Uninterested attackers rely on tools and the expectation that someone, somewhere, will be vulnerable. In most cases, they won't even be aware that a host exists until they take it over. Early examples of uninterested attackers harvested robots for DDoS networks. Botmasters would take over a dozen or so machines, install DDoS software on them, and then launch SYN floods against targets. As connectivity increased, the scope and flexibility of botnets increased as well—attackers started installing software to work as proxies, rob images from attached webcams and sell them to porn sites, install spambots, and carry out a virtually limitless catalog of other abuses.

Uninterested attackers consequently operate more like harvesters than a traditional targeted attacker. A uninterested attacker runs a script, then filters through the results of that script to see what she's pulled in. A host has a webcam, and it's located on a college dorm? Porn feed. A host has a lot of disk space and a fat pipe? Fileserver. A host is a home machine? Keylogger.

This harvest-based approach means that attackers often have little to no idea what they're taking over. In the early days of SCADA exploits, it was apparent that the attackers had no idea what they were looking at, just a Windows host with some weird applications and extra directories. Even now, it's not uncommon to see medical hardware taken over and used as a botnet.

In recent years, a host's "configuration" also includes its role: who owns it, what its used for, and what kind of bragging rights can be acquired by bagging it. For example, if two countries share a hostile border, resident hacker rings will deface sites in the opposing country. The Department of Defense runs literally thousands of websites, ranging from intelligence servers to grade schools. It's not hard to find a vulnerable site and then announce to the world that you've "hacked the DoD!" after the fact. Something to keep in mind.

Fumbling: Misconfiguration, Automation, and Scanning

We'll use the term a *fumble* to refer generically to any failed attempt by a host to access a resource. A fumble in TCP means that a host wasn't able to reach a particular host address/port combination, whereas a fumble in HTTP refers to the inability to access a URL. Individual fumbles are expected and are not automatically suspicious. What's more of a concern is a tendency toward repeated fumbling. Fumbling as an aggregate behavior can happen for several reasons: an error in lookup or configuration, automated software, and scanning.

Lookup Failures

Fumbles usually happen because the destination doesn't exist in the first place. This can be a transient phenomenon due to misaddressing or movement, or it can be due to someone addressing a resource that never existed.

Keep in mind that people *rarely* enter addresses by hand. Most users will never directly enter an IP address, instead relying on DNS to moderate their communications. Similarly, apart from a TLD, users rarely enter URLs by hand, instead copying or clicking them from other applications. When someone does enter a faulty address or URL, it usually means that something further up the chain of lookup protocols that got him there failed.

When a target moves, *misaddressing* is a common phenomenon. In the case of a misaddress, the target *does* exist, but the source is misinformed about the address. For example, an attacker may enter the wrong name or IP address, or use an earlier IP address after a host moves.

Every site has unused IP addresses and port numbers. For instance, a /24 (class C) address space allows 254 addresses (two more are reserved for special purposes), but the network usually uses only a fraction of them. An unused address or port number is called *dark space*. Legitimate users rarely try to access dark space, but attackers almost always do. However, knocking on the door of an usused IP address or port is not dangerous in itself, and is so common that tracking it isn't worthwhile.

Misaddressing is often a common mode failure, meaning that it will not be limited to one or two users, but to a large community. The classic example of a misaddress is somebody sending a messsage to a mailing list, and then mistyping the URL. When this happens, you don't see one or two errors, and you don't see individual errors. You see the exact same meaningless string occurring over and over again, coming from dozens if not hundreds of sites. If you see a large number of fumbles, coming from different sites, all identical and all indicating a misspelling, then it's a good sign that the error has a common cause such as a misconfigured DNS, a faulty redirect on the web server, or an email with the wrong URL.

Automation

People are impatient. Very often, when they can't actually reach a site, they may retry once, but then they'll go off and find something better to do with their time. Conversely, automated systems retry connections as a reliability measure, and will often return after a relatively short interval to see if the target is up and running.

On a network traffic feed, this means that a protocol that is human-driven (SSH, HTTP, Telnet) is likely to have a lower failure rate per connection than protocols that are largely automated (SMTP, peer-to-peer communications).

Scanning

Scanning is *the most common form of attack traffic observed on the network*. If you own a nontrivial chunk of IP space (say a /24 or more), you will literally be scanned thousands of times a day.

Scanning is one of the great sources for bogus security figures. If you classify a scan as an attack, then you can claim to be dealing with thousands of attacks per day. Attacks you're going to do precisely nothing about, but still thousands. Scanning is easy, fun, and stupid amusement for script kiddies.

Imagine that your network is a two-dimensional grid, where the x-axis shows your IP addresses and the y-axis shows the ports. The grid will then have 65,536 by k cells, where k is the total number of IP addresses. Now, every time a scanner hits a target (an IP/port combination), mark a cell. If you're interested in all the capabilities of a single host, you may open up a connection to every port it has, resulting in a single vertical line on the grid, a *vertical scan*. The complement to a vertical scan is a *horizontal scan*, where the attacker communicates with every host on the network, but only a specific port.

As a rule of thumb, defenders scan vertically and attackers horizontally. The difference is primarily opportunistic—an attacker scans a network horizontally because he is uninterested in the targets *outside of the vulnerabilities he can exploit*. An attacker who *is* interested in a specific target may well scan it vertically. Defenders scan vertically because they can't predict what an attacker will hit.

If an attacker knows something about the structure of a network ahead of time, she may use a *hit-list*, a list of IP addresses which she knows or suspects may be vulnerable. An example of a common hit-list attack is described by Alata and Dacier: the attacker begins by using a blind scan of a network to identify SSH hosts and then sometime later uses that list to begin password attacks.[1]

Identifying Fumbling

There are two stages to identifying the process of fumbling. The first is determining what, in a protocol, means that a user failed to correctly access a resource. In other words, what does a failed access "look" like? The second stage is determining whether the failure is consistent or transient, global or local.

TCP Fumbling: The State Machine

Identifying failed TCP connections requires some understanding of the TCP state machine and how it works. As we've discussed before, TCP imposes the illusion of a stream-based protocol on top of the packet-based IP. This simulation of a stream is produced using the TCP state machine, shown in Figure 11-1.

Under normal circumstances, a TCP session consists of a sequence of handshake packets that set up initial state.

- On the client side, the transition is from SYN_SENT (client sends an initial SYN packet) to ESTABLISHED (client receives a SYN|ACK packet from server, sends an ACK in response), and then to normal session operations.

- On the server side, the transition is from LISTEN to SYN_RCVD (receives a SYN, sends a SYN|ACK), and then to ESTABLISHED (receives an ACK).

- For either side, closure consists of at least two packets (CLOSE_WAIT to LAST_ACK or FIN_WAIT_1 to CLOSING/FIN_WAIT_2 to TIME_WAIT).

---

1. Alata, E. et al., "Lessons learned from the deployment of a high-interaction honeypot," EDCC 2006.

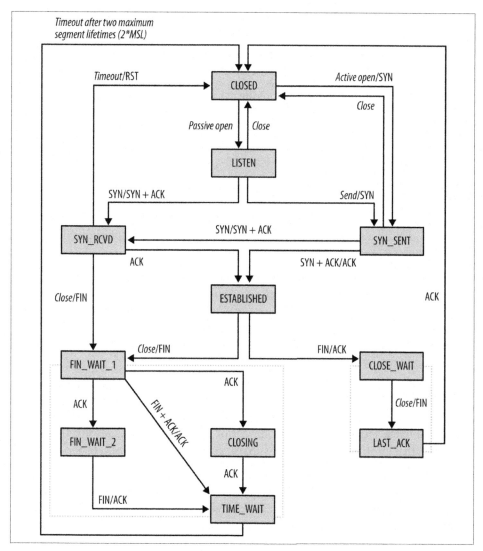

Figure 11-1. The TCP state machine, from texample.net

The net result of these transitions is that a well-behaved TCP/IP session requires *at least* three packets simply to set up the connection. This is overhead required by TCP, and does not include any communications done by the protocol itself. Throw in a standard MTU of 1,500 bytes, and most legitimate sessions are going to consist of at least several dozen packets.

Automated retry attempts add another layer of complexity to the problem. RFC 1122 establishes basic guidelines for TCP retransmission attempts and recommends a minimum of three retransmissions before giving up on a connection. The actual retry value is usually softcoded and stack-dependent; for example, in Linux systems, the number of retries generally defaults to 3 and is controlled by the `tcp_retries1` TCP variable. In Windows systems, the `TcpMaxConnectRetransmissions` registry value in *HKLM\SYSTEM\CurrentControlSet\Services\Tcpip\Parameters* governs this behavior.

An analyst can identify fumbling by looking at a variety of indicators, depending on the type of data the operator has available and the degree of accuracy necessary. These techniques include relying on a network *map*, looking for *bidirectional traffic*, and examining a *unidirectional flow* for activity. Each technique has strengths and weaknesses, which I'll discuss.

Network maps

The best tool for identifying fumbling is a current and accurate network map. Network maps can identify a fumble by looking at a single packet, while examining TCP traffic requires looking for replies and reattempts.

That said, a network map is not relying on actual network information—it's relying on a model of the network that was constructed some time before the event. At the most extreme example, a map of a DHCP network has a limited viable lifetime, but even a statically addressed network will see new services and hosts arrive on a regular basis. When using a network map, make sure to regularly test its integrity using one of the other techniques listed in this section.

Unidirectional flow filtering

If you have access to both sides of a session (i.e., client to server, server to client), identifying complete sessions is simply a matter of joining the two sides together. In the absence of that information, it's still possible to guess whether packets are part of a whole session.

In my personal experience, I find flows to be more effective than individual packets for detecting fumbling. A fumbler doesn't interact with a service proper because there is no payload to examine. At the same time, identifying fumbling involves looking for multiple identically addressed packets that occur around the same time, which is the textbook definition of a flow.

Depending on the amount of information needed and the precision required, a number of different heuristics can identify fumbles in TCP flows. The basic techniques involve looking at flags, packet counts, or payload size and packet count.

Flags are a good indicator of fumbling, but using them is complicated by a messy collection of corner cases happily exploited by scanners to differentiate different IP stack implementations. Recall from the Figure 11-1 that a client sends an ACK flag only after receiving an initial SYN + ACK from the server. In the absence of a response, the client should not send an ACK flag; consequently, flows with a SYN and no ACK flag are a good indicator of a fumble. There exists the *potential* that a response came outside of the timeout of the flow collector, but that's rare in applied cases.

Attackers craft packets with odd flag combinations in order to determine stack and firewall configurations. The best known of these combinations is the "Christmas tree" packet (so called because all flags are lit up like a Christmas tree), setting SYN ACK FIN PUSH URG RST. Combinations of flags with both SYN and FIN high are common as well. When dealing with long-lived protocols (such as SSH), it's not uncommon to encounter a packet consisting solely of an ACK. These packets are TCP keep-alive packets and are not fumbling.

Another odd, non-fumbling behavior is *backscatter*. Backscatter occurs when a host opens a connection to an existing server using a spoofed address, and the server sends the corresponding response to the original spoofed address. Lone SYN, ACK, and RST packets that don't hit a target are likely to be backscatter.

An easy, if rough, indicator of whether a flow shows a complete session is to simply look at the number of packets. A legitimate TCP session requires at least three packets of overhead before it considers transmitting service data. Furthermore, most stacks set their retry value to between three and five packets. These rules provide a simple filter: TCP flows that have five packets or less are likely to be fumbles.

Flow size can be complemented by looking at the ratio of packet size to number of packets. TCP SYN packets contain a number of TCP options (*http://bit.ly/tcp-para*) of variable length. During a failed connection, the host will send the same SYN packet options repeatedly. Consequently, if a flow is an n-packet SYN fumble, we can expect that the total number of bytes sent is $n\times(40 + k)$, where k is the total size of the options.

ICMP Messages and Fumbling

ICMP is actually designed to inform a user that she has failed to make a connection. ICMP type 3 messages (destination unreachable) are supposed to be sent to a host to indicate that the target network (code 0), host (code 1), or port (code 3) cannot be reached by the client packet. ICMP also provides messages indicating that a route is unknown (code 7) or administratively prohibited (code 13).

With the exception of pings, ICMP messages appear in *response* to failures in other protocols. Several messages, such as host or net unreachable, originate from some point other than the destination address—generally the nearest router. ICMP messages may also be filtered, depending on the policies of the network in question, and consequently not received by your sensors.

This asymmetry means that when tracking fumbling from ICMP traffic, it is more productive to look for the *response*. If you see a sudden spike in messages originating from a router, it's a good bet that the target it's sending the messages to has been probing that router's network. You can then look at the host's traffic to identify what it did communicate with that might be suspicious.

You Were Scanned, Here's Your Medal

At this point, scanning is so omnipresent, unstoppable, and obnoxious that it has ceased to be an attack and instead has become a form of Internet weather. I can place a reasonable bet that you're mostly being scanned on TCP ports 80, 443, 22, 25, and 135 without looking at your network.

So, scanning in and of itself is uninteresting, but there is still *value* in scan detection. Primarily, this is an optimization issue. As discussed in Chapter 4, scanning data can be shunted off during postprocessing in order to reduce the number of records that an analyst encounters in the main data flow. As you monitor larger networks, the problem of scan data becomes increasingly more and more important—a dumb scanner on a /16 will generate 65,535 flows for every port he decides to hit. You may see eight flows for a long lived SSH session, if you see them among all the scanning noise.

Scan removal is best done on an IP-by-IP basis, because if a host is scanning the network, it's likely not doing anything legitimate. Identify each scanning address and remove *all* traffic originating from that address. This traffic set can then be trended by identifying the destination ports of the scans, determining the exploits used (if identified by IDS), and comparing the types of scans conducted over time. Top-*n* lists are generally not particularly useful for scan trending because the top five positions have been fairly static for the past five years.

In operational environments, I generally haven't been too fussy about exactly identifying flow traffic, instead opting to use the high-pass filter approach to split TCP traffic into *short* and *long* files, and then using the long files as the default dataset for queries. In occasions when I really need to access the short files, the data is there, and the probability of a short communication actually being meaningful *and all traffic from that host being in the short file* is pretty much nonexistent.

Analytically, scan data is often more useful for identifying who *responded* to a scan rather than who sent it. Attackers are likely to scan your network far more actively and far more often than your own network management staff, meaning that by keeping track of the hosts that responded to scans, you will likely discover new systems and services long before your next audit.

Speculatively, there may be some value in scan trending. SANS, among other organizations, does keep track of current scanning statistics on the Internet storm center (*https://isc.sans.edu*). However, if there is value in trending, it has to get past the overwhelming dominance of the top five ports: ports 22, 25, 80, 443, and 139.

Identifying UDP Fumbling

It's rarely possible to identify a failed UDP connection from the UDP traffic itself. TCP has symmetry baked into the protocol, whereas UDP doesn't provide any guarantees of delivery. If a UDP *service* provides some form of symmetry or other reciprocity, that's a service-specific attribute. In order of preference, network maps and ICMP traffic are the best ways to identify UDP fumbling.

Fumbling at the Service Level

Service-level fumbling commonly results from scanning, automated exploits, and a number of scouting tools. Unlike network-level fumbling, service-level fumbling is usually clearly identifiable as such because there are error codes in most major services that are logged and can be used to differentiate illegitimate connections from legitimate requests.

HTTP Fumbling

Recall that each HTTP transaction returns a three-digit status code, of which the 4xx family of status codes are reserved for client errors. In the 4xx family, the two most important and common access errors are 404 (not found) and 401 (unauthorized).

404 indicates that a resource was not available at the URL specified by the requestor, and is the most common HTTP error in existence. Users will often trigger 404 errors by hand, such as when they mistype a complex URL. Misconfiguration will often cause problems as well, such as when someone publicizes a URL that doesn't exist.

These types of errors, from a misconfigured URL announcement or fat-fingering, are relatively easy to identify. In the first case, fat-fingering should be relatively rare. Fat-fingered URLs will rarely repeat—if one user is mistyping, he'll mistype slightly differently each time. At the same time, since fat-fingering is an *individual* mistake, the same fat-fingering will not appear from multiple locations. If you see the same mistake coming from multiple discrete locations, that is more likely to be a result of a misconfigured URL announcement. Such an announcement may be identifiable by examining the HTTP Referer header. If the Referer points to a site you have control over, then you can identify and fix the error on that site.

The third common source for 404 errors is bots scanning HTTP sites for well-known vulnerabilities. Because most modern HTTP sites are built on top of a collection of other applications, they often carry vulnerabilities from one or more of their component applications. These vulnerabilities are well-known, placed in common locations, and consequently hunted for by bots everywhere. The URLs referenced in Example 11-1 are all associated with phpMyAdmin, a common MySQL database management tool.

Example 11-1. Botnets attempting to fetch common URLs

```
223.85.245.54 - - [16/Feb/2013:20:10:12 -0500]
            "GET /pma/scripts/setup.php HTTP/1.1" 404 390 "-" "ZmEu"
223.85.245.54 - - [16/Feb/2013:20:10:15 -0500]
            "GET /MyAdmin/scripts/setup.php HTTP/1.1" 404 394 "-" "ZmEu"
188.230.44.113 - - [17/Feb/2013:16:54:05 -0500]
             "GET http://www.scanproxy.net:80/p-80.html HTTP/1.0" 404 378 "-"
194.44.28.21 - - [18/Feb/2013:06:20:07 -0500]
            "GET /w00tw00t.at.blackhats.romanian.anti-sec:) HTTP/1.1" 404 410
              "-" "ZmEu"
194.44.28.21 - - [18/Feb/2013:06:20:07 -0500]
            "GET /phpMyAdmin/scripts/setup.php HTTP/1.1" 404 397 "-" "ZmEu"
194.44.28.21 - - [18/Feb/2013:06:20:08 -0500]
            "GET /phpmyadmin/scripts/setup.php HTTP/1.1" 404 397 "-" "ZmEu"
194.44.28.21 - - [18/Feb/2013:06:20:08 -0500]
            "GET /pma/scripts/setup.php HTTP/1.1" 404 390 "-" "ZmEu"
194.44.28.21 - - [18/Feb/2013:06:20:09 -0500]
            "GET /myadmin/scripts/setup.php HTTP/1.1" 404 394 "-"
```

Unlike the 404 errors discussed earlier, 404 scanning is generally identifiable by being *completely unrelated* to the actual structure of a site. Attackers are *guessing* that something is there and are going by the documentation and common practice to try to reach a vulnerable target.

401 errors are authentication errors, and come from HTTP's basic access authentication mechanism—which you should never use. 401 authentication was baked into the HTTP standard early on,[2] and uses unencrypted base64-encoded passwords to authenticate a user's access to protected directories.

Basic access authentication is a disaster and should not be used by any modern web server. If you do see 401 errors in your system logs, you should identify and eliminate the source of them on your server. Unfortunately, basic authentication still occasionally pops up in embedded systems as the only form of authentication available.

Webcrawlers and Robots.txt

Search engines employ automated processes called, variously, *crawlers*, *spiders*, or *robots* to scout out websites and identify searchable content. These crawlers can be phenomenally aggressive in copying site contents; website owners can define what the crawlers access using the *robot exclusion standard*, or *robots.txt*. The standard defines a common file (the aforementioned *robots.txt*), which is accessed by the crawler and provides instructions about which files it can and can't access.

---

2. See RFC 1945 (*http://bit.ly/rfc-1945*) and RFC 2617 (*http://bit.ly/rfc-2617*).

A host that *doesn't* access *robots.txt* and immediately begins poking around the site is suspicious. Furthermore, *robots.txt* is a voluntary standard; there's nothing preventing a crawler from ignoring it, and it's not uncommon for unethical or new crawlers to ignore the instructions.

It's also not uncommon for scanners who want to probe a site to pretend to be a crawler. Crawlers are usually identifiable by two behaviors: they use a User-Agent string unique to the crawler, and they come from a fixed range of IP addresses.[3] Most search engines publish their address ranges to help stop masquerading; these address ranges can change, so regularly checking a site such as the Robots Database (*http://bit.ly/web-robots*) or List of User-Agents (*http://www.user-agents.org*) is a good idea.

SMTP Fumbling

For our purposes, SMTP fumbling occurs when a host sends mail to a nonexistent address. Depending on SMTP server configurations, this will result in one of three actions: a rejection, a bounce, or (in the case of a catch-all configuration) redirection to a catch-all account. All of these events should be logged by the SMTP server that makes the final routing decision.

Analyzing SMTP fumbles runs into the same problem that analyzing all SMTP traffic does: spam. There are a lot of failed addresses sent in SMTP messages because spammers will send mail to every conceivable address.[4] Consequently, the relatively innocuous reasons for fumbling (misaddressing) may exist but are drowned in spam. At the same time, the reasons for attackers to fumble (reconnaissance) are effectively pointless because spammers don't probe to see whether an address exists; they spam it.

There may be one good reason to analyze failed SMTP addresses: uncovering deception. In several APT-type spear-phishing emails, I've seen the attackers seed the To: line with several realistic but fake looking addresses. I assume that the addresses are either out of date due to enterprise turnover or intentionally added to provide the mail with a veneer of legitimacy.

Analyzing Fumbling

> Until some brilliant researcher comes up with a better technique, scan detection will boil down to testing for X events of interest across a Y-sized time window.
>
> — Stephen Northcutt

---

3. Googlebot is a notable exception to this, and includes instructions on how to verify Googlebot (*http://bit.ly/verify-google*).

4. I once logged onto an account I had never used and was greeted by 3,000 spam messages.

Fumbling alarms can be used to detect scans, spams, and other phenomena where the attacker has next to no knowledge about the target network.

Building Fumbling Alarms

When tracking fumbles, the goal is to raise an alarm when there's suspicion that fumbling is not simply accidental. To do so, the alarm must first collect fumbling events using the rules discussed previously in this chapter. These mechanisms include:

1. Creating or consulting a map of targets to determine whether the attacker is reaching a real target.

2. Examining traffic for evidence of a failure to connect. Examples of failures to connect include:

    a. Asymmetric TCP sessions, or TCP sessions without ACK flags

    b. HTTP 404 records

    c. Email bounce logs

Innocuous fumbling, as a false positive, are generally the result of some form of misconfiguration or miscommunication to the target. For example: the DNS name for *destination.com* is moved from IP address A to IP address B; until the change thoroughly propagates through the DNS system, users will accidentally visit address A instead of B. These types of errors, when they occur, will come from multiple sources and will be consistent. Going back to the *destination.com* case, address A is no longer used and address C on the same network is dark (that is, it has no domain name); users may accidentally visit A for a while, but they will not visit C. Suspicious fumbling involves users who visit multiple nonexistent destinations; a host may visit A due to a configuration error, he might possibly visit C due to chance, but if he visits A and C, then he's more likely scouting out a target.

Distinguishing malicious fumbling from innocuous failures is therefore, as Northcutt says, about deciding on a threshold—the number of events tolerated before you raise an alert. There are a number of mechanisms to do this:

1. Calculate an expected value for the number of hosts on the network that a user should contact within a fixed period.

2. An alternative method is to use sequential hypothesis testing, a statistical technique that calculates the likelihood that a phenomenon will pass or fail a particular test multiple times. This approach was pioneered in infosec by Jaeyeoon Jung in her 2004 paper, "Fast Portscan Detection Using Sequential Hypothesis Testing."[5]

---

5. Jung, Jaeyeon et al. "Fast Portscan Detection Using Sequential Hypothesis Testing." Paper presented at the IEEE Symposium on Security and Privacy, Oakland, CA, May 2004.

3. Raise an alert whenever a user visits a dark address.

The thing about malicious fumbling is that the attackers, generally, have no particular reason to be subtle. If someone is scanning a site, she's going to hit everything quickly. Statistical methods are primarily useful to find the attacker *quickly*, and consequently have more use in active defense rather than in alarm generation.

Forensic Analysis of Fumbling

Scanning *qua* scanning is basically of no interest. Every idiot on the planet scans the Internet, and a number of them scan it multiple times daily. There is some worm-based scanning (such as with Code Red and SQLSlammer, if you want to get truly Jurassic), which has gone on for *years* without any noticeable effect. Scanning is like rain: it's going to happen, and the real question is identifying the damage that it causes.

When receiving a scan alarm, there are several basic questions to ask:

1. Who responded to the scanner? As far as I'm concerned, scanners can visit as much of my dark space as they like. What I'm really concerned about is whether anyone in my network talked *back* to the scanner, and what they did afterward. More specific questions include:

    a. Did the scanner have a serious conversation with any host? Attack software usually rolls scanning and exploit into a two-step process. Consequently, my first question about any scan is whether it ended before the true exploit.

    b. Did any responding host have suspicious conversations afterward? Suspicious conversations include communications with external hosts (especially if it's an internal server), receipt of a file, and communications on odd ports.

2. Did the scanner find out something about my network I didn't know? Inventories are always at least *slightly* out of date, and attacks are taking place *all the time*. Given that, it makes sense to take advantage of the scanner's hard work for our own benefit.

    a. Did the scanner identify previously unknown hosts? This is an example of the previous item about unknown information.

    b. Did the scanner identify previously unknown services?

3. What else did the scanner do? Bots usually do multiple things at one time, and it's good to check whether the scanner scanned other ports, engaged in other types of probes, or tried multiple types of attacks.

There are several good questions to ask about fumblers in general:

1. What else did the fumbler do? If the same address or source is sending mail to multiple targets, it's likely to be a spammer and, much like a scanner, is using a bot as a utility knife kind of tool.

2. Are there preferred targets? This particularly applies to fumbling with email addresses, because IP addresses are drawn from a much smaller pool. Are there common target addresses on your network? If so, they're good candidates for further instrumentation.

Engineering a Network to Take Advantage of Fumbling

Fumbling often takes advantage of common network configuration and assumptions. Most obviously, attackers scan common ports like 22 because they expect to encounter services there. You can take advantage of these assumptions to place more sensitive instrumentation on the network, such as full packet capture.

Because malicious scans exploit the regularity of most target sites, you can make the lives of attackers a bit harder by configuring your site in a somewhat irregular way:

Rearrange addresses

Most scanning is linear: the attacker will hit address X, then X+1, and so on. Most administrators and DHCP implementations also assign addresses linearly. It's not uncommon to have a /24 or /27 where the upper half is entirely dark. Rearranging addresses so that they're scattered evenly across the network, or leaving large empty gaps in the network is a simple method that creates dark space.

Move targets

Port assignments are largely a social convention, and most modern applications should be able to handle a service located on an unorthodox port. Especially when dealing with internal services, which shouldn't be accessed by the outside world, port reassignment is a cheap mechanism to frustrate more basic scanners.

Further Reading

1. Jaeyeon Jung, Vern Paxson, Arthur W. Berger, and Hari Balakrishnan, "Fast Portscan Detection Using Sequential Hypothesis Testing," Proceedings of the 2004 IEEE Symposium on Security and Privacy.

## CHAPTER 12

Volume and Time Analysis

In this chapter, we look at phenomena that can be identified by comparing traffic volume against the passage of time. "Volume" may be a simple count of the number of bytes or packets, or it may be a construct such as the number of IP addresses transferring files. Based on the traffic observed, there are a number of different phenomena that can be pulled out of traffic data, particularly:

Beaconing
> When someone contacts your host at regular intervals, it is a possible sign of an attack.

File extraction
> Massive downloads are suggestive of someone stealing your internal data.

Denial of Service (DoS)
> Preventing your servers from providing service.

Traffic volume data is noisy. Most of the observables that you can directly count, such as the number of bytes over time, vary highly and have no real relationship between the volume of the event and its significance. In other words, there's rarely a significant relationship between the number of bytes and the importance of the events. This chapter will help you find unusual behaviors through scripts and visualizations, but a certain amount of human eyeballing and judgment are necessary to determine which behaviors to consider dangerous.

The Workday and Its Impact on Network Traffic Volume

The bulk of traffic on an enterprise network comes from people who are paid to work there, so their traffic is going to roughly follow the hours of the business day. Traffic will trough during the evening, rise around 0800, peak around 1300, and drop off around 1800.

To show how dominant the workday is, consider Figure 12-1, a plot showing the progression of the SoBIG.F email worm across the SWITCH network (*http://www.switch.ch*) in 2003. SWITCH is Switzerland and Lichtenstein's educational network, and makes up a significant fraction of the national traffic for Switzerland. In Figure 12-1, the plot shows the total volume of SMTP traffic over time for a two-week period. SoBIG propagates at the end of the plot. But what I want to highlight is the normal activity during the earlier part of the week on the left. Note that each weekday is a notched peak, with the notch coming at lunchtime. Note also that there is considerably less activity over the weekend.

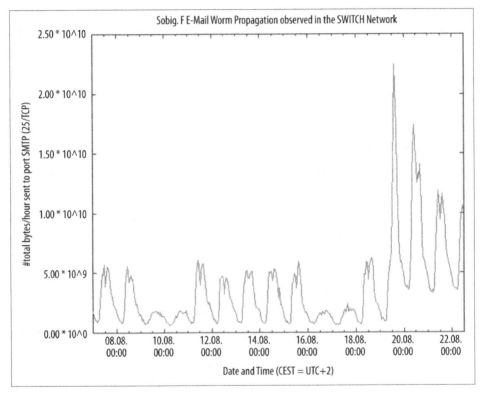

Figure 12-1. Mail traffic and propagation of a worm across Switzerland's SWITCH network (image courtesy of Dr. Arno Wagner)

This is a social phenomenon; knowing roughly where the address you're monitoring is (home, work, school), and the local time zone can help predict both events and volumes. For example, in the evening, streaming video companies become a more significant fraction of traffic as people kick back and watch TV.

There are a number of useful rules of thumb for working with workday schedules to identify, map, and manage anomalies. These include tracking active and inactive periods, tracking the internal schedule of an organization, and keeping track of the time zone. The techniques covered in this section are a basic, empirical approach to time series analysis; considerably more advanced techniques are covered in the books cited.

When working with site data, I usually find that it's best to break traffic into "on" (people are working) and "off" (people are at home) periods. The histogram in Figure 12-2 shows how this phenomenon can affect the distribution of traffic volume—in this case, the two distinct peaks correspond to the on-periods and off-periods. Modeling the two periods separately will provide a more accurate volume estimate without pulling out the heavier math used for time series analysis.

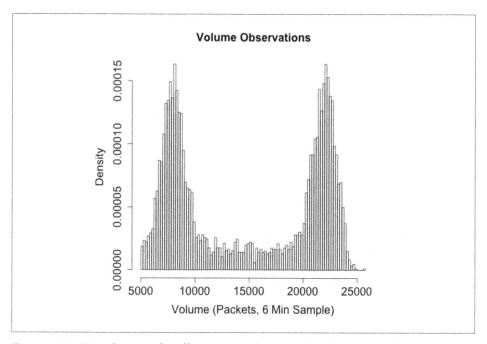

Figure 12-2. Distribution of traffic in a sample network, where the peak on the right is workday and the peak on the left is evening

When determining on-periods and off-periods, consider the schedule of the organization itself. If your company has any special or unusual holidays, such as taking a founder's birthday off, keep track of those as potential off-days. Similarly, are there parts of the organization that are staffed constantly and other parts that are only 9 to 5? If something is constantly staffed, keep track of the shift changes, and you'll often see traffic repeat at the start of a shift as everyone logs on, checks email, meets, and then starts working.

The Value of Off-Days

Off-time is valuable. If I want to identify dial-homes, file exfiltration, and other suspicious activity, I like to do so by watching off-hours. There's less traffic, there are fewer people, and if someone is ignorant of a company's internal circadian rhythm, she'll be a lot easier to identify during those periods than if she's hiding in the crowd.

This is the reason I like to keep track of a company's own special off-times. It's easy enough for someone to hide his traffic by keeping all activity in 9–5/M–F, but if the attacker doesn't know the company gives St. Swithin's Day off, then he's more likely to stick out.

I've seen this particular phenomenon show up when dealing with insiders, particularly people worried about shoulder surfing or physical surveillance. They'll move their activity to evenings and weekends in order to make sure their neighbors don't ask what they're doing, and then show up fairly visibly in the traffic logs.

Business processes are a common source of false positives with volume analysis. For example, I've seen a corporate site where there's a sudden biweekly spike in traffic to a particular server. The server, which covered company payroll, was checked by every employee every other Friday and never visited otherwise. Phenomena that occurs weekly, biweekly, or on multiples of 30 days is likely to be associated with the business's own processes and should be identified as such for future reference.

Beaconing

Beaconing is the process of systematically and regularly contacting a host. For instance, botnets will poll their command servers for new instructions periodically. This is particularly true of many modern botnets that use HTTP as a moderator. Such behavior will appear to you as information flows at regular intervals between infected systems on your site and an unknown address off-site.

However, there are many legitimate behaviors that also generate routine traffic flows. Examples include:

Keep alives
> Long-lived sessions, such as an interactive SSH session, will send empty packets at regular intervals in order to maintain a connection with the target.

Software updates

Most modern applications include some form of automated update checkup. AV, in particular, regularly downloads signature updates to keep track of the latest malware.

News and weather

Many news, weather, and other interactive sites regularly refresh the page as long as a client is open to read it.

Beacon detection is a two-stage process. The first stage involves identifying consistent signals. An example process for doing so is the *find_beacons.py* script shown in Example 12-1. *find_beacons.py* takes a sequence of flow records and dumps them into equally sized bins. Each input consists of two fields: the IP address where an event was found and the starting time of the flow, as returned by *rwcut*. *rwsort* is used to order the traffic by source IP and time.

The script then checks the median distance between the bins and scores each IP address on the fraction of bins that fall within some tolerance of that median. If a large number of flows are near the median, you have found a regularly recurring event.

Example 12-1. A simple beacon detector

```
#!/usr/bin/env python
#
#
# find_beacons.py
#
# input:
#        rwsort --field=1,9 | rwcut --no-title --epoch --field=1,9 | <stdin>
# command line:
# find_beacons.py precision tolerance [epoch]
#
# precision: integer expression for bin size (in seconds)
# tolerance: floating point representation for tolerance expressed as
# fraction from median, e.g. 0.05 means anything within (median -
# 0.5*median, median + 0.5*median) is acceptable
# epoch: starting time for bins; if not specified, set to midnight of the first
# time read.

# This is a very simple beacon detection script which works by breaking a traffic
# feed into [precision] length bins.  The distance between bins is calculated and
# the median value is used as representative of the distance.  If all the distances
# are within tolerance% of the median value, the traffic is treated as a beacon.

import sys

if len(sys.argv) >= 3:
    precision = int(sys.argv[1])
    tolerance = float(sys.argv[2])
else:
```

```
        sys.stderr.write("Specify the precision and tolerance\n")

starting_epoch = -1
if len(sys.argv) >= 4:
    starting_epoch = int(sys.argv[3])

current_ip = ''

def process_epoch_info(bins):
    a = bins.keys()
    a.sort()
    distances = []
    # We create a table of distances between the bins
    for i in range(0, len(a) -1):
        distances.append(a[i + 1] - a[i])

    distances.sort()
    median = distances(len(distances)/2)
    tolerance_range = (median - tolerance * median, median + tolerance *median)
    # Now we check bins
    count = 0
    for i in distances:
        if (i >= tolerance_range[0]) and (i <= tolerance_range[1]):
            count+=1
    return count, len(distances)


bins = {}    # Checklist of bins hit during construction; sorted and
             # compared later.  AA be cause it's really a set and I
             # should start using those.
results = {} # Associate array containing the results of the binning
             # analysis, dumped during the final report

# We start reading in data; for each line I'm building a table of
# beaconing events.  The beaconing events are simply indications that
# traffic 'occurred' at time X.  The size of the traffic, how often it occurred,
# how many flows is irrelevant.  Something happened, or it didnt.
for i in sys.stdin.readlines():
    ip, time = i.split('|')[0:2]
    if ip != current_ip:
        results[ip] = process_epoch_info(bins)
        bins = {}

    if starting_epoch == -1:
        starting_epoch = time - (time % 86400) # Sets it to midnight of that day
    bin = (time - starting_epoch) / precision
    bins[bin] = 1

a = bins.sort()
for i in a:
    print "%15s|%5d|%5d|%8.4f" % (ip, bins[a][0], bins[a][1],
                                  100.0 * (float(bins[a[0]])/float(bins[a[1]])))
```

The second stage of beacon detection (as usual) is inventory management. An enormous number of legitimate applications, as we saw earlier, transmit data periodically. NTP, routing protocols, and AV tools all dial home on a regular basis for information updates. SSH also tends to show periodic behavior, because administrators run periodic maintenance tasks via the protocol.

File Transfers/Raiding

Data theft is still the most basic form of attack on a database or website, *especially* if the website is internal or an otherwise protected resource. For lack of a better term, I'll use *raiding* to denote copying a website or database in order to later disseminate, dump, or sell the information. The difference between raiding and legitimate access is a matter of degree, as the point of any server is to serve data.

Obviously, raiding should result in a change in traffic volume. Raiding is usually conducted quickly (possibly while someone is packing up her cubicle) and often relies on automated tools such as *wget*. It's possible to subtly raid, but that would require the attacker to have both the time to slowly extract data and the patience to do so.

Volume is one of the easiest ways to identify a raid. The first step is building up a model of the normal volume originating from a host over time. The *calibrate_raid.py* script in Example 12-2 provides thresholds for volume over time, as well as a table of results to plot.

Example 12-2. A raid detection script

```python
#!/usr/bin/env python
#
# calibrate_raid.py
#
# input:
#       Nothing
# output:
#       writes a report containing a time series and volume estimates to stdout
# command_line
# calibrate_raid.py start_date end_date ip_address server_port period_size
#
# start_date: The date to begin the query on
# end_date: The date to end the query on
# ip_address: the server address to query
# server_port: the port of the server to query
# period_size: the size of the periods to use for modeling the time
#
# Given a particular IP address, this generates a time series (via rwcount)
# and a breakdown on what the expected values at the 90-100% thresholds would
# be.  The count output can then be run through a visualizer in order to
# check for outliers or anomalies.
#
import sys,os,tempfile
```

```
start_date = sys.argv[1]
end_date = sys.argv[2]
ip_address = sys.argv[3]
server_port = int(sys.argv[4])
period_size = int(size.arg[5])


if __name__ == '__main__':
    fh, temp_countfn = tempfile.mkstemp()
    os.close(fh)
    # Note that the filter call uses the IP address as the source, and the
    # server port as the source.  We're pulling out flows that originated
    # FROM the server, which means that they should be the data from the
    # file transfer.  If we used daddress/dport, we'd be logging the
    # (much smaller) requests to the server from the clients.
    #
    os.system(('rwfilter --saddress=%s --sport=%d --start-date=%s ',
               '--end-date=%s --pass=stdout | rwcount --epoch-slots',
               ' --bin-size=%d --no-title > %s') % (
                    ip_address, server_port, start_date, end_date, period_size,
                    temp_countfn))

    # A note on the filtering I'm doing here.  You *could* rwfilter to
    # only include 4-packet or above sessions, therefore avoiding the
    # scan responses.  However, those *should* be minuscule, and
    # therefore I elect not to in this case.


    # Load the count file into memory and add some structure
    #
    a = open(temp_countfn, 'r')
    # We're basically just throwing everything into a histogram, so I need
    # to establish a min and max
    min = 99999999999L
    max = -1
    data = {}
    for i in a.readlines():
        time, records, bytes, packets = map(lambda x:float(x),
                                            i[:-1].split('|')[0:4])
        if bytes < min:
            min = bytes
        if bytes > max:
            max = bytes
        data[time] = (records, bytes, packets)
    a.close()
    os.unlink(temp_countfn)
    # Build a histogram with hist_size slots
    histogram = []
    hist_size = 100
    for i in range(0,hist_size):
        histogram.append(0)
    bin_size = (max - min) / hist_size
```

```
total_entries = len(data.values)
for records, bytes, packets in data.values():
    bin_index = (bytes - min)/bin_size
    histogram[bin_index] += 1

# Now we calculate the thresholds from 90 to 100%
thresholds = []
for i in range(90, 100):
    thresholds.append(0.01 * i * total_entries)
total = 0
last_match = 0 # index in thresholds where we stopped
# Step 1, we dump the thresholds
for i in range(0, hist_size):
    total += histogram[i]
    if total >= thresholds[last_match]:
        while thresholds[last_match] < total:
            print "%3d%% | %d" % (90 + last_match, (i * bin_size) + min)
a = data.keys()
a.sort()
for i in a:
    print "%15d|%10d|%10d|%10d" % (i, data[i][0], data[i][1], data[i][2])
```

Visualization is critical when calibrating volume thresholds for detecting raiding or other raiding anomalies. We've discussed the problem with standard deviations in Chapter 10, and a histogram is the easiest way to determine whether a distribution is even remotely Gaussian. In my experience, a surprising number of services regularly raid hosts—web spiders and the Internet archive being among the more notable examples. If a site is strictly internal, backups and internal mirroring are common false positives.

Visualization can identify these outliers. The example in Figure 12-3 shows that the overwhelming majority of traffic occurs below about 1000 MB/10 min, but those few outliers above 2000 MB/10 min will cause problems for *calibrate_raid.py* and most training algorithms. Once you have identified the outliers, you can record them in a whitelist and remove them from the filter command using --not-dipset. You can then use *rwcount* to set up a simple alert mechanism.

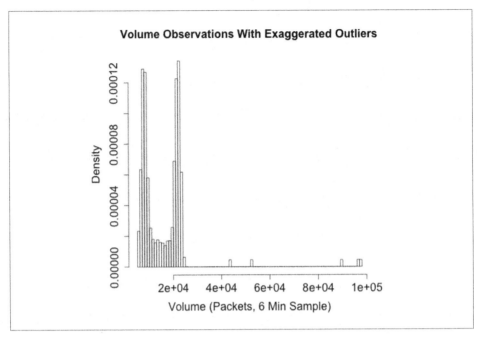

Figure 12-3. Traffic volume with outliers; determining the origin and cause of outliers will reduce alerts

Locality

Locality is the tendency of references (memory locations, URLs, IP addresses) to cluster together. For example, if you track the web pages visited by a user over time, you will find that the majority of pages are located in a small and predictable number of sites (spatial locality), and that users tend to visit the same number of sites over and over (temporal locality). Locality is a well understood concept in computer science, and serves as the foundation of caching, CDNs, and reverse proxies.

Locality is particularly useful as a complement to volumetric analysis because users are generally predictable. Users visit a small number of sites and talk to a small number of people, and while there are occasional changes, we can model this behavior using a *working set*.

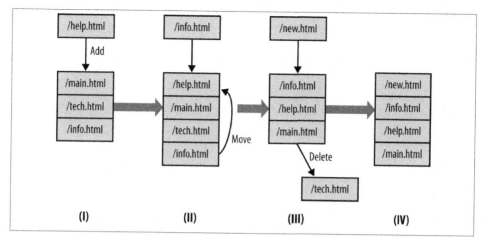

Figure 12-4. A Working Set in Operation

Figure 12-4 is a graphical example of a working set in operation. In this example, the working set is implemented as an LRU (Least Recently Used) queue of fixed size (in this case, four references in the queue). This working set is tracking web surfing, so it gets fed URLs from an HTTP server logfile and adds them to the stack. Working sets only keep one copy of every reference they see, so a four-reference set like the one shown in Figure 12-4 will only show four references. When a working set receives a reference, it does one of three things:

1. If there are empty references left, the new reference is enqueued at the back of the queue (I to II).

2. If the queue is filled AND the reference is present, the reference is moved to the back of the queue.

3. If the queue is filled AND the reference is NOT present, then the reference is enqueued at the back of the queue, and the reference at the front of the queue is removed.

The code in Example 12-3 shows an LRU working set model in python.

Example 12-3. Calculating working set characteristics

```
#!/usr/bin/env python
#
#
# Describe the locality of a host using working_set depth analysis.
# Inputs:
#        stdin - a sequence of tags
#
# Command line args:
#        first: working_set depth
```

```python
import sys

try:
    working_set_depth = int(sys.argv[1])
except:
    sys.stderr.write("Specify a working_set depth at the command line\n")
    sys.exit(-1)

working_set = []

i = sys.stdin.readline()
total_processed = 0
total_popped = 0
unique_symbols = {}
while i != '':
    value = i[:-1] #Ditch the obligatory \n
    unique_symbols[value] = 1 # Add in the symbol
    total_processed += 1
    try:
        vind = working_set.index(value)
    except:
        vind = -1

    if (vind == -1):
        # Value isn't present as an LRU cache; delete the
        # least recently used value and store this at the end
        working_set.append(value)
        if len(working_set) > working_set_depth:
            del working_set[0]
        working_set.append(value)
        total_popped +=1
    else:
        # Most recently used value; move it to the end of the working_set
        del working_set[vind]

# Calculate probability of replacement stat
p_replace = 100.0 * (float(total_popped)/float(total_processed))

print "%10d %10d %10d %8.4f" % (total_processed, unique_symbols,
                                working_set_depth, p_replace)
```

Figure 12-5 shows an example of what working sets will look like. This figure plots the probability of replacing a value in the working set as a function of the working set size. Two different sets are compared here: a completely random set where references are picked from a set of 10 million symbols, and a model of user activity using a Pareto distribution. The Pareto model is adequate for modeling normal user activity, if actually a bit *less* stable than users under normal circumstances.

Note the "knee" in the Pareto model, while the random model remains consistent at a 100% replacement rate. Working sets generally have an ideal size after which increasing the set's size is counterproductive. This knee is representative of this phenomenon—you can see that the probability of replacement drops slightly before the knee, but remains effectively stable afterward.

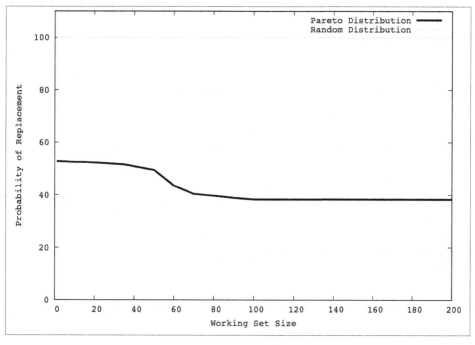

Figure 12-5. Working set analysis

The value of working sets is that once they're calibrated, they reduce user habit down to two parameters: the size of the queue modeling the set and the probability that a reference will result in a queue replacement.

DDoS, Flash Crowds, and Resource Exhaustion

Denial of Service (DoS) is a goal, not a specific strategy. A DoS results in a host that cannot be reached from remote locations. Most DoS attacks are implemented as a Distributed Denial of Service (DDoS) attack in which the attacker uses a network of captured hosts in order to implement the DoS. There are several ways an attacker can implement DoS, including but not limited to:

Service level exhaustion
> The targeted host runs a publicly accessible service. Using a botnet, the attacker starts a set of clients on the target, each conducting some trivial but service-specific interaction (such as fetching the home page of a website).

SYN flood

The SYN flood is the classic DDoS attack. Given a target with an open TCP port, the attacker sends clients against the attacker. The clients don't use the service on the port, but simply open connections using a SYN packet and leave the connection open.

Bandwidth exhaustion

Instead of targeting a host, the attacker sends a massive flood of garbage traffic towards the host, intending to overwhelm the connection between the router and the target.

And you shouldn't ignore a simple insider attack: the attacker walks over to the physical server and disconnects it.

All these tactics produce the same result, but each tactic will appear differently in network traffic and may require different mitigation techniques. Exactly how many resources the attacker needs is a function of how the attacker implements DDoS. As a rule of thumb, the higher up an attack is on the OSI model, the more stress it places on the target and the fewer bots are required by the attacker. For example, bandwidth exhaustion hits the router and basically has to exhaust the router interface. SYN flooding, the classic DDoS attack, has to simply exhaust the target's TCP stack. At higher levels, tools like Slowloris (*http://ha.ckers.org/slowloris*) effectively create a partial HTTP connection, exhausting the resources of the web server.

This has several advantages from an attacker's perspective. Fewer resources consumed means fewer bots involved and a legitimate session is more likely to be allowed through by a firewall that might block a packet crafted to attack the IP or TCP layer.

DDoS and Routing Infrastructure

DDoS attacks aimed specifically at routing infrastructure will produce collateral damage. Consider a simple network like the one in Figure 12-6; the heavy line shows the path of the attack to subnetwork C. The attacker hitting subnetwork C is exhausting not just the connection at C, but also the router's connection to the Internet. Consequently, hosts on networks A and B will not be able to reach the Internet and will see their incoming Internet traffic effectively drop to zero.

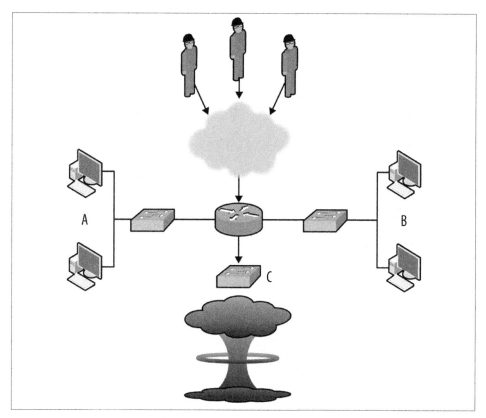

Figure 12-6. DDoS collateral damage

This type of problem is not uncommon on colocated services, and emphasizes that DDoS defense is rooted at network infrastructure. I am, in the long run, deeply curious to see how cloud computing and DDoS are going to marry. Cloud computing enables defenders to run highly distributed services across the Internet's routing infrastructure. This, in turn, increases the resources the attacker needs to take out a single defender.

With DoS attacks, the most common false positives are *flash crowds* and cable cuts. A flash crowd is a sudden influx of legitimate traffic to a site in response to some kind of announcement or notification. Alternate names for flash crowds such as *SlashDot effect*, *farking*, or *Reddit effect* provide a good explanation of what's going on.

These different classes of attacks are usually easily distinguished by looking at a graph of incoming traffic. Some idealized images are shown in Figure 12-7, which explain the basic phenomena.

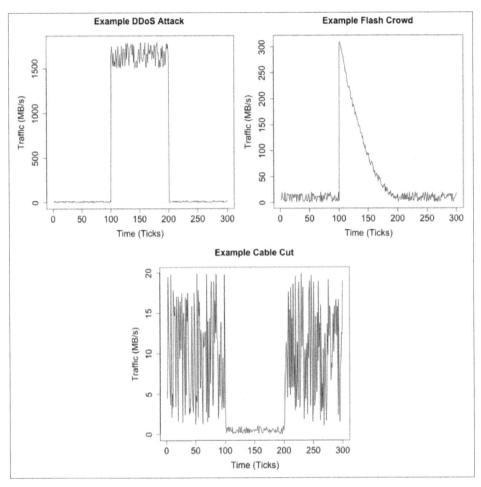

Figure 12-7. Different classes of bandwidth exhaustion

The images in Figure 12-7 describe three different classes of bandwidth exhaustion: a DDoS, a flash crowd, and a cable cut or other infrastructure failure. Each plot is of incoming traffic and equivalent to sitting right at the sensor. The differences between the plots reflect the phenomena causing the problems.

DDoS attacks are mechanical. The attack usually switches on and off instantly, as the attacker is issuing commands remotely to a network of bots. When a DDoS starts, it almost instantly consumes as much bandwidth as available. In many DDoS plots, the upper limit on the plot is dictated by the networking infrastructure: if you have a 10 GB pipe, the plot maxes at 10 GB. DDoS attacks are also *consistent*. Once they start, they generally keep humming along at about the same volume. Most of the time, the attacker has grossly overprovisioned the attack. Bots are being removed while the attack goes on, but there's more than enough to consume all available bandwidth even if a significant fraction are knocked offline.

DDoS mitigation is an endurance contest. The best defense is to provision out bandwidth before the attack starts. Once an attack actually occurs, the best you can do at any particular location is to try to identify patterns in the traffic and block the ones causing the most damage. Examples of patterns to look for include:

- Identifying a core audience for the target and limiting traffic to the core audience. The audience may be identified by using IP address, netblock, country code, or language, among other attributes. What is critical is that the audience has a limited overlap with the attacker set. The script in Example 12-4 provides a mechanism for ordering /24s by the difference between two sets: historical users that you trust and new users whom you suspect of being part of a DDoS attack.

- Spoofed attacks are *occasionally* identifiable by some flaw in the spoofing. The random number generator for the spoof might set all addresses to x.x.x.1, as an example.

Example 12-4. An example script for ordering blocks

```
#!/usr/bin/env python
#
# ddos_intersection.py
#
# input:
#       Nothing
# output:
#       A report comparing the number of addresses in two sets, ordered by the
#       largest number of hosts in set A which are not present in set B.
#
# command_line
# ddos_intersection.py historical_set ddos_set
#
# historical_set: a set of historical data giving external addresses
# which have historically spoken to a particular host or network
# ddos_set: a set of data from a ddos attack on the host
# This is going to work off of /24's for simplicity.
#
import sys,os,tempfile

historical_setfn = sys.argv[1]
ddos_setfn = sys.argv[2]
blocksize = int(sys.argv[3])

mask_fh, mask_fn = tempfile.mkstemp()
os.close(mask_fh)
os.unlink(mask_fn)

os.system(('rwsettool --mask=24 --output-path=stdout %s | ' +
                    ' rwsetcat | sed 's/$/\/24/' | rwsetbuild stdin %s') %
```

```
                    (historical_setfn, mask_fn))

bins = {}
# Read and store all the /24's in the historical data
a = os.popen(('rwsettool --difference %s %s --output-path=stdout | ',
              'rwsetcat --network-structure=C') % (mask_fn, historical_setfn),'r')
# First column is historical, second column is ddos
for i in a.readlines():
    address, count = i[:-1].split('|')[0:2]
    bins[address] = [int(count), 0]

a.close()
# Repeat the process with all the data in the ddos set
a = os.popen(('rwsettool --difference %s %s --output-path=stdout | ',
              'rwsetcat --network-structure=C') % (mask_fn, ddos_setfn),'r')
for i in a.readlines():
    address, count = i[:-1].split('|')[0:2]
    # I'm intersecting the maskfile again, since I originally intersected it against
    # the file I generated the maskfile from, any address that I find in the file
    # will already be in the bins associative array
    bins[address][1] = int(count)

#
# Now we order the contents of the bins.  This script is implicitly written to
# support a whitelist-based approach -- addresses which appear in the historical
# data are candidates for whitelisting, all other addresses will be blocked.
# We order the candidate blocks in terms of the number of historical addresses
# allowed in, decreasing for every attacker address allowed in.
address_list = bins.items()
address_list.sort(lambda x,y:(y[1][0]-x[1][0])-(y[1][1]-x[1][1]))
print "%20s|%10s|%10s" % ("Block", "Not-DDoS", "DDoS")
for address, result in address_list:
    print "%20s|%10d|%10d" % (address, bins[address][0], bins[address][1])
```

This type of filtering works more effectively if the attack is focused on striking a specific
service, such as DDoSing a web server with HTTP requests. If the attacker is instead
focused on traffic flooding a router interface, the best defenses will normally lie up-
stream from you.

As discussed in Chapter 11, people are impatient where machines are not, and this
behavior is the easiest way to differentiate flash crowds from DDoS attacks. As the flash
crowd plot in Figure 12-7 shows, when the event occurs, the initial burst of bandwidth
is followed by a rapid falloff. The falloff is because people have discovered that they can't
reach the targeted site and have moved on to more interesting pastures until some later
time.

Flash crowds are public affairs—for some reason, *somebody* publicized the target. As a
result, it's often possible to figure out the origin of the flash crowd. For example, HTTP
referrer logs will include a reference to the site. Googling the targeted site is often a good

option. If you are familiar with the press and news associated with your site, this is also a good option.

Cable cuts and mechanical failures will result in an actual drop in traffic. This is shown in the cable cut figure, where all of a sudden traffic goes to zero. When this happens, the first follow-up step is to try to generate some traffic *to* the target, and ensure that the problem is actually a failure in traffic and not a failure in the detector. After that, you need to bring an alternate system online and then research the cause of the failure.

DDoS and Force Multipliers

Functionally, DDoSes are wars of attrition: how much traffic can the attacker throw at the target, and how can the target compensate for that bandwidth? Attackers can improve the impact of their attack through a couple of different strategies: they can acquire more resources, attack at different layers of the stack, and rely on Internet infrastructure to inflict additional damage. Each of these techniques effectively serves as a force multiplier for attackers, increasing the havoc with the same number of bots under their control.

The process of resource acquisition is really up to the attacker. The modern Internet underground provides a mature market for the rental and use of botnets. An alternative approach, used notably by some of Anonymous, involves volunteers. Anonymous has developed a family of JavaScript and C# DDoS tools under the monicker "LOIC" (Low Orbit Ion Cannon) to conduct DDoS attacks. The LOIC family of tools are, in comparison to hardcore malware, fairly primitive. Arguably, they're not intended to be anything more than that given their hacktivist audience.

These techniques rely on processing asymmetry: the attacker in some way juggles operations so that the processing demand on the server per connection is higher than the processing demand on the client. Development decisions will impact a system's vulnerability to a higher-level DDoS.[1]

Attackers can also rely on Internet infrastructure to conduct attacks. This is generally done by taking a response service and sending the response to a forged target address. The classic example of this, the smurf attack, consisted of a ping where the host A, wanting to DDoS site B, sends a spoofed ping to a broadcast address. Every host receiving the ping (i.e., everything sharing the broadcast address) then drowns the target in responses. The most common modern form of this attack uses *DNS reflection*: the attacker sends a spoofed request to a DNS resolver, which then sends an inordinately informative and helpfully large packet in response.

---

1. This is true historically as well. Fax machines are subject to *black fax* attacks, where the attacker sends an entirely black page and wastes toner.

Applying Volume and Locality Analysis

The phenomena discussed in this chapter are detectable using a number of different approaches. In general, the problem is not so much detecting them as differentiating malicious activity from legitimate but similar-appearing activity. In this section, we discuss a number of different ways to build detectors and limit false positives.

Data Selection

Traffic data is noisy, and there's little correlation between the volume of traffic and the malice of a phenomenon. An attacker can control a network using *ssh* and generate much less traffic than a legitimate user sending an attachment over email. The basic noisiness of the data is further exacerbated by the presence of garbage traffic such as scanning and other background radiation (see Chapter 11 for more information on this).

The most obvious values to work with when examining volume are byte and packet counts over a period. They are also generally so fantastically noisy that you're best off using them to identify DDoS and raiding attacks and little else.

Because the values are so noisy and so easily disrupted, I prefer working with constructed value such as a flow. NetFlow groups traffic into session approximations; I can then filter the flows on different behaviors, such as:

- Filtering traffic that talks only to legitimate hosts and not to dark space, this approach requires access to a current map of the network, as discussed in Chapter 15.

- Splitting short TCP sessions (four packets or less) from longer sessions, or looking for other indications that a session is legitimate, such as the presence of a PSH flag. See Chapter 11 for more discussion on this behavior.

- Further partitioning traffic into command, fumble, and file transfers. This approach, discussed in Chapter 14, extends the filtering process to different classes of traffic, some of which should be rare.

- Using simple volume thresholds. Instead of recording the byte count, for example, record the number of 100, 1000, 10000, and 100000+ byte flows received. This will reduce the noise you're dealing with.

Whenever you're doing this kind of filtering, it's important to not simply throw out the data, but actually partition it. For example, if you count thresholded volume, record the 1–100, 100+, 1000+, 10000+ and 100000+ values as separate time series. The reason for partitioning the data is purely paranoia. Any time you introduce a hard rule for what data you're going to ignore, you've created an opening for an attacker to imitate the ignored data.

A less noisy alternative to volume counts are values such as the number of IP addresses reaching a network or the number of unique URLs fetched. These values are more computationally expensive to calculate as they require distinguishing individual values; this can be done using a tool like *rwset* in the SiLK suite or with an associative array. Address counts are generally more stable than volume counts, but at least splitting off the hosts who are only scanning is (again) a good idea to reduce the noise.

Example 12-5 illustrates how to apply filtering and partitioning to flow data in order to produce time series data.

Example 12-5. A simple time series output application

```
#
#
# gen_timeseries.py
#
# Generates a timeseries output by reading flow records and partitioning
# the data in this case, into short (<=4 packet) TCP flows, and long
# (>4 packet) TCP flows.
#
# Output
# Time <bytes> <packets> <addresses> <long bytes> <long packets> <long addresses>
#
# Takes as input
# rwcut --fields=sip,dip,bytes,packets,stime --epoch-time --no-title
#
# We assume that the records are chronologically ordered, that is, no record
# will produce an stime earlier than the records preceding it in the
# output.

import sys
current_time = sys.maxint
start_time = sys.maxint
bin_size = 300 # We'll use five minute bins for convenience
ip_set_long = set()
ip_set_short = set()
byte_count_long = 0
byte_count_short = 0
packet_count_long = 0
packet_count_short = 0
for i in sys.stdin.readlines():
    sip, dip, bytes, packets, stime = i[:-1].split('|')[0:5]
    # convert the non integer values
    bytes, packets, stime = map(lambda x: int(float(x)), (bytes, packets, stime))
    # Now we check the time binning; if we're onto a new bin, dump and
    # reset the contents
    if (stime < current_time) or (stime > current_time + bin_size):
        ip_set_long = set()
        ip_set_short = set()
        byte_count_long = byte_count_short = 0
    packet_count_long = packet_count_short = 0
```

```
            if (current_time == sys.maxint):
                # Set the time to a 5 minute period at the start of the
                # currently observed epoch.  This is done in order to
                # ensure that the time values are always some multiple
                # of five minutes apart, as opposed to dumping something
                # at t, t+307, t+619 and so on.
                current_time = stime - (stime % bin_size)
            else:
                # Now we output results
                print "%10d %10d %10d %10d %10d %10d %10d" % (
                    current_time, len(ip_set_short), byte_count_short,
                    packet_count_short,len(ip_set_long), byte_count_long,
                    packet_count_long)
                current_time = stime - (stime % bin_size)
        else:
            # Instead of printing, we're just adding up data
            # First, determine if the flow is long or short
            if (packets <= 4):
                # flow is short
                byte_count_short += bytes
                packet_count_short += packets
                ip_set_short.update([sip,dip])
            else:
                byte_count_long += bytes
                packet_count_long += packets
                ip_set_long.update([sip,dip])

if byte_count_long + byte_count_short != 0:
    # Final print line check
    print "%10d %10d %10d %10d %10d %10d %10d" % (
                    current_time, len(ip_set_short), byte_count_short,
                packet_count_short,len(ip_set_long), byte_count_long,
                    packet_count_long)
```

Keep track of what you're partitioning and analyzing. For example, if you decide to calculate thresholds for a volume-based alarm only on sessions from Bulgaria that have at least 100 bytes, then you need to make sure that approach is used to calculate future thresholds, but that it's also documented, and why.

Using Volume as an Alarm

The easiest way to construct a volume-based alarm is to calculate a histogram and then pick thresholds based on the probability that a sample will exceed the observed threshold. *calibrate_raid* in Example 12-2 is a good example of this kind of threshold calculation. When generating alarms, consider the time of day issues discussed in "The Workday and Its Impact on Network Traffic Volume" on page 237, and whether you want multiple models; a single model will normally cost you precision. Also, when considering thresholds, consider the impact of unusually *low* values and whether they merit investigation.

Given the noisiness of traffic volume data, expect a significant number of false positives. Most false positives for volume breaches come from hosts that have a legitimate reason for copying or archiving a target, such as a web crawler or archiving software. Several of the IDS mitigation techniques discussed in "Enhancing IDS Response" on page 143 are useful here; in particular, whitelisting anomalies after identifying that the source is innocuous and rolling up events.

Using Beaconing as an Alarm

Beaconing is used to detect a host that is consistently communicating with other hosts. To identify malicious activity, beaconing is primarily used to identify communications with a botnet command and control server. To detect beacons, you identify hosts that communicate *consistently* over a time window, as done with *find_beacons.py*.

Beacon detection runs into an enormous number of false positives because software updates, AV updates, and even SSH cron jobs have consistent and predictable intervals. Beacon detection consequently depends heavily on inventory management. After receiving an alert, you will have to determine whether a beaconing host has a legitimate justification, which you can do if the beaconing is from a known protocol, is communicating with a legitimate host, or provides other evidence that the traffic is *not* botnet C&C traffic. Once identified as legitimate, the indicia of the beacon (the address and likely the port used for communication) should be recorded to prevent further false positives.

Also of import are hosts that are *supposed* to be beaconing, but don't. This is particularly critical when dealing with AV software, because attackers often disable AV when converting a newly owned host. Checking to see that all the hosts that are supposed to visit an update site do so is a useful alternative alarm.

Using Locality as an Alarm

Locality measures user habits. The advantage of the working set model is that it provides room for those habits to break. Although people are predictable, they do mail new contacts or visit new websites at irregular intervals. Locality-based alarms are consequently useful for measuring changes in user habits, such as differentiating the normal user of a website from someone who is raiding it, or identifying when a site's audience changes during a DDoS.

Locality is a useful complement to volume-based detection for identifying raiding. A host that is raiding the site or otherwise scanning it will demonstrate minimal locality, as it will want to visit all the pages on the site as quickly as possible. In order to determine whether or not a host is raiding, look at what the host is fetching and the speed at which the host is working.

The most common false positives in this case are search engines and bots such as Googlebot. A well-behaved bot can be identified by its User-Agent string, and if the host is *not* identified as a bot by that string, you have a dangerous host.

A working set model can also be applied to a server rather than individual users. Such a working set is going to be considerably larger than a user profile, but it is possible to use that set to track the core audience of a website or an SSH server.

Engineering Solutions

Raid detection is a good example of a scenario in which you can apply analysis and are probably better off *not* building a detector. The histograms generated by *calibrate_raid.py* or analysis done by counting the expected volume a user pulls over a day is ultimately about determining how much data a user will realistically access from a server.

This same information can be used to impose rate limits on the servers. Instead of firing off an alert when a user exceeds this threshold, use a rate limiting module (such as Apache's Quota) to cut the user off. If you're worried about user revolt, set the threshold to 200% of the maximum you observe and identify outliers who need special permissions to exceed even that high threshold.

This approach is going to be most effective when you've got a server whose data radically exceeds the average usage of any one user. If people access a server and use less than a megabyte of traffic a day, whereas the server has gigabytes of data, you've got an easily defensible target.

Further Reading

1. Avril Coghlan, "A Little Book of R for Time Series" (*http://bit.ly/bookofr*)
2. John McHugh and Carrie Gates, "Locality: A New Paradigm in Anomaly Detection," Proceedings of the 2003 New Security Paradigms Workshop.

## CHAPTER 13

Graph Analysis

A *graph* is a mathematical construct composed of one or more *nodes* (or *vertices*) connected together by one or more *links* (or *edges*). Graphs are an effective way to describe communication without getting lost in the weeds. They can be used to model connectivity and provide a comprehensive view of that connectivity while abstracting away details such as packet sizes and session length. Additionally, graph attributes such as centrality can be used to identify critical nodes in a network. Finally, many important protocols (in particular, SMTP and routing) rely on algorithms that model their particular network as a graph.

The remainder of this chapter is focused on the analytic properties of graphs. We begin by describing what a graph is and then developing examples for major attributes: shortest paths, centrality, clusters, and clustering coefficient.

Graph Attributes: What Is a Graph?

A graph is a mathematical representation of a collection of objects and their interrelationships. Originally developed in 1736 by Leonhard Euler to address the problem of crossing the bridges of Konigsberg, graphs have since been used to model everything from the core members of conspiracies to the frequency of sounds uttered in the English language. Graphs are an extremely powerful and flexible descriptive tool, and that power comes because they are extremely fungible. Researchers in mathematics, engineering, and sociology have developed an extensive set of constructed and observed graph attributes that can be used to model various behaviors. The first challenge in using graphs is deciding which attributes you need and how to derive them. The following attributes represent a subset of what can be done with graphs, and are chosen for their direct relevance to the traffic models built later. Any good book on graph theory will include more attributes because at some point, someone has tried just about anything with a graph.

At the absolute minimum, a graph is composed of *nodes* and *links*, where a link is a connection between exactly two nodes. A link can be *directed* or *undirected*; if a link is directed, then it has an *origin* and a *destination*. Conventionally, a graph is either composed entirely of directed links, or entirely of undirected links. If a graph is undirected, then each node has a *degree*, which is the number of links connected to that node. Nodes in a directed graph have an *indegree*, which is the number of links with a destination that is that node, and an *outdegree*, which is the number of links whose origin is the node.

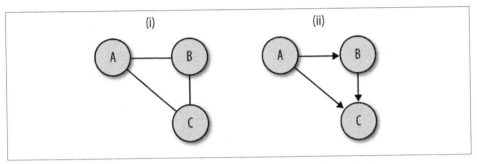

Figure 13-1. Directed and undirected graphs: in (i), the graph is undirected and each node has degree 2; in (ii), the graph is directed: node a has outdegree 2, indegree 0; node b has outdegree 1, indegree 1; node c has outdegree 0, indegree 2

In network traffic logs, there are a number of candidates for conversion to graphs. In flow data, IP addresses can be used as nodes and the existence of a flow between them can be used as links. In HTTP server logs, nodes can be individual pages linked together by `Referer` headers. In mail logs, email addresses can be nodes, and the links between them can be expressed as mail. Anything expressed as a communication from point A to point B is a suitable candidate.

A disclaimer about code in this section of the book: it is intended primarily for educational purposes, so in the interests of clearly pointing out how various algorithms or numbers work, I've avoided optimization and a lot of the exception trapping I'd use in production code. This is particularly important when dealing with graph analysis, since graph algorithms are notoriously expensive. There are a number of good libraries available for doing graph analysis, and they will process complex graphs much more efficiently than anything I hack together here.

The script in Example 13-1 can create directed or undirected graphs from lists of pairs (for example, the output of rwcut `--field=1,2 --no-title --delim=' '`). There are a couple of methods under the hood for implementing graphs; in this case, I'm using *adjacency lists*, which I feel are the most intuitively obvious. In an adjacency list implementation, each node maintains a table of all the links adjacent to it.

Example 13-1. Basic graphs

```python
#!/usr/bin/env python
#
# basic_graph.py
#
# Library
# Provides:
#         Graph Object, which as a constructor takes a flow file
#
import os, sys

class UndirGraph:
    """ An undirected, unweighted graph class. This also serves as the base class
    for all other graph implementations in this chapter """
    def add_node(self, node_id):
        self.nodes.add(node_id)

    def add_link(self, node_source, node_dest):
        self.add_node(node_source)
        self.add_node(node_dest)
        if not self.links.has_key(node_source):
            self.links[node_source] = {}
        self.links[node_source][node_dest] = 1
        if not self.links.has_key(node_dest):
            self.links[node_dest] = {}
        self.links[node_dest][node_source] = 1
        return

    def count_links(self):
        total = 0
        for i in self.links.keys():
            total += len(self.links[i].keys())
        return total/2 # Compensating for link doubling in undirected graph

    def neighbors(self, address):
        # Returns a list of all the nodes adjacent to the node address,
        # returns an empty list of there are no ndoes (technically impossible with
        # these construction rules, but hey).
        if self.nodes.has_key(address):
            return self.links[address].keys()
        else:
            return None

    def __str__(self):
        return 'Undirected graph with %d nodes and %d links' % (len(self.nodes),
                                                        self.count_links())

    def adjacent(self, sip, dip):
        # Note, we've defined the graph as undirected during construction,
        # consequently links only has to return the source.
        if self.links.has_key(sip):
```

```
                if self.links[sip].has_key(dip):
                    return True

        def __init__(self):
            #
            # This graph is implemented using adjacency lists; every node has
            # a key in the links hashtable, and the resulting value is another hashtable.
            #
            # The nodes table is redundant for undirected graphs, since the existence of
            # a link between X and Y implies a link between Y and X, but in the case of
            # directed graphs it'll providea speedup if I'm just looking for a
            # particular node.
            self.links = {}
            self.nodes = set()

class DirGraph(UndirGraph):
    def add_link(self, node_source, node_dest):
        # Note that in comparison to the undirected graph, we only
        # add links in one direction
        self.add_node(node_source)
        self.add_node(node_dest)
        if not self.links.has_key(node_source):
            self.links[node_source] = {}
        self.links[node_source][node_dest] = 1
        return

    def count_links(self):
        # This had to be changed from the original count_links since I'm now
        # using an undirected graph.
        total = 0
        for i in self.links.keys():
            total += len(self.links[i].keys())
        return total


if __name__ == '__main__':
    #
    # This is a stub executable that will create and then render an
    # undirected graph assuming that it receives some kind of
    # space delimited set of (source, dest) pairs on input
    #
    a = sys.stdin.readlines()
    tgt_graph = DirGraph()
    for i in a:
        source, dest = i.split()[0:2]
        tgt_graph.add_link(source, dest)
    print tgt_graph
    print "Links:"
    for i in tgt_graph.links.keys():
        dest_links = ' '.join(tgt_graph.links[i].keys())
        print '%s: %s' % (i, dest_links)
```

Labeling, Weight, and Paths

On a graph, a *path* is a set of links connecting two nodes. In a directed graph, paths follow the direction of the link, while in an undirected graph they can move in either direction. Of particular importance in graph analysis are *shortest paths*, which as the name implies are the shortest set of links required to get from point A to point B (see Example 13-2).

Example 13-2. An shortest path algorithm

```python
#!/usr/bin/env python
#
# apsp.py -- implemented weighted paths and dijkstra's algorithm

import sys,os,basic_graph

class WeightedGraph(basic_graph.UndirGraph):
    def add_link(self, node_source, node_dest, weight):
        # Weighted bidirectional link aid, note that
        # we keep the aa, but now instead of simply setting the value to
        # 1, we add the weight value.  This reverts to an unweighted
        # graph if we always use the same weight.
        self.add_node(node_source)
        self.add_node(node_dest)
        if not self.links.has_key(node_source):
            self.links[node_source] = {}
        if not self.links[node_source].has_key(node_dest):
            self.links[node_source][node_dest] = 0
```

```
        self.links[node_source][node_dest] += weight
        if not self.links.has_key(node_dest):
            self.links[node_dest] = {}
        if not self.links[node_dest].has_key(node_source):
            self.links[node_dest][node_source] = 0
        self.links[node_dest][node_source] += weight

    def dijkstra(self, node_source):
        # Given a source node, create a map of paths for each vertex
        D = {}  # Tentative distnace table
        P = {}  # predecessor table

        # The predecessor table exploits a unique feature of shortest paths,
        # every subpath of a shortest path is itself a shortest path, so if
        # you find that (B,C,D) is the shortest path from A to E, then
        # (B,C) is the shortest path from A to D.  All you have to do is keep
        # track of the predecessor and walk backwards.

        infy = 999999999999  # Shorthand for infinite
        for i in self.nodes:
            D[i] = infy
            P[i] = None

        D[node_source] = 0
        node_list = list(self.nodes)
        while node_list != []:
            current_distance = infy
            current_node = None
            # Step 1, find the node with the smallest distance, that'll
            # be node_source in the first call as it's the only one
            # where D =0
            for i in node_list:
                if D[i] < current_distance:
                    current_distance = D[i]
                    current_node = i
            node_index = node_list.index(i)
            del node_list[node_index] # Remove it from the list
            if current_distance == infy:
                break # We've exhausted all paths from the node,
                    # everything else is in a different component
            for i in self.neighbors(current_node):
                new_distance = D[current_node] + self.links[current_node][i]
                if new_distance < D[i]:
                    D[i] = new_distance
                    P[i] = current_node
                    node_list.insert(0, i)
        for i in D.keys():
            if D[i] == infy:
                del D[i]
        for i in P.keys():
            if P[i] is None:
                del P[i]
```

```
    return D,P

def apsp(self):
    # Calls dijkstra repeatedly to create an all-pairs shortest paths table
    apsp_table = {}
    for i in self.nodes:
        apsp_table[i] = self.dijkstra(i)
    return apsp_table
```

An alternative formulation of shortest paths uses *weighting*. In a *weighted graph*, links are assigned a numeric weight. When weight is assigned, the shortest path is no longer simply the smallest number of connected links from point A to point B, but the set of links whose total weight is smallest. Figure 13-2 shows these attributes in more detail.

Shortest paths are a fundamental building block in graph analysis. In most routing services, such as Open Shortest Path First (OSPF), finding shortest paths is the goal. As a result, a good number of graph analyses begin by building a table of shortest paths between all the nodes using an All Pairs, Shortest Paths (APSP) algorithm on the graph in order to create a table of all of them. The code in the following sidebar provides an example of using *Dijkstra's Algorithm* on a weighted, undirected, graph to calculate shortest paths.

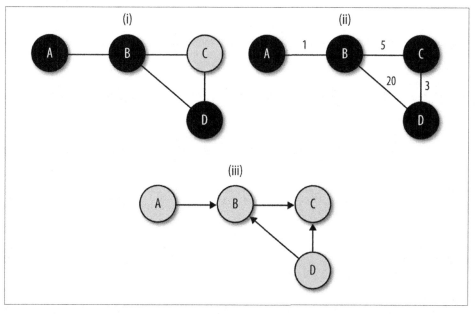

Figure 13-2. Weighting and paths, the shortest path from a to d: (i) in an undirected, unweighted graph, the shortest path involves the least nodes, (ii) in a weighted graph, the shortest path generally has the lowest total weight, (iii) in a directed graph, the shortest path might not be achievable

Dijkstra's algorithm is a good shortest path algorithm that can handle any graph whose link weights are positive. Shortest path algorithms are critical in a number of fields, and there are consequently a huge number of algorithms available depending on the structure of the graph, the construction of the nodes, and the amount of knowledge of the graph that the individual nodes have.

Shortest paths effectively define the distance between nodes on a graph, and serve as the building blocks for a number of other attributes. Of particular importance are *centrality* attributes (see Example 13-3). Centrality is a concept originating in social network analysis; social network analysis models the relationships between entities using graphs and mines the graphs for attributes showing the relationship between these entities in bulk. Centrality, for which there are several measures, is an indicator of how important a node is to that graph's structure.

Example 13-3. Centrality calculation

```
#/usr/bin/env python
#
#
# centrality.py
#
# script which generates centrality statistics for a dataset
#
# input:
# A table of pairs in the form source, destination with a space separating them
# Weight is implicit, the weight of a link is the number of times a pair appears
#
# command_line
# calc_centrality.py n
# n: integer value, the number of elements to return in the report
#
# Output
# 7 Column report of the form rank | betweenness winner | betweenness
# score | degree winner | degree score | closeness winner | closeness
# score
import sys,string
import apsp

n = int(sys.argv[1])

closeness_results = []
degree_results = []
betweenness_results = []

target_graph = apsp.WeightedGraph()

# load up the graph
for i in sys.stdin.readlines():
    source, dest = i[:-1].split()
    target_graph.add_link(source, dest, 1)
```

```
# Calculate degree centrality; the easiest of the bunch since it's just the
# degree
for i in target_graph.nodes:
    degree_results.append((i, len(target_graph.neighbors(i))))

apsp_results = target_graph.apsp()

# Now, calculate the closeness centrality scores
for i in target_graph.nodes:
    dt = apsp_results[i][0] # This is the distance table
    total_distance = reduce(lambda a,b:a+b, dt.values())
    closeness_results.append((i, total_distance))

# Now, we calcualte betweenness centrality scores

bt_table = {}
for i in target_graph.nodes:
    bt_table[i] = 0

for current_node in target_graph.nodes:
    # Reconstruct the shortest paths from the predecessor table;
    # for every entry in the distance table, walk backwards from that
    # entry to the corresponding origin to get the shortest path, then
    # count the nodes in that path on the master bt table
    pred_table = apsp_results[i][1] # We have the predecessor table
    sp_list = apsp_results[i][0]
    if current_node in sp_list.keys():
        path = []
        for working_node in sp_list.keys():
            if working_node != current_node:
                # We should be done with working node at this point, count
                # the nodes there for bt score
                for i in path:
                    bt_table[i] += 1
            else:
                path.append(working_node)
                working_node = pred_table[working_node]

for i in bt_table.keys():
    betweenness_results.append((i,bt_table[i]))

# Order the tables, remember that betweenness and degree use higher score, closeness
# lower score

degree_results.sort(lambda a,b:b[1]-a[1])
betweenness_results.sort(lambda a,b:b[1]-a[1])
closeness_results.sort(lambda a,b:a[1]-b[1])

print "%5s|%15s|%10s|%15s|%10s|%15s|%10s" %
  ("Rank", "Between", "Score", "Degree", "Score","Close", "Score")
for i in range(0, n):
    print "%5d|%15s|%10d|%15s|%10d|%15s|%10d" % ( i + 1,
```

```
                                       str(betweenness_results[i][0]),
                                       betweenness_results[i][1],
                                       str(degree_results[i][0]),
                                       degree_results[i][1],
                                       str(closeness_results[i][0]),
                                       closeness_results[i][1])
```

We're going to consider three metrics for centrality in this book: *degree, closeness*, and *betweenness*. Degree is the simplest centrality measure; in an undirected graph, the degree centrality of a node is the node's degree.

Closeness and betweenness centrality are both associated with shortest paths. The closeness centrality represents the ease of transmitting information from a particular node to any other node on the graph. To calculate the closeness of a node, you calculate the sum total distance between that node and every other node in the graph. The node with the *lowest* total value has the highest closeness centrality.

Like closeness centrality, betweenness centrality is a function of the shortest paths. Betweenness centrality repersents the likelihood that a node will be part of the shortest path between any two particular nodes. Betweenness centrality is calculated by generating a table of all the shortest paths and then counting the number of paths using that node.

Centrality algorithms are all relative measures. Operationally, they're generally best used as ranking algorithms. For example, finding that a particular web page has a high betweenness centrality means that most users when surfing are going to visit that page, possibly because it's a gatekeeper or an important index. Observing user surfing patterns and finding that a particular node has a high closeness centrality can be useful for identifying important news or information sites.

Components and Connectivity

If two nodes in an undirected graph have a path between them, then they are *connected*. The set of all nodes that have paths to each other composes a *connected component*. In directed graphs, the corresponding terms are *weakly connected* (if the paths exist when direction is ignored), and *strongly connected* (if the paths exist when direction is accounted for).

A graph can be broken into its components by using a breadth-first search. A *breadth-first search* (BFS) is a search that progresses by picking a node, examining all the neighbors of that node, and then examining each of those neighbors in turn. This contrasts with a *depth-first search* (DFS), which examines a single neighbor, then a neighbor of that neighbor, and so on. The code in Example 13-4 shows how to use a breadth-first search to break a graph into components.

Example 13-4. Calculating components and clustering coefficient

```python
#!/usr/bin/env python
#
#
import os,sys, basic_graph

def calculate_components(g):
    # Creates a table of components via a breadth first search.
    component_table = {}
    unfinished_nodes = {}
    for i in g.nodes.keys():
        unfinished_nodes[i] = 1
    node_list = [g.nodes.keys()[0]]
    component_index = 1
    while node_list != []:
        current_node = node_list[0]
        del node_list[0]
        del unfinished_nodes[current_node]
        for i in g.neighbors(current_node):
            component_table[i] = component_index
            node_list.insert(0, i)
        if node_list == [] and len(unfinished_nodes) > 0:
            node_list = [unfinished_nodes.keys()[0]]
    return component_table
```

Clustering Coefficient

Another mechanism for measuring the relationship between nodes on a graph is the *clustering coefficient*. The clustering coefficient is the probability that any two neighbors of a particular node on a graph are neighbors of each other. Example 13-5 shows a code snippet for calculating the clustering coefficient.

Example 13-5. Calculating clustering coefficient

```python
def calculate_clustering_coefficients(g):
    # Clustering coefficient for a node is the
    # fraction of its neighbors who are also neighbors with each other
    node_ccs = {}
    for i in g.nodes.keys():
        mutual_neighbor_count = 0
        neighbor_list = g.neighbors(i)
        neighbor_set = {}
        for j in neighbor_list:
            neighbor_set[j] = 1
        for j in neighbor_list:
            # We grab his neighbors and find out how many of them are in the
            # set
            new_neighbor_list = g.neighbors[j]
            for k in new_neighbor_list:
                if k != i and neighbor_list.has_key(k):
                    mutual_neighbor_count += 1
```

```
# We now calculate the coefficient by dividing by d*(d-1) to get the
# fraction
cc = float(mutual_neighbor_count)/((float(len(neighbor_list) *
                                        (len(neighbor_list) -1 ))))
    node_ccs[i] = cc
total_cc = reduce(lambda a,b:node_ccs[a] + node_ccs[b], node_ccs.keys())
total_cc = total_cc/len(g.nodes.keys())
return total_cc
```

The clustering coefficient is a useful measure of "peerishness." A graph of a pure client server network will have a clustering coefficient of zero—a client talks only to servers, and servers talk only to clients. We've had some success using clustering as a measure of the impact of spam on large networks. As an example of this, Figure 13-3 shows the impact of the shutdown of McColo, a bulletproof hosting provider on SMTP network structure on a large network. Following McColo's shutdown, the clustering coefficient for SMTP rose by about 50%.

The relationship between peerishness and spam may be a bit obscure; SMTP, like DNS and other early Internet services, is very sharing-oriented. An SMTP client in one interaction may operate as a server for another interaction, and there should be interactions between each other. Spammers, however, operate effectively as *superclients*—they talk to servers, but never operate as a server for anyone else. This behavior manifests as a low clustering coefficient. Remove the spammers, and the SMTP network starts to look more like a peer-to-peer network and the clustering coefficent rises.

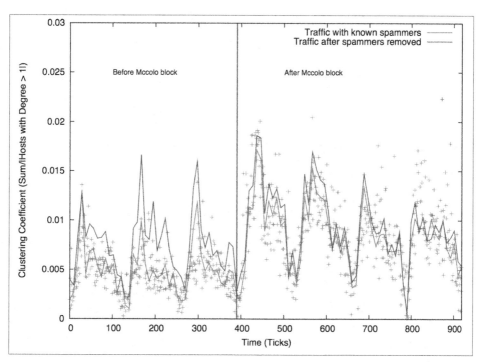

Figure 13-3. Clustering coefficient and large email networks

Analyzing Graphs

Graph analysis can be used for a number of purposes. Centrality metrics are a useful tool both for engineering and for forensic analysis, while components and graph attributes can be used to generate a number of alarms.

Using Component Analysis as an Alarm

In Chapter 11 we discussed detection mechanisms that relied on the attacker's ignorance of a particular network, such as blind scanning and the like. Connected components are a good way of modeling a different type of attacker ignorance. An attacker might know *where* various servers and systems are located on a network, but he doesn't know how they relate to each other. Organizational structure can be identified by looking at connected components, and a number of attacks such as APT and hit-list attacks, which may know the target but not how targets relate to each other, can be identified by examining these components.

To understand how this phenomenon can be used as an alarm, consider the graphical example in Figure 13-4. In this example, a network is composed of two discrete components (say, engineering and marketing), and there is little interaction between them.

When an attacker appears and tries to communicate with the hosts on the network, he combines these two components to produce one huge component that does not appear under normal circumstances.

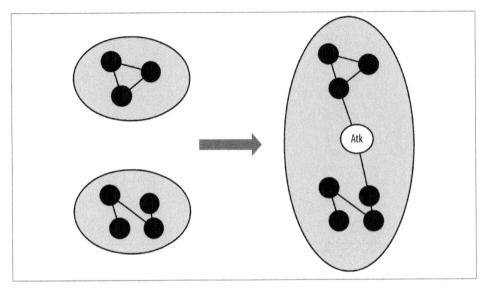

Figure 13-4. An attacker artifically links discrete components

To implement this type of alarm, you must first identify a service that can be divided into multiple components. Good candidates are services such as SSH that require some form of user login; permissions mean that certain users won't have access, which breaks the network into discrete components. SMTP and HTTP are generally bad candidates, though HTTP is feasible if you are looking exclusively at servers that require user login, and you limit your analysis to *just* those servers (e.g., by using an IPSet).

After you've identified your set of servers, identify components to monitor. And after you identify a component, calculate its size—the number of nodes within the component as a function of the time taken to collect it (for example, 60 seconds of netflow). The distribution is likely to be sensitive not only to the time taken to collect the traffic, but also the time of day. Breaking traffic at least into on/off periods (as discussed in Chapter 12) is likely to help.

There are two ways to identify components: either by size order or by tracking hosts within the components. In the case of size order, you simply track the size of the largest component, the second largest component, and so on. This approach is simple, robust, and relatively insensitive to subtle attacks. It's not uncommon for the largest component to make up more than one-third of the total nodes in the graph, so you need a fairly aggressive attack to disrupt the size of the component. The alternative approach involves identifying nodes by their component (e.g., component A is the component containing address 127.0.1.2).

Using Centrality Analysis for Forensics

Centrality is a useful tool for identifying important nodes in a network, and for identifying nodes that communicate at much lower volumes than traffic analysis can identify.

Consider an attack where the attacker infects one or more hosts on a network with malware. These infected hosts now communicate with a command and control server that was previously not present. Figure 13-5 shows this scenario in more depth; before hosts A, B, and C are infected, one node shows some degree of centrality. Following infection, a new node (*Mal*) is the most central node in the set.

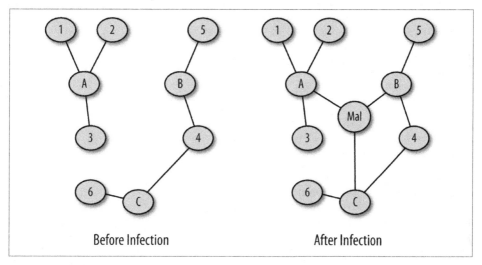

Figure 13-5. Centrality in forensics

This kind of analysis can be done by isolating traffic data into two sets, a *pre-event set* and a *post-event set*. For example, after finding out that the network received a malicious attachment at a particular time, I can pull traffic before that time to produce a pre-event set and traffic after that time to find a post-event set. Looking for newly central nodes gives me a reasonable chance of identifying the command and control server.

Using Breadth-First Searches Forensically

Once you've identified that a malicious host is communicating on your network, the next step is to find out who he's talking to, such as the host's C&C or other infected hosts on the network. Once you've found that out, you can repeat the process to find out who *they* talked to in order to identify other targets.

This iterative investigation is a breadth-first search. You start with a single node, look at all of its neighbors for suspicious behavior, and then repeat the process on *their* neighbors (see Example 13-6). This type of graph-based investigation can help identify other infected hosts, suspicious targets, and other systems on the network that need investigation or analysis.

Example 13-6. Examining a site's neighbors

```python
#!/usr/bin/env python
#
# This is a somewhat ginned-up example of how to use breadth-first searches to
# crawl through a dataset and identify other hosts that are using BitTorrent.
# The crawling criteria are as follows:
#      A communicates to B on ports 6881-6889
#      A and B send a large file between each other (> 1 MB)
#
# The point of the example is that you could use any criteria you want and put
# multiple criteria into constructing the graph.
#
#
# Comand line
#
# crawler.py seed_ip datafile
#
# seed_ip is the ip address of a known bittorrent user
# datafile
import os, sys, basic_graph

def extract_neighbors(ip_address, datafile):
    # Given an ip_address, identify the nodes adjacent to that
    # address by finding flows that have that address as either a source or
    # destination.  The other address in the pair is considered a neighbor.
    a = os.popen("""rwfilter --any-address=%s --sport=1024-65535 --dport=1024-65535 \
--bytes=1000000- --pass=stdout %s | rwfilter --input=stdin --aport=6881-6889 \
--pass=stdout | rwuniq --fields=1,2 --no-title""" % (ip_address,datafile), 'r')
    # In the query, note the fairly rigorous port definitions I'm using -- everything
    # starts out as high.  This is because, depending on the stack implementation,
    # ports 6881-6889 (the BT ports) may be used as ephemeral ports.  By breaking
    # out client ports in the initial filtering call, I'm guaranteeing that I
    # don't accidently record, say, a web session to port 6881.
    # The 1 MB limit is also supposed to constrain us to actual BT file transfers.
    neighbor_set = set()
    for i in a.readlines():
        sip, dip = i.split('|')[0:2].strip()
        # I check to see if IP address is the source or destination of the
        # flow; whichever one it is, I add the complementary address to the
        # neighbor set (e.g., if ip_address is sip, I add the dip)
        if sip == ip_address:
            neighbor_set.add(dip)
        else:
            neighbor_set.add(sip)
    a.close()
```

```
        return neighbor_set

if __name__ == '__main__':
    starting_ip = sys.argv[1]
    datafile = sys.argv[2]
    candidate_set = set([starting_ip])
    while len(candidate_set) > 0:
        target_ip = candidate_set.pop()
        target_set.add(target_ip)
        neighbor_set = extract_neighbors(target_ip, datafile)
        for i in neighbor_set:
            if not i in target_set:
                candidate_set.add(i)
    for i in target_set:
        print i
```

Using Centrality Analysis for Engineering

Given limited monitoring resources and analyst attention, effectively monitoring a network requires identifying mission-critical hosts and assigning resources to protecting and watching them. That said, in any network, there's a huge difference between the hosts that people *say* they need and the hosts they actually use. Using traffic analysis to identify critical hosts helps differentiate between what's important on paper and what users actually visit.

Centrality is one of a number of metrics that can be used to identify criticality. Alternatives include counting the number of hosts that visit a site (which is effectively degree centrality) and looking at traffic volume. Centrality is a good complement to volume.

Further Reading

1. Michael Collins and Michael Reiter, "Hit-list Worm Detection and Bot Identification in Large Networks Using Protocol Graphs," Proceedings of the 2007 Symposium on Recent Advances in Intrusion Detection.

2. Thomas Cormen, Charles Leiserson, Ronald Rivest, and Clifford Stein, *Introduction to Algorithims, Third Edition* (MIT Press, 2009).

3. igraph (*http://bit.ly/igraph-pack*) (R graph library)

4. Lun Li, David Alderson, Reiko Tanaka, John C. Doyle, and Walter Willinger, "Towards a Theory of Scale-Free Graphs: Definition, Properties, and Implications (Extended Version)."

5. Neo4j (*http://www.neo4j.org*)

6. Networkx (*http://networkx.github.io/*) (Python graph library)

## CHAPTER 14

Application Identification

It used to be so easy to identify applications in network traffic; you looked at the port number, or if that failed, you looked at a couple of header packets for identification information. But these identifiers have become muddier over the past decade, in particular as users seek to hide certain classes of traffic (BitTorrent!) and as privacy advocates push for increased encryption.

There are still methods for identifying traffic that do not rely on payload. Most protocols have a well-defined sequence and certain predictable behaviors that mark them so you don't have to look at payload. By looking at the hosts to which a session talks and at packet sizes, a surprising amount of information is available.

This chapter is broken into two major sections. The first section focuses on techniques for identifying a protocol, starting with the most obvious methods and moving toward more complex techniques such as behavioral analysis. The second section discusses the contents of application banners and discusses some methods for finding behavioral and payload information for analysis.

Mechanisms for Application Identification

In a perfectly safe and secure computing environment, you could just examine the configuration file on each server and it would tell you all the traffic that the server allows. Unfortunately, there are many hidden ways of starting traffic that undermine this simple strategy. You may have hosts on your system you don't know about that were started by users with innocent or not-so-innocent goals of their own. Services can be started by administrators or ordinary users outside of your startup configuration. And legitimate servers can be taken over by intruders and used for things you never intended. Although many of the techniques in this section are commonly run by snoopers who don't have access to your servers' configuration files, you should be using the techniques as well so you know what is really happening.

Port Number

Port numbers are the first way to check what a service is, and while there's no technical requirement that a particular service runs on a particular port, there are social conventions that tend to make it so. IANA maintains a public registry (*http://bit.ly/port-list*) of port numbers and their associated services. Although port number assignment is effectively arbitrary, and users have an active interest in evading detection by using previously untouched port numbers (or, slightly more deviously, by using common port numbers), the well-known ports still carry enough official and innocent traffic to make them the first-pass mechanism for identifying protocols. Techniques we'll discuss later in this section often use port numbers as an assertion on the user's part. For example, a user talking on port 80 is effectively asserting that she's talking to a web server.

Port number assignment is chaotic because all anyone really has to do is pick a number and hope nobody else is using it. The official registry maintained by IANA (*http://bit.ly/iana-port*) focuses on protocols designed as part of the RFC process. Other registries and lists include a Wikipedia page (*http://bit.ly/tcp-udp-ports*), speedguide (*http://bit.ly/sg-ports*), and the SANS Internet Storm Center (*http://bit.ly/sans-isc*), which provides a mini-messageboard per port with useful insights.

So a huge number of ports are reserved for certain applications, and another huge number are used conventionally for other applications—but there are a small set of applications that actually matter. Table 14-1 lists the ports that I worry about the most with a short description explaining why in each case.

Table 14-1. Ports to care about

Port	Name	Meaning
The Holy Trinity		
80/tcp	HTTP	Not only is HTTP the basic protocol for nearly everything on the Internet now, it's also the most commonly imitated protocol. Users will drop traffic on port 80 to evade firewall rules.
25/tcp	SMTP	Email is the most critical service after HTTP and also one of the most attacked.
53/udp	DNS	Another critical foundational protocol; DNS attacks will seriously damage networks.
Infrastructure and Management		
179/tcp	BGP	A core protocol for inter-network routing.
161-162/udp	SNMP	System Network Management Protocol; used to manage routers and other devices.
22/tcp	SSH	The administrative workhorse.
23/tcp	Telnet	If I see Telnet, I kill the connection. It is obsolete and should be replaced by other protocols, notably SSH.

Port	Name	Meaning
123/udp	NTP	Network Time Protocol; used to coordinate clocks on networks.
389/tcp	LDAP	Lightweight Directory Access Protocol; manages directory services.

File Transfer

Port	Name	Meaning
20/tcp	FTP-data	Along with 21, makes up FTP.
21/tcp	FTP	The FTP control port. Another service I kill if I see it. Use SFTP.
69/tcp	TFTP	Trivial file transfer; largely used by system administrators and hopefully never seen crossing a border router.
137-139/tcp & udp	NETBIOS	NetBios is the infrastructure used for Service Message Block (SMB) and in particular provides sharing features for Windows and (via Samba) Unix systems. Pounded by attacks over its history.

Email

Port	Name	Meaning
143/tcp	IMAP	Internet Message Access Protocol; one of the two standard email client protocols.
110/tcp	POP3	Post Office Protocol; the other standard email client protocol.

Databases

Port	Name	Meaning
1521/tcp	Oracle	The primary Oracle server port.
1433/tcp & udp	SQL Server	Microsoft SQL Server's port.
3306/tcp	MySQL Server	MySQL's default port.
5432/tcp	Postgresql Server	Postgres's default port.

File Sharing

Port	Name	Meaning
6881-6889/tcp	BitTorrent	The default BitTorrent client ports.
6346-6348/tcp & udp	Gnutella	Bearshare and Limewire's default gnutella ports.
4662/tcp & udp	eDonkey	Default port for eDonkey clients.

On Unix and Windows systems, port assignment is supposed to be controlled by the */etc/services* file (*\WINDOWS\SYSTEM32\DRIVERS\ETC\SERVICES* on Windows hosts). A dump of the file, shown in Example 14-1, shows that it's a simple database listing a service name and the corresponding host.

Example 14-1. The contents of /etc/services

```
$ # Catting /etc/services without header info
$ cat /etc/services | egrep -v '^#' | head -10
rtmp            1/ddp    #Routing Table Maintenance Protocol
tcpmux          1/udp     # TCP Port Service Multiplexer
tcpmux          1/tcp     # TCP Port Service Multiplexer
nbp             2/ddp    #Name Binding Protocol
```

```
compressnet    2/udp     # Management Utility
compressnet    2/tcp     # Management Utility
compressnet    3/udp     # Compression Process
compressnet    3/tcp     # Compression Process
echo           4/ddp     #AppleTalk Echo Protocol
rje            5/udp     # Remote Job Entry
```

The names in the *services* file are used by getportbyname and any other port lookup functions to identify protocols. This does *not*, of course, mean that the users are really invoking those services, just that *services* says the ports are supposed to be used by the services. For example, to get a list of all the services I have listening on a host, I use netstat -a, as shown in Example 14-2:

Example 14-2. Netstat and /etc/services/

```
# I'm running a django web server on port 8000, and I run netstat
$ netstat -a | grep LISTEN
tcp4    0    0  localhost.irdmi      *.*                LISTEN
tcp46   0    0  *.8508               *.*                LISTEN
tcp46   0    0  *.8507               *.*                LISTEN
$ cat /etc/services | grep irdmi
irdmi2         7999/udp     # iRDMI2
irdmi2         7999/tcp     # iRDMI2
irdmi          8000/udp     # iRDMI
irdmi          8000/tcp     # iRDMI
```

netstat consults */etc/services* to determine what the port number is named, and you can always find the real port number in */etc/services*. However, there is no guarantee that the service is actually what the named service is—in my example, I'm running a Django web server.

It's appropriate at this point to make a digression into the raving paranoia characteristic of a network traffic analyst. *netstat* is obviously a great tool for identifying which ports are open on your host, but if you want more certainty, scan the machine vertically and compare the results.

Port Assignment

Any symmetric TCP or UDP transaction uses two port numbers: the *server port* is used by the client to send traffic to the server, and the *client port* used by the server to respond. Client ports are short-lived and recycled from a pool of *ephemeral ports*; the size and allocation of the pool is a function of the TCP stack in question and user configuration.

There are several conventions regarding port assignment. The most important is the distinction between port numbers 1024 and below: nearly every operating system requires that has a socket on one of these requires root or administrative access. When used legitimately, this means only the administrator can start a service such as a web or

---

email server. But this property also makes services on those ports attractive to attackers, because subverting those processes grants root privileges.

Generally, ports below 1024 are used only to run server sockets. This isn't to say that you couldn't use them for clients, only that it would be contrary to standard practice and mildly insane because you're using a client port with root access. Technically, an ephemeral port can be any port above 1024, but there are a number of conventions in their assignment.

IANA has assigned a standard range (49152 to 65535) for ephemeral ports (*http://bit.ly/iana-port*). However, this range is still in the process of being adopted, and different operating systems will have different default ranges. Table 14-2 lists common port assignments.

Table 14-2. Port assignment rules for various operating systems

Operating system	Default range	Controllable
Windows, through XP	1025-5000	Partly, through MaxUserPort in *Tcpip\Parameters*
Windows, Vista onward	49152-65535	Yes, via netsh
Mac OS X	49152-65535	Yes, through `net.inet.ip.portrange` family in sysctl
Linux	32768-65535	Yes, through */proc/sys/net/ipv4/ip_local_port_range*
FreeBSD	49152-65535	Yes, through `net.inet.ip.portrange` family in sysctl

Application Identification by Banner Grabbing

Banner grabbing and its companion function, OS fingerprinting, are scanning techniques used to determine server and operating system information. They rely on the convention that the first thing most applications do when woken up is identify themselves. Most server applications respond to an open socket by passing their protocol, their current version, or other configuration information. If they don't do it automatically, they will often do so with a little prodding.

Banner grabbing can easily be done manually using any "keyboard to the socket" tool, such as *netcat* (see Chapter 9 for more information). Example 14-3 shows active banner grabbing using *netcat* to collect some data. Note that I am able to pull information from several servers without actually using the protocol in question.

Example 14-3. Examples of active banner grabbing with netcat

```
# Open a connection to an SSH server
# Note that I receive information without the need for actual
# interaction with the server.
$ netcat 192.168.2.1 22
SSH-2.0-OpenSSH_6.1
```

```
^C
# Open an IMAP connection.
# Again, note that I have to do nothing with mail itself.
$ netcat 192.168.2.1 143
* OK [CAPABILITY IMAP4rev1 LITERAL+ SASL-IR LOGIN-REFERRALS
  ID ENABLE STARTTLS AUTH=PLAIN AUTH=LOGIN] Dovecot ready.
```

An alternative to active banner grabbing is passive banner grabbing, which can be done using *tcpdump*. Since a banner is really just text that appears at the beginning of a session, grabbing the payload of the first five or six packets will provide banner data as well.

bannergrab.py is a very simple banner grabbing script using Scapy (from Chapter 9). It's not trying to parse banner contents—it's just grabbing the first load of information it sees. This can be quite informative. Example 14-4 shows the contents from the SSH dump.

Example 14-4. Grabbing client and server banners using scapy

```
#!/usr/bin/env python
#
#
# bannergrab.py
# This is a Scapy application that loads up a banner file and drops
# out the client and server banners.  To do so, it
# reads the contents of the client and server files from the session,
# extracts ASCII text, and dumps it to screen.
#
from scapy.all import *
import sys
sessions = {}

packet_data = rdpcap(sys.argv[1])
for i in packet_data:
    if not sessions.has_key(i[IP].src):
        sessions[i[IP].src] = ''
    try:
        sessions[i[IP].src] += i[TCP].payload.load
    except:
        pass

for j in sessions.keys():
    print j, sessions[j][0:200]


$ bannergrab.py ssh.dmp
WARNING: No route found for IPv6 destination :: (no default route?)
192.168.1.12
216.92.179.155 SSH-2.0-OpenSSH_6.1
```

Example 14-5 shows a pull from *www.cnn.com*:

Example 14-5. A pull from cnn.com

```
57.166.224.246 HTTP/1.1 200 OK
Server: nginx
Date: Sun, 14 Apr 2013 04:34:36 GMT
Content-Type: application/javascript
Transfer-Encoding: chunked
Connection: keep-alive
Vary: Accept-Encoding
Last-Modified: Sun
157.166.255.216
157.166.241.11 HTTP/1.1 200 OK
Server: nginx
Date: Sun, 14 Apr 2013 04:34:27 GMT
Content-Type: text/html
Transfer-Encoding: chunked
Connection: keep-alive
Set-Cookie: CG=US:DC:Washington; path=/
Last-Modified

66.235.155.19 HTTP/1.1 302 Found
Date: Sun, 14 Apr 2013 04:34:35 GMT
Server: Omniture DC/2.0.0
Access-Control-Allow-Origin: *
Set-Cookie: s_vi=[CS]v1|28B31B23851D063C-60000139000324E4[CE];
            Expires=Tue, 14 Apr 2
23.6.20.211 HTTP/1.1 200 OK
x-amz-id-2: 287KOoW3vWNpotJGpn0RaXExCzKkFJQ/hkpAXjWUQTb6hSBzDQioFUoWYZMRCq7V
x-amz-request-id: 8B6B2E3CDBC2E300
Content-Encoding: gzip
ETag: "e5f0fa3fbe0175c47fea0164922230d4"
Acc

192.168.1.12 GET / HTTP/1.1
Host: www.cnn.com
Connection: keep-alive
Accept: text/html,application/xhtml+xml,application/xml;q=0.9,*/*;q=0.8
User-Agent: Mozilla/5.0 (Macintosh; Intel Mac OS X 10_8_3) AppleWebK
23.15.9.160 HTTP/1.1 200 OK
Server: Apache
Last-Modified: Wed, 10 Apr 2013 13:44:28 GMT
ETag: "233bf1-3e803-4da01de67a700"
Accept-Ranges: bytes
Content-Type: text/css
Vary: Accept-Encoding
Content-Encoding

63.85.36.42 HTTP/1.1 200 OK
Content-Length: 43
Content-Type: image/gif
Date: Sun, 14 Apr 2013 04:34:36 GMT
Connection: keep-alive
Pragma: no-cache
```

```
Expires: Mon, 01 Jan 1990 00:00:00 GMT
Cache-Control: priv

138.108.6.20 HTTP/1.1 200 OK
Server: nginx
Date: Sun, 14 Apr 2013 04:34:35 GMT
Content-Type: image/gif
Transfer-Encoding: chunked
Connection: keep-alive
Keep-Alive: timeout=20
```

In the previous example, the client is midway through the dump (at 192.168.1.12). Note the sheer number of web servers; this is a common feature with modern websites, and you can expect to see dozens of servers involved in constructing a single page. Also note the information provided: the server sends content information, the server name, and a bunch of configuration data. The client string includes a variety of acceptable formats, and the User-Agent string, which we'll discuss in more depth later.

Banner grabbing is fairly simple. The challenge lies in identifying what the banners *mean*. Different applications have radically different banners, which are often complete languages in themselves.

Application Identification by Behavior

In the absence of payload, it's often difficult to tell what an application *is*, but an enormous amount of information is still available about what an application *does*. Behavioral analysis focuses on finding cues for the application's behavior by examining features such as the packet sizes and connection failures.

Packet sizes in any IP protocol are bound by the *maximum transmission unit* (MTU), the maximum frame size defined by the layer 2 protocol. When IP attempts to send a packet larger than the MTU, the original packet is split into the number of MTU-sized packets that are required to transmit it. In *tcpdump* and NetFlow data, this means that the maximum packet size you will ever see is controlled by the shortest MTU of the route taken by that packet so far. Because the Internet is dominated by Ethernet, this imposes an effective limit of 1,500 bytes on packet sizes.

We can use this limit to split network traffic into four major categories:

Fumbling
Covered in Chapter 11, this consists of failed attempts to open connections to targets.

Control traffic
Small, fixed-size packets sent by clients and servers at the beginning of a session.

Chatter

Packets less than the MTU in size, of varying size and sent back and forth between clients and servers. Chatter messages are characteristic of chat protocols like ICQ and AIM, as well as the command messages for many protocols such as SMTP and BitTorrent.

File transfer

Asymmetric traffic where one side sends packets almost entirely of MTU size and the other side sends ACKs in response. Characteristic of SMTP, HTTP, and FTP.

Control packets are, when available, the most interesting information you can find on a service because their sizes are often specified by the service itself. Control messages are often implemented as templates of some form, with specific areas to fill in the blanks. As a result, even with the payload obscured, the sizes can often be used to identify them.

Histograms, presented in "Histograms" on page 198, are useful for comparing protocols via the lengths of their control messages. As an example, consider Figure 14-1. This is a plot of histograms for short flows (less than 1,000 bytes in total) from clients to Bit-Torrent and web servers.

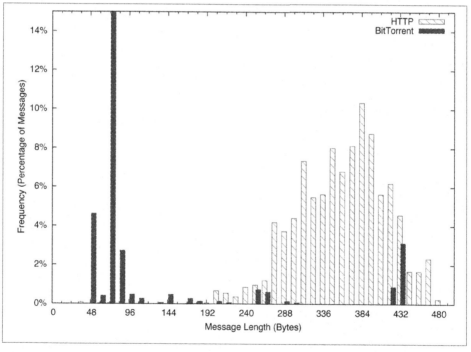

Figure 14-1. Histogram comparing BitTorrent and HTTP short flow sizes

For a web client, this consists primarily of issuing the HTTP GET request and then receiving a file. The GET requests, as you can see in Figure 14-1, are spread over a somewhat normalized distribution between about 200 and 400 bytes. Conversely, the BitTorrent packets have a huge peak between 48 and 96 bytes, a function of the 68-byte BitTorrent handshake message.

Histograms can be checked visually, as in Figure 14-1, or numerically by calculating the L1 (or Manhattan) distance (*http://bit.ly/l1-norm*). In a histogram, calculate the L1 distance as the sum of the differences between each bin. Normalized to percentages, this provides a value between 0 and 2, with 0 indicating that the two histograms are identical, and 2 indicating that the two histograms are complete opposites. Example 14-6 shows how to calculate the L1 distance in Python.

Example 14-6. Calculating L1 distance in Python

```
#!/usr/bin/env python
#
#
# calc_l1.py
#
# Given two data files consisting purely of sizes and a histogram
# specification (bin size, max bin size), calculate the l1 distance
# between two histograms
#
# command line;
#          calc_l1 size min max file_a file_b
#
# size: the size of a histogram bin
# min: the minimum size to bin
# max: the maximum size to bin
#
#
import sys

bin_size = int(sys.argv[1])
bin_min = int(sys.argv[2])
bin_max = int(sys.argv[3])
file_1 = sys.argv[4]
file_2 = sys.argv[5]

bin_count = 1 + ((bin_max - bin_min)/bin_size)
histograms = [[],[]]
totals = [0,0]

for i in range(0, bin_count):
    for j in range(0,2):
        histograms[j].append(0)

# Generate histograms
for h_index, file_name in ((0, file_1), (1,file_2)):
    fh = open(file_name, 'r')
```

```
results = map(lambda x:int(x), fh.readlines())
fh.close()
for i in results:
    if i <= bin_max:
        index = (i - bin_min)/bin_size
        histograms[h_index][index] += 1
        totals[h_index] += 1

# Compare and calculate l1 distance
l1_d = 0.0
for i in range(0, bin_count):
    h0_pct = float(histograms[0][i])/float(totals[0])
    h1_pct = float(histograms[1][i])/float(totals[1])
    l1_d += abs(h0_pct - h1_pct)

print l1_d
```

Chatting and file transfers can be examined by identifying the individual packet sizes or, in the case of flow files, comparing the mean packet sizes for the flow (flow bytes divided by flow packets). If one side is close to MTU, odds are that it's a file transfer, and if both sides are roughly asymmetric and greater than 40 bytes per packet, some form of chatter may be going on. To illustrate this graphically, consider the plots in Figure 14-2 and Figure 14-3. These show the packet sizes for a file transfer (HTTP) and chat (AIM) session, respectively.

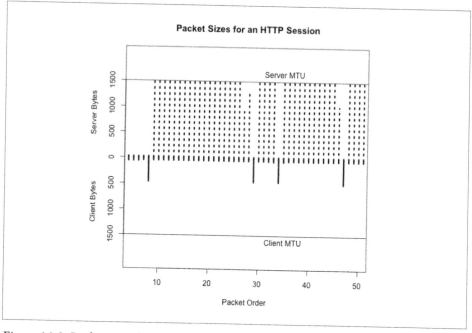

Figure 14-2. Packet sizes for an HTTP session

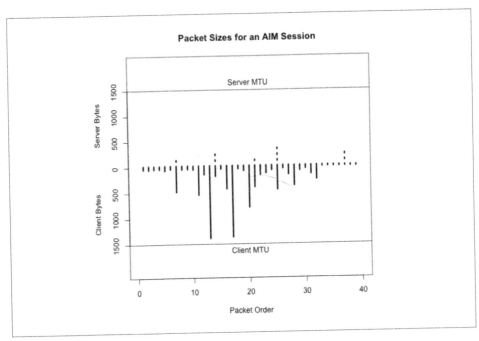

Figure 14-3. Packet sizes for an AIM session

Application Identification by Subsidiary Site

Network-aware applications rarely exist in a vacuum. Software updates, registration servers, database updates, advertising, and user tracking are all examples of network-based functionality that an application can conduct without a user being aware of them. At the same time, users may visit support forums, talk on message boards, or require access to information just to run the application.

As example of this behavior, consider two applications: antivirus and BitTorrent. Any antivirus application needs to contact its home servers on a regular basis in order to update the knowledgebase. This activity is so predictable that it's not uncommon for malware to explicitly disable the update addresses on the local host. Any host running AV should be contacting these addresses on a regular basis, and anyone who does is likely to be running AV.

Now consider BitTorrent. BitTorrent has done a considerable amount of work in recent years to decentralize the protocol. In the late 2000s, it was possible to identify trackers and then identify users by finding out who was communicating with the tracker. Although tracker ID is less effective now, BitTorrent users still need to find their files, and the relevant magnet links are concentrated on sites such as the Pirate Bay, KickAssTorrents, and other specialized torrent sites. Find a user who visits the Pirate Bay, then find someone engaging in huge file downloads on weird ports, and you have probably found a BitTorrent user. Once you've identified a server or host running a particular service, look at who else is talking to it.

Application Banners: Identifying and Classifying

Application banners can provide a lot of information about applications, servers, operating systems, and versions of all these things. Unfortunately, the format of these banners changes radically with each service, almost like a different language. The good news is that, with the exception of web browsers, most application banners are relatively simple. The bad news is that web browsers will make most of the banners you see.

Non-Web Banners

This section discusses server banners for servers not using the Web. Banners can provide information on the operating system and the protocol, or can be obfuscated to prevent scanners from acquiring intelligence.

SMTP banners are defined in RFC 5321. On client login, an SMTP server should respond with a 220 status code (the greeting), along with some domain information. Given that SMTP servers are one of the most commonly targeted services by scanners, it's not unusual to find SMTP banners reduced to a bare minimum by system administrators.

Microsoft defines the default banner for MS Exchange as:

```
220 <Servername> Microsoft ESMTP MAIL service ready at
    <RegionalDay-Date-24HourTimeFormat> <RegionalTimeZoneOffset>
```

with optional customization. An example banner for Exchange is:

```
220 mailserver.bogodomain.com Microsoft ESMTP MAIL service ready at
    Sat, 16 Feb 2013 08:34:14 +0100
```

SSH is defined in RFC 4253. On client login, an SSH server sends a brief message providing an identification string. According to the protocol definition, the identification string will be of the form:

```
SSH-protoversion-softwareversion SP comments CR LF
```

where SP is a space, CR is a carriage return, and LF is a line feed. All modern implementations of SSH should use 2.0 for the protocol version, but a server that supports previous versions of SSH should identify its version as 1.99. Comments are optional.

The following banner is an example of SSH before version 2.0, which should be rare:

```
SSH-1.99-OpenSSH_3.5p1
```

Everything else should be 2.0 or above:

```
SSH-2.0-OpenSSH_4.3
```

As these two examples show, the first step to identifying a banner is usually to find the relevant technical documentation. This may be an RFC for an IETF-engineered protocol such as IMAP, POP3, SSH, or SMTP. For protocols that do not involve the IETF, some searching may be required to identify the developer of the protocol and any support sites. For example, BitTorrent's protocol is currently specified at the *theory.org* wiki (*http://bit.ly/bt-spec*).

Web Client Banners: The User-Agent String

Web clients send browsers a complicated configuration string defining their capabilities and preferences: the platform the browser runs on, the operating system, and a variety of configuration details. This string, `User-Agent`, is defined in RFC 2616, but can become phenomenally complicated (as well as informative) fairly quickly.

Some user-agent strings are shown sorted by broswer in Example 14-7.

Example 14-7. Example user-agent strings by browser

```
Firefox:
Mozilla/5.0 (X11; U; Linux x86_64; en-US; rv:1.8.1.12) Gecko/20080214
          Firefox/2.0.0.12
Mozilla/5.0 (Windows; U; Windows NT 5.1; cs; rv:1.9.0.8) Gecko/2009032609
          Firefox/3.0.8
Mozilla/5.0 (X11; U; Linux i686; en-US; rv:1.8) Gecko/20051111 Firefox/1.5


Internet Explorer:
Mozilla/5.0 (compatible; MSIE 9.0; Windows NT 6.1; WOW64; Trident/5.0; SLCC2;
          Media Center PC 6.0; InfoPath.3; MS-RTC LM 8; Zune 4.7)
Mozilla/5.0 (compatible; MSIE 10.0; Windows NT 6.1; Trident/6.0)
Mozilla/5.0 (compatible; MSIE 9.0; Windows NT 6.1; Trident/5.0; Xbox)


Safari:
Mozilla/5.0 (Macintosh; Intel Mac OS X 10_6_8) AppleWebKit/534.57.1
          (KHTML, like Gecko) Version/5.1.7 Safari/534.57.1
Mozilla/5.0 (iPad; CPU OS 6_0 like Mac OS X) AppleWebKit/536.26
          (KHTML, like Gecko) Version/6.0 Mobile/10A403 Safari/8536.25


Opera:
Opera/9.80 (Windows NT 6.0) Presto/2.12.388 Version/12.11
Opera/9.80 (Macintosh; Intel Mac OS X 10.8.2) Presto/2.12.388 Version/12.11
Opera/9.80 (X11; Linux i686; U; ru) Presto/2.8.131 Version/11.11
Mozilla/5.0 (Windows NT 6.1; rv:2.0) Gecko/20100101 Firefox/4.0 Opera 12.11


Chrome:
Mozilla/5.0 (Windows NT 6.2; WOW64) AppleWebKit/535.24
          (KHTML, like Gecko) Chrome/19.0.1055.1 Safari/535.24
Mozilla/5.0 (Macintosh; Intel Mac OS X 10_7_3) AppleWebKit/535.19
          (KHTML, like Gecko) Chrome/18.0.1025.151 Safari/535.19
Mozilla/5.0 (Linux; Android 4.0.4; Galaxy Nexus Build/IMM76B)
          AppleWebKit/535.19 (KHTML, like Gecko) Chrome/18.0.1025.133
```

```
        Mobile Safari/535.19
Mozilla/5.0 (iPhone; U; CPU iPhone OS 5_1_1 like Mac OS X; en)
        AppleWebKit/534.46.0 (KHTML, like Gecko) CriOS/19.0.1084.60
        Mobile/9B206 Safari/7534.48.3

Googlebot:
Mozilla/5.0 (compatible; Googlebot/2.1; +http://www.google.com/bot.html)

Bingbot:
Mozilla/5.0 (compatible; bingbot/2.0; +http://www.bing.com/bingbot.htm)

Baiduspider:
Mozilla/5.0 (compatible; Baiduspider/2.0; +http://www.baidu.com/search/
spider.html)
```

The user agent strings in Example 14-7 follow a basic structure that is derived from the original RFC 2616 specification along with various detritus from the browser wars. These attributes are broken down as follows:

1. An initial tag, usually `Mozilla/4.0` or higher. The use of Mozilla as the default string is a relic of the browser wars. Suffice it to say that almost every browser automatically masquerades as Mozilla.

2. A set of values in parentheses that will tell you what the browser *really* is. These values vary based on the browser make and configuration, but usually contain the actual browser name, the OS, and a number of optional parameters.

3. Following the parentheses (usually) is a tag naming the layout engine for the software; the layout engine is the browser's toolkit for rendering HTML, and the same engine can be used by multiple browsers. Common engines include Gecko (used by Firefox, Mozilla, and SeaMonkey), WebKit (used by Safari and Chrome), Presto (Opera), and Trident (IE).

As Example 14-7 shows, the actual composition of the string is very much a function of the browser, the OS, and the idiosyncratic whims of the implementor.

Further Reading

1. Michael Collins and Michael Reiter, "Finding Peer-to-Peer File Sharing Using Coarse Network Behaviors," Proceedings of the 2007 ESORICS Conference.

2. Hajime Inoue, Dana Jansens, Abdulrahman Hijazi, and Anil Somayaji, "NetAD-HICT: A Tool for Understanding Network Traffic," Large Installation System Administration Conference (LISA '07). November, 2007.

3. NetADHICT Homepage (*http://bit.ly/netADHICT*)

4. Michael Zalewski's p0f (*http://bit.ly/p0fv3*)

5. UserAgentString.com (*http://bit.ly/browserlist*)

## CHAPTER 15

Network Mapping

In this chapter, we discuss mechanisms for managing the rate of false positives produced by detection systems by reducing make-work. Consider this scenario: I create a signature today to identify the IIS exploit of the week, and sometime tomorrow afternoon it starts firing off like crazy. Yay, somebody's using an exploit! I check the logs, and I find out that I am not in fact being attacked by this exploit because my network *actually doesn't run IIS*. Not only have I wasted analyst time dealing with the alert, I've wasted *my* time writing the original alert for something to which the network isn't vulnerable.

The process of inventory is the foundation of situational awareness. It enables you to move from simply reacting to signatures to continuous audit and protection. It provides you with baselines and an efficient anomaly detection strategy, it identifies critical assets, and it provides you with contextual information to speed up the process of filtering alerts.

Creating an Initial Network Inventory and Map

Network mapping is an iterative process that combines technical analysis and interviews with site administrators. The theory behind this process is that any inventory generated by design is inaccurate to some degree, but accurate enough to begin the process of instrumentation and analysis. Acquiring this inventory begins with identifying the personnel responsible for managing the network.

The mapping process described in this book consists of four distinct phases, which combine iterative traffic analysis and asking a series of questions of network administrators and personnel. These questions inform the traffic analyses, and the analyses lead to more queries. Figure 15-1 shows how the process progresses: in phase I, you identify the space of IP addresses you are monitoring, and in each progressive phase you partition the space into different categories.

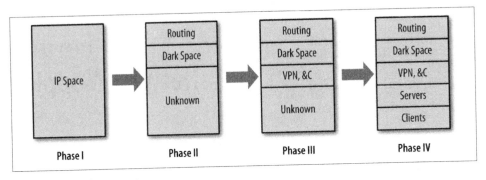

Figure 15-1. The mapping process

Creating an Inventory: Data, Coverage, and Files

In a perfect world, a network map should enable you to determine, based on addresses and ports, the traffic you are seeing on any host on the network. The likelihood of producing such a perfect map on an enterprise network is pretty low because by the time you finish the initial inventory, *something* on the network will have changed. Maps are dynamic and consequently have to be updated on a regular basis. This updating process provides you with a facility for continuously auditing the network.

A security inventory should keep track of every addressable resource on the network (that is, anything an attacker could conceivably reach if she had network access, even if that means access inside the network). It should keep track of which services are running on the resource, and it should keep track of how that system is monitored. An example inventory is shown in Table 15-1.

Table 15-1. An example worksheet

Address	Name	Protocol	Port	Role	Last seen	Sensors	Comments
128.2.1.4	www.server.com	tcp	80	HTTP Server	2013/05/14	Flow 1, Log	Primary web server
128.2.1.4	www.server.com	tcp	22	SSH Server	2013/05/14	Flow 1, Log	Administrators only
128.2.1.5-128.2.1.15	N/A	N/A	N/A	Client	2013/05/14	Flow 2	Workstations
128.2.1.16-128.2.1.31	N/A	N/A	N/A	Empty	2013/05/14	Flow 2	Dark space

Table 15-1 has an entry for each unique observed port and protocol combination on the network, along with a role, an indicator of when the host was last seen in the sensor data, and the available sensor information. These fields are the *minimum* set that you should consider if generating an inventory. Additional potential items to consider include the following:

- The Role field should be enumerable, rather than an actual text field. Enumerating the roles will make searching much less painful. A suggested set of categories is:

  — Service Server, where Service is HTTP, SSH, etc.

— Workstation, to indicate a dedicated client

— NAT, to indicate a network address translator

— Service Proxy for any proxies

— Firewall for Firewalls

— Sensor for any sensors

— Routing for any routing equipment

— VPN for VPN concentrators and other equipment

— DHCP for any dynamically addressed space

— Dark for any address that is allocated in the network but has no host on it

- Identifying VPNs, NATs, DHCP, and proxies, as we'll discuss in a moment, is particularly important—they mess up the address allocation and increase the complexity of analysis.

- Keeping centrality or volume metrics is also useful. A five-number summary of volume over a month is a good starting point for anomaly detection.

- Per-host whitelists are a useful tool for anomaly management (see Chapter 2 for a more extensive discussion). The inventory is a good place to track per-host whitelist and rule files.

- Ownership and point of contact information is critical. One of the most time-consuming steps after identifying an attack is usually finding out who owns the victim.

- Keeping track of the specific services on hosts, and the versions of those services, helps track the risk that a particular system has to current exploits. This can be identified by banner grabbing, but it's more effective to just scan the network using the inventory as a guideline.

Table 15-1 could be kept on paper or a spreadsheet, but it really should be kept in an RDBMS or other storage system. Once you've created the inventory, it will serve as a simple anomaly detection system, and should be updated regularly by automated processes.

Phase I: The First Three Questions

The first step of any inventory process involves figuring out what is already known and what is already available for monitoring. For this reason, instrumentation begins at a meeting with the network administrators.[1] The purpose of this initial meeting is to determine what is monitored, specifically:

---

1. Preferably at a brewpub.

- What addresses make up the network?
- What sensors do I have?
- How are the sensors related to traffic?

Start with addresses, because they serve as the foundation of the inventory. More specific questions to ask include:

Is the network IPv4 or IPv6?
> If the network is IPv6, there's going to be a lot more address space to play with, which reduces the need for DHCP and NAT. The network is more likely to be IPv4, however, and that means that if it is of any significant size, there's likely to be a fair degree of aliasing, NAT, and other address conservation tricks.

How many addresses are accessible or hidden behind NATs?
> Ideally, you should be able to get a map showing the routing on the network, whether there are DMZs, and what information is hidden behind NATs. These individual subnets are future candidates for instrumentation.

How many hosts are on the network?
> Determine how many PCs, clients, servers, computers, and embedded systems are on the network. These systems are the things you're defending. Pay particular attention to embedded systems such as printers and teleconferencing tools because they often have network servers, are hard to patch and update, and are often overlooked in inventories.

This discussion should end with a list of all your potential IP addresses. This list will probably include multiple instances of the same ephemeral spaces over and over again. For example, if there are six subnets behind NAT firewalls, expect to see 192.168.0.0/16 repeated six times. You should also get an estimate of how many hosts are in each subnet and in the network as a whole.

The next set of questions to ask involves current instrumentation. Host-based instrumentation (e.g., server logs and the like, as discussed in Chapter 3) are not the primary target at this point. Instead, the goal is to identify *whether* network-level collection is available. If it is available, determine what is collected, and if not, determine whether it can be turned on. More specific questions to ask include:

What is currently being collected?
> A source doesn't have to be collected "for security purposes" to be useful. NetFlow, for example, has been primarily used as a billing system, but can be useful in monitoring as well.

Are there NetFlow-capable sensors?
> For example, if Cisco routers with built-in NetFlow instrumentation are available, use them as your initial sensors.

Is any IDS present?

An IDS such as Snort can be configured to just dump packet headers. Depending on the location of the IDS (such as if it's on the border of a network), it may be possible to put up a flow collector there as well.

At the conclusion of this discussion, you should come up with a plan for initially instrumenting the network. The goal of this initial instrumentation should be to capitalize on any existing monitoring systems and to acquire a systematic monitoring capability for cross-border traffic. As a rule of thumb, on most enterprise networks, it's easiest to turn on deactivated capabilities such as NetFlow, while it's progressively more difficult, respectively, to add new software and hardware.

The Default Network

Throughout this chapter, I use sidebars to discuss more concrete methods to answer the high-level questions in the text. These sidebars involve a hefty number of SiLK queries and at least a little understanding of how SiLK breaks down data.

The default network is shown in Figure 15-2. As described by SiLK, this network as two sensors: R1 (Router 1) and R2 (Router 2). There are three types of data: in (coming from the cloud into the network), out (going from the network to the cloud), and internal (traffic that doesn't cross the border into the cloud).

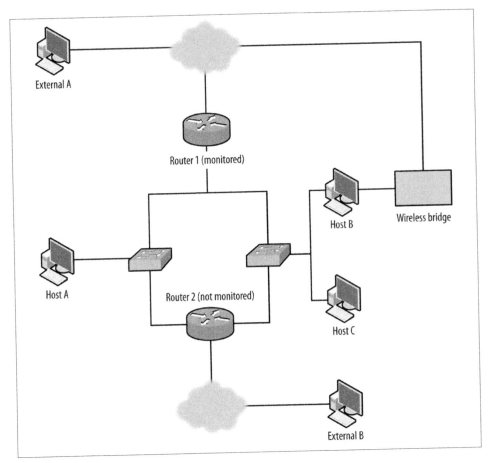

Figure 15-2. Unmonitored routes in action

In addition, there exist a number of IP sets. `initial.set` is a list of hosts on the network provided by administrators during the initial interview. This set is composed of `servers.set` and `clients.set`, comprising the clients and servers. `servers.set` contains `webservers.set`, `dnsservers.set`, and `sshservers.set` as subsets. These sets are accurate at the time of the interview, but will be updated as time passes.

Phase II: Examining the IP Space

You'll need to consider the following questions:

- Are there unmonitored routes?
- What IP space is dark?
- Which IP addresses are network appliances?

Following phase I, you should have an approximate inventory of the network and a live feed of, at the minimum, cross-border traffic data. With this information, you can begin to validate the inventory by comparing the traffic you are receiving against the list of IP addresses that the administrators provided you. Note the use of the word *validate*—you are comparing the addresses that you observe in traffic against the addresses you were told would be there.

Your first goal is to determine whether instrumentation is complete or incomplete, in particular, whether you have any unmonitored routes to deal with—that is, legitimate routes where traffic is not being recorded. Figure 15-2 shows some common examples of dark routes. In this figure, a line indicates a route between two entities:

- The first unmonitored route occurs when traffic moves through router 2, which is not monitored. For example, if host A communicates with external address B using router 2, you will not see A's traffic to B or B's traffic to A.
- A more common problem in modern networks is the present of wireless bridges. Most modern hosts have access to multiple wireless networks, especially in shared facilities. Host B in the example can communicate with the Internet while bypassing router 1 entirely.

The key to identifying unmonitored routes is to look at *asymmetric* traffic flow. Routing protocols forward traffic with minimal interest in the point of origin, so if you have n access points coming into your network, the chance of any particular session going in and out of the same point is about $1/n$. You can expect *some* instrumentation failures to result on any network, so there are always going to be broken sessions, but if you find *consistent* evidence of asymmetric sessions between pairs of addresses, that's good evidence that the current monitoring configuration is missing something.

The best tool for finding asymmetric sessions is TCP traffic, because TCP is the most common protocol in the IP suite that guarantees a response. To identify legitimate TCP sessions, take the opposite approach from Chapter 11: look for sessions where the SYN, ACK, and FIN flags are high, with multiple packets or with payload.

Identifying Asymmetric Traffic

To identify asymmetric traffic, look for TCP sessions that carry payload and don't have a corresponding outgoing session. This can be done using `rwuniq` and `rwfilter`:

```
$ rwfilter --start-date=2013/05/10:00 --end-date=2013/05/10:00 --proto=6 \
  --type=out --packets=4- --flags-all=SAF/SAF --pass=stdout | \
  rwuniq --field=1,2 --no-title --sort | cut -d '|' -f 1,2 > outgoing.txt
# Note that I use 1,2 for the rwuniq above, and 2,1 for the rwuniq below.
# This ensures that the
# fields are present in the same order when I compare output.
$ rwfilter --start-date=2013/05/10:00 --end-date=2013/05/10:00 --proto=6 \
```

```
        --type=in --packets=4- --flags-all=SAF/SAF --pass=stdout | rwuniq \
        --field=2,1 --no-title --sort | cut -d '|' -f 2,1 > incoming.txt
```

Once these commands finish, I will have two files of internal IP and external IP pairs.
I can compare these pairs directly using -cmp or a hand-written routine. Example 15-1
shows a python example that generates a report of unidirectional flows:

Example 15-1. Generating a report of unidirectional flows

```
#!/usr/bin/env python
#
#
# compare_reports.py
#
# Command line: compare_reports.py file1 file2
#
# Reads the contents of two files and checks to see if the same
# IP pairs appear.
#
import sys, os
def read_file(fn):
    ip_table = set()
    a = open(fn,'r')
    for i in a.readlines():
        sip, dip = map(lambda x:x.strip(), i.split('|')[0:2])
        key = "%15s:%15s" % (sip, dip)
        ip_table.add(key)
    a.close()
    return ip_table

if __name__ == '__main__':
    incoming = read_file(sys.argv[1])
    outgoing = read_file(sys.argv[2])
    missing_pairs = set()
    total_pairs = set()
    # Being a bit sloppy here, run on both incoming and outgoing to ensure
    # that if there's an element in one not in the other, it gets caught
    for i in incoming:
        total_pairs.add(i)
        if not i in outgoing:
            missing_pairs.add(i)
    for i in outgoing:
        total_pairs.add(i)
        if not i in incoming:
            missing_pairs.add(i)
    print missing_pairs, total_pairs
    # Now do some address breakdowns
    addrcount = {}
    for i in missing_pairs:
        in_value, out_value = i.split(':')[0:2]
        if not addrcount.has_key(in_value):
            addrcount[in_value] = 0
        if not addrcount.has_key(out_value):
```

```
        addrcount[out_value] = 0
    addrcount[in_value] += 1
    addrcount[out_value] += 1
# Simple report, number of missing pairs, list of most commonly occurring
# addresses
print "%d missing pairs out of %d total" % (len(missing_pairs),
                                    len(total_pairs))
s = addrcount.items()
s.sort(lambda a,b:b[1] - a[1]) # lambda just guarantees order
print "Most common addresses:"
for i in s[0:10]:
    print "%15s %5d" % (i[0],addrcount[i[0]])
```

This approach is best done using passive collection because it ensures that you are observing traffic from a number of locations outside the network. Scanning is also for identifying dark spaces and back doors. When you scan and control the instrumentation, not only can you see the results of your scan on your desktop, but you can compare the traffic from the scan against the data provided by your collection system.

Although you can scan the network and check whether all your scanning sessions match your expectations (i.e., you see responses from hosts and nothing from empty space), you are scanning from only a single location, when you really need to look at traffic from multiple points of origin.

If you find evidence of unmonitored routes, you need to determine whether they can be instrumented and why they aren't being instrumented right now. Unmonitored routes are a security risk: they can be used to probe, exfiltrate, and communicate without being monitored.

Unmonitored routes and dark spaces have similar traffic profiles to each other; in both cases, a TCP packet sent to them will not elicit a reply. The difference is that in an unmonitored route, this happens due to incomplete instrumentation, while a dark space has nothing to generate a response. Once you have identified your unmonitored routes, any monitored addresses that behave in the same way should be dark.

Identifying Dark Space

Dark spaces can be found either passively or actively. Passive identification requires collecting traffic to the network and progressively eliminating all address that respond or are unmonitored—at that point, the remainder should be dark. The alternative approach is to actively probe the addresses in a network and record the ones that don't respond; those addresses should be dark.

Passive collection requires gathering data over a long period. At the minimum, collect traffic for at least a week to ensure that dynamic addressing and business processes are handled.

```
$ rwfilter --type=out --start-date=2013/05/01:00 --end-date=2013/05/08:23 \
    --proto=0-255 --pass=stdout | rwset --sip-file=light.set
# Now remove the lit addresses from our total inventory
$ rwsettool --difference --output=dark.set initial.set light.set
```

An alternative approach is to ping every host on the network to determine whether it is present.

```
$ for i in `rwsetcat initial.set`
    do
    # Do a ping with a 5 second timeout and 1 attempt to each target
        ping -q -c 1 -t 5 ${i} | tail -2 >> pinglog.txt
    done
```

pinglog.txt will contain the summary information from the ping command, which will look like this:

```
--- 128.2.11.0 ping statistics ---
1 packets transmitted, 0 packets received, 100.0% packet loss
```

The contents can be parsed to produce a dark map.

Of these two options, scanning will be faster than passive mapping, but you have to make sure the network will return ECHO REPLY ICMP messages to your pings.

Another way to identify dynamic spaces through passive monitoring is to take hourly pulls and compare the configuration of dark and light addresses in each hour.

"Network appliances" in this context really means router interfaces. Router interfaces are identifiable by looking for routing protocols such as BGP, RIP, and OSPF. Another mechanism to use is to check for "ICMP host not found" messages (also known as network unreachable messages), which are generated only by routers.

Finding Network Appliances

Identifying network appliances involves either using *traceroute*, or looking for specific protocols used by them. Every host mentioned by *traceroute* except the endpoint is a router. If you check for protocols, candidates include:

BGP

> BGP is commonly spoken by routers that route traffic across the Internet, and won't be common inside corporate networks unless you have a very big network. BGP runs on TCP port 179.

```
# This will identify communications from the outside world with BGP speakers
# inside.
$ rwfilter --type=in --proto=6 --dport=179 --flags-all=SAF/SAF \
    --start-date=2013/05/01:00 --end-date=2013/05/01:00 --pass=bgp_speakers.rwf
```

OSPF and EIGRP

> Common protocols for managing routing on small networks. EIGRP is protocol number 88, OSPF protocol number 89.

```
# This will identify communications between OSPF and EIGRP speakers,
# note the use of internal, we don't expect this traffic to be cross-border
$ rwfilter --type=internal --proto=88,89 --start-date=2013/05/01:00 \
  --end-date=2013/05/01:00 --pass=stdout | rwfilter --proto=88 \
    --input-pipe=stdin --pass=eigrp.rwf --fail=ospf.rwf
```

RIP

Another internal routing protocol, RIP is implemented on top of UDP using port 520.

```
# This will identify communications with RIP speakers
$ rwfilter --type=internal --proto=17 --aport=520 \
  --start-date=2013/05/01:00 --end-date=2013/05/01:00 --pass=rip_speakers.rwf
```

ICMP

Host unreachable messages (ICMP Type 3, Code 7) and time exceeded messages (ICMP Type 11) both originate from routers.

```
# Filter out icmp messages, the longer period is because ICMP is much rarer
$ rwfilter --type=out --proto=1 --icmp-type=3,11 --pass=stdout \
  --start-date=2013/05/01:00 \
  --end-date=2013/05/01:23 | rwfilter --icmp-type=11 --input-pipe=stdin \
  --pass=ttl_exceeded.rwf --fail=stdout | rwfilter --input-pipe=stdin \
  --icmp-code=7 --pass=not_found.rwf
$ rwset --sip=routers_ttl.set ttl_exceeded.rwf
$ rwset --sip=routers_nf.set not_found.rwf
$ rwsettool --union --output-path=routers.set routers_nf.set routers_ttl.set
```

The results of this step will provide you with a list of router interface addresses. Each router on the network will control one or more of these interfaces. At this point, it's a good idea to go back to the network administrators in order to associate these interfaces with actual hardware.

Phase III: Identifying Blind and Confusing Traffic

You'll need to consider the following questions:

- Are there NATs?
- Are there proxies, reverse proxies, or caches?
- Is there VPN traffic?
- Are there dynamic addresses?

After completing phase II, you will have identified which addresses within your network are active. The next step is to identify which addresses are going to be problematic. Life would be easier for you if every host were assigned a static IP address, that address were used by exactly one host, and the traffic were easily identifiable by port and protocol.

Obviously, these constraints don't hold. Specific problems include:

NATs

These are a headache because they alias multiple IP addresses behind a much smaller set of addresses.

Proxies, reverse proxies, and caches

Like a NAT, a proxy hides multiple IP addresses behind a single proxy host address. Proxies generally operate at higher levels in the OSI stack and often handle specific protocols. Reverse proxies, as the name implies, provide aliases for multiple server addresses and are used for load balancing and caching. Caches store repeatedly referenced results (such as web pages) to improve performance.

VPNs

Virtual Private Network (VPN) traffic obscures the contents of protocols, hiding what's being done and hiding how many hosts are involved. VPN traffic includes IPv6-over-IPv4 protocols such as 6to4 and Teredo, and encrypted protocols such as SSH and TOR. All of these protocols encapsulate traffic, meaning that the addresses seen at the IP layer are relays, routers, or concentrators rather than the actual hosts doing something.

Dynamic addresses

Dynamic addressing, such as that assigned through DHCP, causes a single host to migrate through a set of addresses over time. Dynamic addressing complicates analysis by introducing a lifetime for each address. You can never be sure whether the host you're tracking through its IP address did something after its DHCP lease expired.

These particular elements should be well-documented by network administrators, but there are a number of different approaches for identifying them. Proxies and NATs can both be identified by looking for evidence that a single IP address is serving as a frontend for multiple addresses. This can be done via packet payload or flow analysis, although packet payload is more certain.

Identifying NATs

NATs are an enormous pain to identify unless you have access to payload data, in which case they simply become a significant pain. The best approach for identifying NATs is to quiz the network administrators. Failing that, you have to identify NATs through evidence that there are multiple addresses hidden behind the same address. A couple of different indicia can be used for this.

Variant User-Agent *strings*

The best approach I've seen to identify NAT is to pull the User-Agent strings from web sessions. Using a script such as *bannergrab.py* from Chapter 14, you can pull and dump all instances of the User-Agent string issuing from the NAT. If you see different instances of the same browser, or multiple browsers, you are likely looking at a NAT.

There is a *potential* false positive here. A number of applications (including email clients) include some form of HTTP interaction these days. Consequently, it's best to restrict yourself to explicit browser banners, such as those output by Firefox, IE, Chrome, and Opera.

Multiple logons to common servers
Identify major internal and external services used by your network. Examples include the company email server, Google, and major newspapers. If a site is a NAT, you should expect to see redundant logins from the same address. Email server logs and internal HTTP server logs are the best tool for this kind of research.

TTL behavior
Recall that time-to-live (TTL) values are assigned by the IP stack and that initial values are OS-specific. Check the TTLs coming from a suspicious address and see if they vary. Variety suggests multiple hosts behind the address. If values are the same *but below the initial TTL for an OS*, you're seeing evidence of multiple hops to reach that address.

Identifying Proxies

Proxy identification requires you to have both sides of the proxy instrumented. Figure 15-3 shows the network traffic between clients, proxies, and servers. As this figure shows, proxies take in requests from multiple clients, and send those requests off to multiple servers. In this way, a proxy behaves as *both* a server (to the clients it's proxying for) and as a client (to the servers it's proxying to). If your instrumentation lets you see both the client-to-proxy and proxy-to-server communication, you can identify the proxy by viewing this traffic pattern. If you don't, you can use the techniques discussed in the previous cookbook on NAT identification. The same principles apply because, after all, a proxy is a frontend to multiple clients like a NAT firewall.

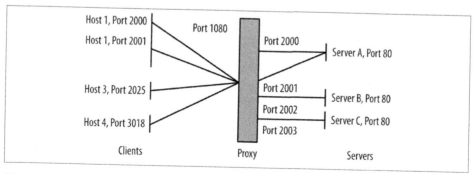

Figure 15-3. Network connections for a proxy

To identify a proxy using its connectivity, first look for hosts that are acting like clients. You can tell a client because it uses multiple ephemeral ports. For example, using *rwuniq*, you can identify clients on your network as follows:

```
$ rwfilter --type=out --start-date=2013/05/10:00 --end-date=2013/05/10:01 \
    --proto=6,17 --sport=1024-65535 --pass=stdout | rwuniq --field=1,3 \
    --no-title | cut -d '|' -f 1 | sort | uniq -c | egrep -v '^[ ]+1' |\
    cut -d ' ' -f 3 | rwsetbuild stdin clients.set
```

That command identifies all combinations of source IP address (sip) and source port number (sport) in the sample data and eliminates any situation where a host only used one port. The remaining hosts are using multiple ports. It's possible that hosts that are using only seven or eight ports at a time are running multiple servers, but as the distinct port count rises, the likelihood of them running multiple services drops.

Once you've identified clients, the next step is to identify which of the clients are *also* behaving as servers (see "Identifying Servers" on page 309).

VPN traffic can be identified by looking for the characteristic ports and protocols used by VPNs. VPNs obscure traffic analysis by wrapping all of the traffic they transport in another protocol such as GRE. Once you've identified a VPN's endpoints, instrument there. Once the wrapper has been removed from VPN traffic, you should be able to distinguish flows and session data.

Identifying VPN Traffic

The major protocols and ports used by VPN traffic are:

IPSec
>   IPSec refers to a suite of protocols for encrypted communications over VPNs. The two key protocols are AH (authentication header, protocol 51) and ESP (Encapsulating Security Payload, protocol 50):

```
$ rwfilter --start-date=2013/05/13:00 --end-date=2013/05/13:01 --proto=50,51 \
    --pass=vpn.rwf
```

GRE
>   GRE (generic routing encapsulation) is the workhorse protocol for a number of VPN implementations. It can be identified as protocol 47.

```
$ rwfilter --start-date=2013/05/13:00 --end-date=2013/05/13:01 --proto=47 \
    --pass=gre.rwf
```

A number of common tunneling protocols are also identifiable using port and protocol numbers, although unlike standard VPNs, they are generally software-defined and don't require special assets specifically for routing. Examples include SSH, Teredo, 6to4, and TOR.

Phase IV: Identifying Clients and Servers

After identifying the basic structure of the network, the next step is to identify what the network does, which requires profiling and identifying clients and servers on the network. Questions include:

- What are the major internal servers?
- Are there servers running on unusual ports?
- Are there FTP, HTTP, SMTP, or SSH servers that are not known to system administration?
- Are servers running as clients?
- Where are the major clients?

Identifying Servers

Servers can be identified by looking for ports that receive sessions and by looking at the spread of communications to ports.

To identify ports that are receiving sessions, you need either access to *pcap* data or flow instrumentation that distinguishes the initial flags of a packet from the rest of the body (which you can get through YAF, as described in "YAF" on page 96). In a flow, the research then becomes a matter of identifying hosts that respond with a SYN and ACK:

```
$ rwfilter --proto=6 --flags-init=SA|SA --pass=server_traffic.rwf \
    --start-date=2013/05/13:00 --end-date=2013/05/13:00 --type=in
```

This approach won't work with UDP, because a host can send UDP traffic to any port it pleases without any response. An alternate approach, which works with both UDP and TCP, is to look at the *spread* of a port/protocol combination. I briefly touched on this in "Identifying Proxies" on page 307, and we'll discuss it in more depth now.

A server is a public resource. This means that the address has to be sent to the clients, and that, over time, you can expect multiple clients to connect to the server's address. Therefore, over time, you will see multiple flows with distinct source IP/source port combinations all communicating with the same destination IP/destination port combination. This differs from the behavior of a client, which will issue multiple sessions from different source ports to a number of distinct hosts. Figure 15-4 shows this phenomenon graphically.

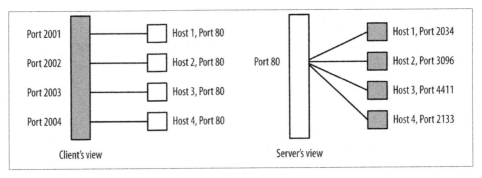

Figure 15-4. A graphical illustration of spread

Spread can easily be calculated with flow data by using the `rwuniq` command. Given a candidate file of traffic originating from one IP address, use the following:

```
$rwuniq --field=1,2 --dip-distinct candidate_file | sort -t '|' -k3 -nr |\
        head -15
```

The more distinct IP addresses talk to the same host/port combination, the more likely is it that the port represents a server. In this script, servers will appear near the top of the list.

By using spread and direct packet analysis, you should have a list of most of the IP:port combinations that are running servers. This is always a good time to scan those IP:port combinations to verify what's actually running: in particular, search for servers that are *not* running on common ports. Servers are a public resource (for some limited definition of "public"), and when they appear on an unusual port, it may be an indication that a user didn't have permissions to run the server normally (suspicious behavior) or was trying to hide it (also suspicious behavior, especially if you've read Chapter 11).

Once you've identified the servers on a network, determine which ones are most important. There are a number of different metrics for doing so, including:

Total volume over time
    This is the easiest and most common approach.

Internal and external volume
    This differentiates servers accessed only by your own users from those accessed by the outside world.

Graph centrality
    Path and degree centrality often identify hosts that are important and that would be missed using pure degree statistics (number of contacts). See Chapter 13 for more information.

The goal of this exercise is to produce a list of servers ordered by priority, from the ones you should watch the most to the ones that are relatively low profile or, potentially, even removable.

Once you have identified all the servers on a network, it's a good time to go back to talk to the network administrators.[2] This is because you will almost invariably find servers that nobody knew were running on the network, examples of which include:

- Systems being run by power users
- Embedded web servers
- Occupied hosts

Identifying Sensing and Blocking Infrastructure

Questions to consider:

- Are there any IDS or IPS systems in place? Can I modify their configuration?
- What systems do I have log access to?
- Are there any firewalls?
- Are there any router ACLs?
- Is there an antispam system at the border, or is antispam handled at the mail server, or both?
- Is AV present?

The final step of any new instrumentation project is to figure out what security software and capabilities are currently present. In many cases, these systems will be identifiable more from an *absence* than a presence. For example, if no hosts on a particular network show evidence of BitTorrent traffic (ports 6881–6889), it's likely that a router ACL is blocking BitTorrent.

Updating the Inventory: Toward Continuous Audit

Once you've built an initial inventory, queue up all the analysis scripts you've written to run on a regular basis. The goal is to keep track of what's changed on your network over time.

This inventory provides a handy anomaly-detection tool. The first and most obvious approach is to keep track of changes in the inventory. Sample questions to ask include:

---

2. Preferably at a place that serves vodka.

- Are there new clients or servers on the network?
- Have previously existing addresses gone dark?
- Has a new service appeared on a client?

Changes in the inventory can be used as triggers for other analyses. For example, when a new client or server appears on the network, you can start analyzing its flow data to see who it communicates with, scan it, or otherwise experiment on it in order to fill the inventory with information on the new arrival.

In the long term, keeping track of what addresses are known and monitored is a first approximation for how well you're protecting the network. It's impossible to say "X is more secure than Y"; we just don't have the ability to quantitatively measure the X factor that is attacker interest. By working with the map, you can track coverage either as a strict number (out of X addresses on the network, Y are monitored) or as a percentage.

Further Reading

1. Umesh Shankar and Vern Paxson, "Active Mapping: Resisting NIDS Evasion Without Altering Traffic," Proceedings of the 2003 IEEE Symposium on Security and Privacy.

2. Austin Whisnant and Sid Faber, "Network Profiling Using Flow," CMU/SEI-2012-TR-006, Software Engineering Institute.

Index

A

actions
    control, 11
    event production, 11, 129
    reporting, 10
active banner grabbing, 283
active security analysis, 180
Address and Routing Parameter area, 167
address filtering, 27, 78
Address Resolution Protocol (ARP), 23, 149
addressing
    address classes and CIDR blocks, 29
    address exhaustion, 150
    checking connectivity, 153
    DNS lookup, 167
    dynamic addresses, 306
    identifying geolocation/demographics, 157
    identifying routers, 155
    IPv4 address structure and function, 150
    IPv6 address structure and function, 152
    network layers and, 23
    network mapping and, 298
    notable addresses, 153
    researching chain of ownership, 152
    unused addresses, 224
address_types.pmap, 94
adjacency lists, 262
aggregation tools, 12
Akamai, 166

alarm construction, 193
alert processing, steps of, 137
All Pairs, Shortest Paths (APSP), 267
analytics
    achieving effective, 1, 55, 188
    application identification, 279–293
    common mistakes in, 203
    exploratory data analysis (EDA), 191–219
    for fumbling behaviors, 221–236
    graph analysis, 261–277
    network mapping, 295–312
    space and query times, 2
    streaming analytics, 63
    volume/time analysis, 237–260
animation, drawbacks of, 213
annotated data logs, 41, 43
anomaly-based IDS, 132–141
Anonymous, 255
Anscombe Quartet, 192
Apache
    log configuration in, 46
    Quota rate limiting module, 260
appliance-based generation, 32
application identification
    banner identification/classification, 291
    by banner grabbing, 283
    by behavior, 286
    by subsidiary site, 290
    challenges in, 279

We'd like to hear your suggestions for improving our indexes. Send email to index@oreilly.com.

About the Author

Michael Collins is the chief scientist for RedJack, LLC, a network security and data analysis company located in the Washington, D.C., area. Prior to his work at RedJack, Dr. Collins was a member of the technical staff at the CERT/Network Situational Awareness group at Carnegie Mellon University. His primary focus is on network instrumentation and traffic analysis, in particular on the analysis of large traffic datasets. Dr. Collins graduated with a PhD in Electrical Engineering from Carnegie Mellon University in 2008. He holds Master's and Bachelor's degrees from the same institution.

Colophon

The animal on the cover of *Network Security Through Data Analysis* is a European Merlin (*Falco columbarius*). There is some debate as to whether the North American and the European/Asian varieties of Merlin are actually different species. Carl Linnaeus was the first to classify the bird in 1758 using a specimen from America, then in 1771 the ornithologist Marmaduke Tunstall assigned a separate taxon to the Eurasian Merlin, calling it *Falco aesalon* in his book *Ornithologica Britannica*.

Recently, it has been found that there are significant genetic variations between North American and European types of Merlin, supporting the idea that they should be officially classified as distinct species. It is believed that the separation between the two kinds happened more than a million years ago, and since then the birds have existed completely independently of each other.

The Merlin is more heavily built than most other small falcons and can weigh almost a pound, depending on the time of year. Females are generally larger than males, which is common among raptors. This allows the male and female to hunt different types of prey animals and means that less territory is required to support a mating pair. Merlins normally inhabit open country, such as scrubland, forests, parks, grasslands, and moorland. They prefer areas with low and medium-height vegetation because it allows them to hunt easily and find the abandoned nests that they take on as their own. During the winter, European Merlins are known to roost communally with Hen Harriers, another bird of prey.

Breeding occurs in May and June, and pairs are monogamous for the season. The Merlins will often use the empty nests of crows or magpies, but it is also common, especially in the UK, to find Merlins nesting in crevices in cliffs or buildings. Females lay three to six eggs, which hatch after an incubation period of 28 to 32 days. The chicks will be dependent on their parents for up to 4 weeks before starting out on their own.

In medieval times, chicks were taken from the nest and hand-reared to be used for hunting. *The Book of St. Albans*, a handbook of gentleman's pursuits, included Merlins in the "Hawking" section, calling the species, "the falcon for a lady." Today, they are still trained by falconers for hunting smaller birds, but this practice is declining because of conservation efforts. The most serious threat to Merlins is habitat destruction, especially in their breeding areas. However, since the birds are highly adaptable and have been successful at living in settled areas, their population remains stable around the world.

The cover image is from Wood's *Animate Creation*. The cover fonts are URW Typewriter and Guardian Sans. The text font is Adobe Minion Pro; the heading font is Adobe Myriad Condensed; and the code font is Dalton Maag's Ubuntu Mono.

Get even more for your money.

Join the O'Reilly Community, and register the O'Reilly books you own. It's free, and you'll get:

- $4.99 ebook upgrade offer
- 40% upgrade offer on O'Reilly print books
- Membership discounts on books and events
- Free lifetime updates to ebooks and videos
- Multiple ebook formats, DRM FREE
- Participation in the O'Reilly community
- Newsletters
- Account management
- 100% Satisfaction Guarantee

Signing up is easy:

1. **Go to: oreilly.com/go/register**
2. **Create an O'Reilly login.**
3. **Provide your address.**
4. **Register your books.**

Note: English-language books only

To order books online:
oreilly.com/store

For questions about products or an order:
orders@oreilly.com

To sign up to get topic-specific email announcements and/or news about upcoming books, conferences, special offers, and new technologies:
elists@oreilly.com

For technical questions about book content:
booktech@oreilly.com

To submit new book proposals to our editors:
proposals@oreilly.com

O'Reilly books are available in multiple DRM-free ebook formats. For more information:
oreilly.com/ebooks

Spreading the knowledge of innovators   oreilly.com

Have it your way.

CPSIA information can be obtained at www.ICGtesting.com
Printed in the USA
BVOW08s1849180315

392288BV00016B/59/P